INVENTING THE SKYLINE

THE ARCHITECTURE OF CASS GILBERT

FRONTISPIECE.

Drafting room in Cass Gilbert's office, 1 East Twenty-fourth Street, New York City, during the Woolworth Building project, ca. 1912.

(Courtesy Museum of the City of New York, Wurts Collection)

INVENTING THE SKYLINE

THE ARCHITECTURE OF CASS GILBERT

Edited by Margaret Heilbrun

With an introduction by Hugh Hardy

COLUMBIA UNIVERSITY PRESS NEW YORK

COLUMBIA UNIVERSITY PRESS
Publishers Since 1893
New York Chichester, West Sussex

Library of Congress Cataloging-in-Publication Data
Gilbert, Cass, 1859-1934.
Inventing the skyline : the architecture of Cass Gilbert / edited by Margaret Heilbrun ; with an introduction by Hugh Hardy.
p. cm.
Published on the occasion of an exhibition held at the New-York Historical Society, summer–fall 2000.
Includes bibliographical references and index.
ISBN 0-231-11872-4 (cloth : alk. paper)
1. Gilbert, Cass, 1859-1934—Exhibitions. 2. Eclecticism in architecture—United States—Exhibitions. 3. Architectural drawing—Private collections—New York (State)—New York—Exhibitions. 4. Architectural drawing—New York (State)—New York—Exhibitions. 5. New-York Historical Society—Exhibitions. I. Heilbrun, Margaret. II. New-York Historical Society. III. Title.

NA737.G5 A4 2000
720′.92—dc21
99-086736

Casebound editions of Columbia University Press books are printed on permanent and durable acid-free paper.
Printed in the United States of America
1 2 3 4 5 6 7 8 9 c

To Henry Hope Reed

CONTENTS

FOREWORD

Betsy Gotbaum

Dear Reader:
Welcome to the New-York Historical Society and this overdue look at one of its most important treasures of architectural history: the Cass Gilbert Collection.

I am grateful to Columbia University Press for sharing our belief that this catalog deserved publication as a complement to and commemoration of the exhibition *Inventing the Skyline: The Architecture of Cass Gilbert*, on view at the society during the summer and fall of 2000.

The significance of the publication of this book, coming as it does in the sixth year of my role as custodian of this great public trust, is threefold.

First, *Inventing the Skyline* is another example of our revival as New York's oldest cultural institution. As part of this rebirth we are preparing for a third century of service through comprehensive online cataloging and digitization of both museum and library holdings, including those relating to architecture; total reconstruction and refurbishing of our landmark headquarters on Central Park West; and development of a growing presence on the World Wide Web.

Second, this publication reveals the richness of the society's collections. Both the exhibition and the book draw most of their wealth from this remarkable resource and make it available to scholars and the general public alike.

Finally, *Inventing the Skyline* helps rekindle our commitment to a program of publication, whether in traditional or electronic format. The society is proud to play a part in increasing an appreciation for the study of the American experience by supporting the fine scholarship taking place in that field both in New York and around the globe.

I salute the writer and civic gadfly Henry Hope Reed for persuading the Gilbert family to donate Cass Gilbert's New York files to the society in 1956 and 1957 and, even more fundamentally, for his prescient recognition of the significance of the collection to the history of architecture.

I also thank Joan Davidson and the Publication Program of the J. M. Kaplan Fund for launching this catalog, as well as the New York State Council on the Arts for its subsequent support. Appreciation goes too to the Andy Warhol Foundation for helping catalog and conserve this collection and to Arthur Ross, who shares our regard for Henry Reed and the many New York treasures he has helped rescue. It is due to supporters such as these that the historic achievements of the last and the current centuries will be known in the next.

Sincerely,
Betsy Gotbaum, President
New-York Historical Society
July 2000

PREFACE

Margaret Heilbrun

In 1923 the monthly journal *Architecture* wondered how many of the "hurrying crowd" on New York City's lower Broadway could name the architect of the Woolworth Building. The architect in question received clippings of the piece from a number of people who knew the answer, including C. S. Woolworth, F. W. Woolworth's brother, who suggested that something be done to assure proper attribution on the building itself.[1] Thus prompted, Cass Gilbert wrote to Hubert T. Parson, president of the F. W. Woolworth Company, giving the address simply as "Woolworth Building, New York City."

> A number of my clients in recent years have asked me to sign their buildings and it has increasingly become a custom on important works that the architect's name should appear in some modest way. As time goes on people forget who the architect was and yet it is a subject of very general interest. I recall when I was building the new Custom House the great difficulty we had in ascertaining who was the architect of the old Custom House on Wall Street and after months of inquiry succeeded in locating him as one named Rogers.[2]

To this day, the Woolworth Building offers no plaque acknowledging its architect. However, since 1923, New York's "hurrying crowd," not to mention the rest of us, have grown far more aware of the pedigrees of the city's

FIGURE P.1

One portion of the Cass Gilbert Collection in the stacks of the New-York Historical Society library. *(Photograph courtesy New-York Historical Society)*

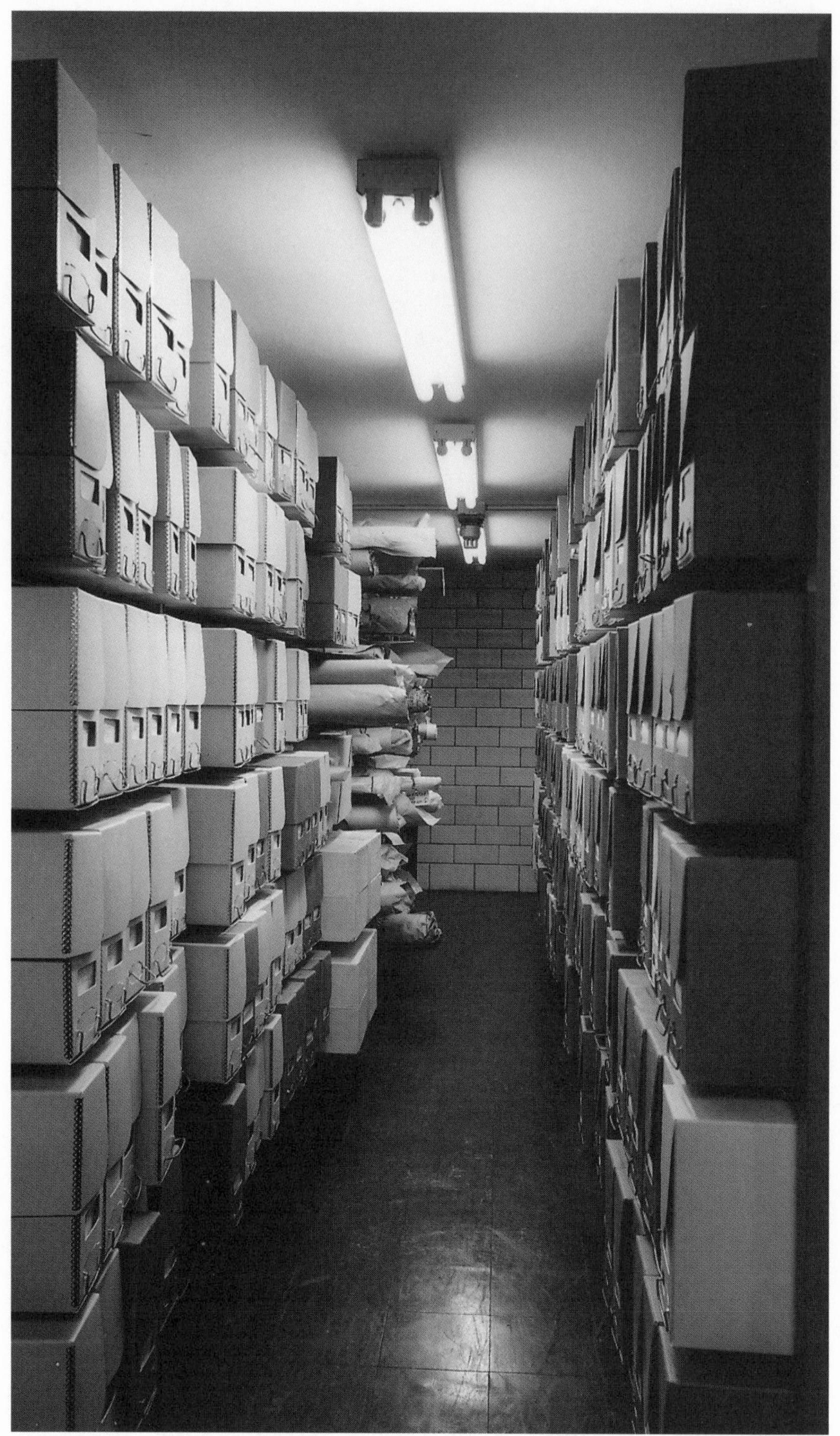

notable buildings and attuned to the attendant issues of preservation that their survival entails. The process, needless to say, took several decades and the destruction of a number of architectural masterpieces, including finally, McKim, Mead, and White's Pennsylvania Station.

In 1955 Henry Hope Reed, the architectural historian and advocate for historic preservation, organized and curated an exhibit at the University Club of New York called *Monuments of Manhattan: An Exhibition of Great Buildings in New York City, 1800–1918.* Cosponsored by the Municipal Art Society, the show encompassed seventy-nine plans, elevations, and drawings, several from the permanent collections of the University Club, and many lent by the New-York Historical Society, the Avery Architectural and Fine Arts Library at Columbia University, the Museum of the City of New York, the New York Public Library, and the American Institute of Architects, among others. In addition, Mr. Reed's exhibit offered the first public viewing of some architectural drawings still held in private hands, including selections from the office of McKim, Mead, and White, and from the families of George B. Post and Cass Gilbert. Thanks in great part to the efforts of Henry Hope Reed, working with Wayne Andrews, curator of manuscripts at the New-York Historical Society, these last three collections later came to the society to form the dazzling core of its architectural holdings, today numbering in the hundreds of thousands of items.

Cass Gilbert's daughter, Emily Gilbert, and son, Cass Gilbert Jr., donated their father's entire New York City office files to the society in 1956 and 1957. They stipulated that "all drawings, renderings, sketches and the like, relating to standing structures . . . shall be preserved so long as the structures to which they relate shall remain standing." Such was their perception of historic preservation at the time, both regarding buildings and archival records.[3]

In linear footage on the shelves of the New-York Historical Society, the Cass Gilbert Collection approximates the height of the Woolworth Building and contains his firm's records for all its work around the country, as well as the personal files maintained at the office by Gilbert. Files from his home were donated by his family to the Library of Congress, which also received several hundred Gilbert sketches. The records of his St. Paul office went to the Minnesota Historical Society. Smaller collections are held at other repositories, including the National Archives and Records Administration, the Missouri Historical Society, and the Oberlin College Archives.

The bulk of the society's Cass Gilbert Collection covers the years of his New York practice, 1899–1934, but it also includes earlier materials that were maintained in Gilbert's New York files. The collection contains more than 63,000 drawings, sketches, blueprints, and watercolor renderings, 245 cubic feet of incoming letters and personal desk files, 469 letter books holding copies of outgoing correspondence, 75 volumes of specifications, 11 cubic feet of photographs, and an assortment of cash books, journals, payroll ledgers, appointment diaries, and scrapbooks.

In the 1990s the curator of architectural collections at the society, Mary Beth Betts, made a priority of strengthening the society's intellectual control of the George B. Post, McKim, Mead, and White, and Cass Gilbert collections and of improving physical access to them, both for researchers by appointment and for a more general audience by means of exhibit. She curated *McKim, Mead, and White's New York* in 1991. Sarah Bradford Landau, of New York University, guest-curated an exhibit on George B. Post in 1998, using the society's collections. Post was the subject of a book by her, published at the same time.[4] Now the society has prepared an exhibit, and this accompanying volume, to illuminate the depth and glories of its Cass Gilbert Collection: *Inventing the Skyline: The Architecture of Cass Gilbert.* Both the exhibit and the book owe much to the work of Mary Beth Betts before she moved on to become director of research at the New York City Landmarks Preservation Commission.

This volume contains an introduction by Hugh Hardy and essays by Cass Gilbert specialists Sharon Irish, Mary Beth Betts, Barbara Christen, and Gail Fenske. Sharon Irish offers a look at Gilbert's overall architectural practice; in chapter 2 Mary Beth Betts studies the evolution of Gilbert's use of architectural drawings; in the next section she narrates the history of twelve of Gilbert's major projects. Barbara Christen's essay considers Gilbert's work as a planner at Oberlin College in Ohio and in New Haven, Connecticut. Gail Fenske analyzes Cass Gilbert's skyscrapers in New York and their role in the making of a modern city.

Just over one hundred years ago, on the threshold of the twentieth century, Cass Gilbert returned from St. Paul to New York City, where, in the early 1880s he had worked as an assistant at McKim, Mead, and White. He opened his own office at 111 Fifth Avenue. Over the next several decades he rigorously and systematically maintained extensive documentation of his architectural practice. That documentation is the basis for the essays in this volume. In this preface, to round out the reader's sense of the breadth of the Cass Gilbert Collection, I touch upon some of the other materials that we find in his files.

Gilbert's personal desk files contain a typescript of an untitled poem, signed and dated by him early in his independent career: "New York, De-

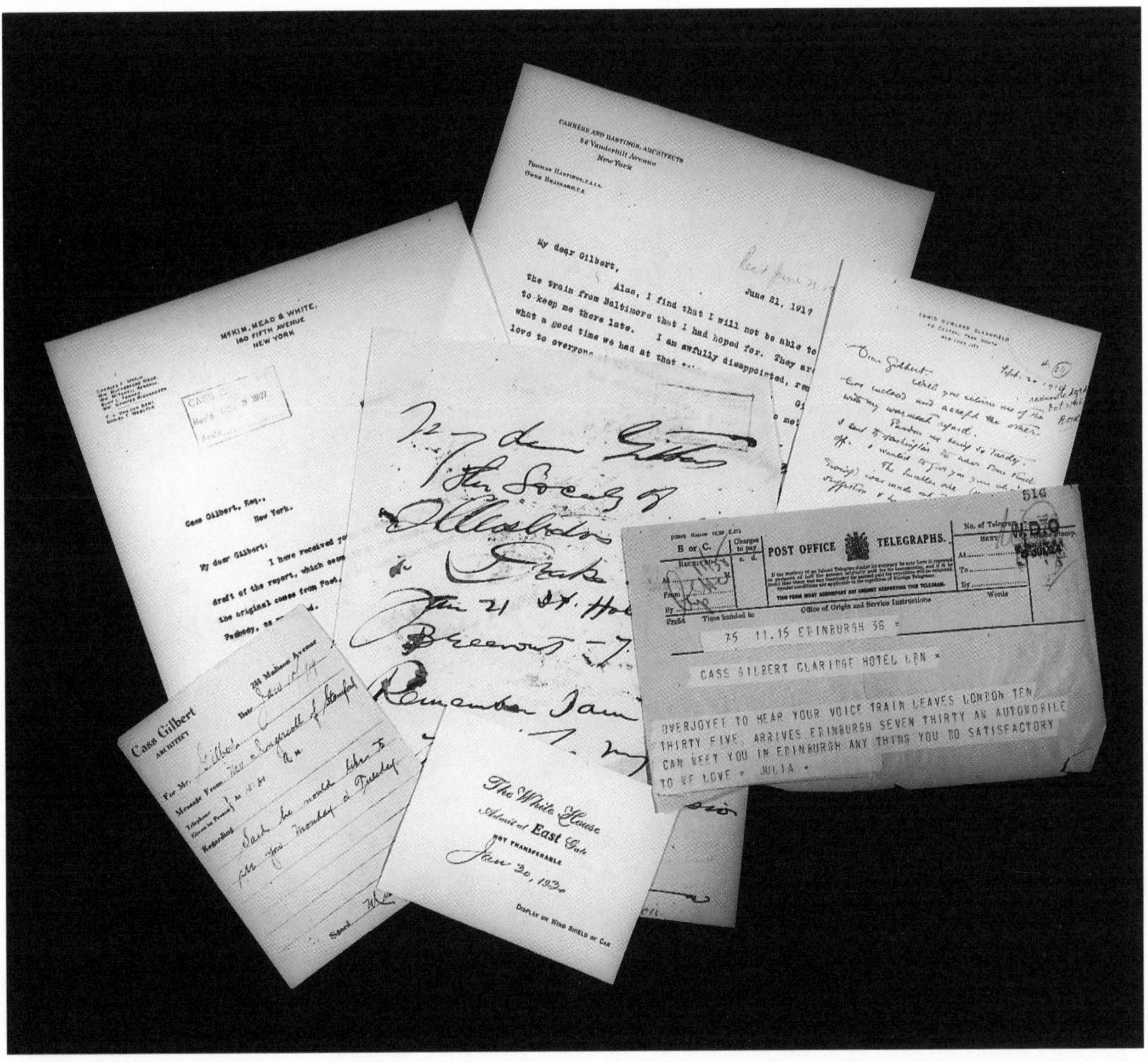

FIGURE P.2

Some items in Cass Gilbert's personal papers at the New-York Historical Society. Clockwise from top: letter from Thomas Hastings, letter from Edwin Howland Blashfield, telegram from Julia Finch Gilbert, White House admission ticket, office message form, letter from Charles F. McKim; center, invitation from Charles Dana Gibson.

(Photograph courtesy New-York Historical Society, neg. no. 72886)

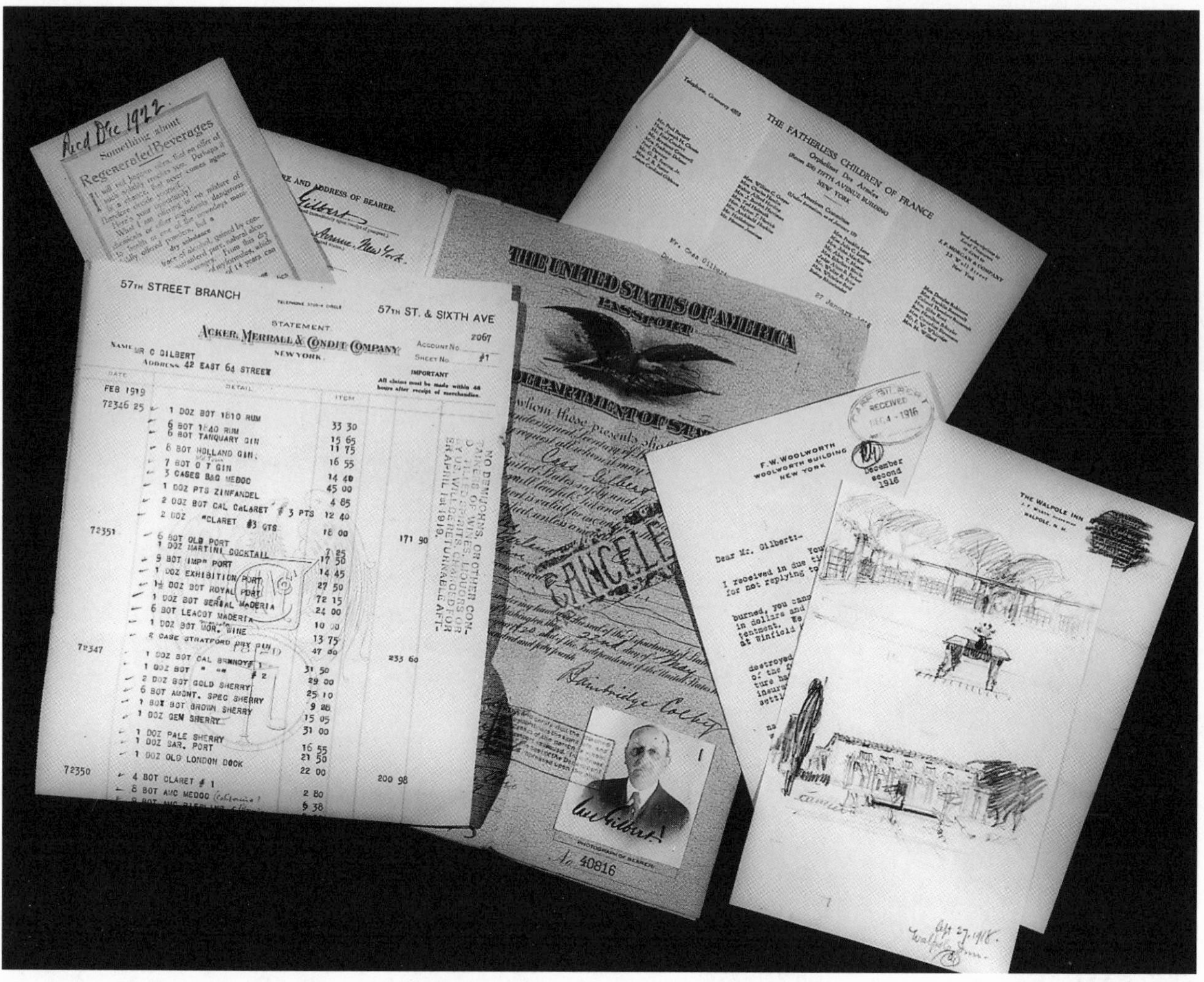

FIGURE P.3

Some items in Cass Gilbert's personal papers at the New-York Historical Society. Clockwise from top: World War I relief letter, letter from F. W. Woolworth, Gilbert sketches on blank stationery, Acker, Merrall, and Condit Company statement of account, "Regenerated Beverages" flyer; center, Gilbert's passport. *(Photograph courtesy New-York Historical Society, neg. no. 72887)*

cember 20, 1901." It is the poem of a man who, though perhaps not much of a poet, obviously cares for form and tradition, a man simultaneously conservative and brimming with benevolent expectation. It begins:

Oh, the Architect bold,
In brave days of old,
Wore a dagger and broad-sword long;
In his hat was a feather,
His coat was of leather,
His buskins were laced with a thong.

And ends, three verses later:

Then, with faith in the right,
Let us enter each fight
With a hope of good fortune to share;
God give us success,
But, nevertheless,
Keep us modest, chivalrous and fair.[5]

Other verses, typed or handwritten, turn up in Gilbert's papers. Some unattributed ones are similar to the above in style and may have also been composed by him. The poetry is but one example of writings in his files showing preoccupations that seem to stray from the professional architectural focus of most of the collection. Yet upon further study, it becomes clear that these writings, too, define the man and even illuminate his career. At the height of his career, Cass Gilbert and his works formed a whole that was invested with the kind of symmetry that opposites, in balance, can achieve. He was both Old World gentleman and brash salesman; he produced works simultaneously serious and fanciful; he was a technician and an artist, capable of expressing power, but always with grace.

Gilbert's personal office files are rich with letters from artists whom he considered his colleagues and friends. By and large they were men who shared Gilbert's traditional outlook, who were gaining greater and greater prominence in their field, and who, like Gilbert, were assiduous committee men in numerous professional associations and private clubs. Several contributed to his major projects. The sculptor Daniel Chester French was a frequent correspondent. The illustrator Charles Dana Gibson sent him hasty invitations in an astonishing, rampant scrawl. There are letters received from the muralist Edwin Howland Blashfield over the course of four decades, ranging from the dejected notes of an unhappy vacationer ("We hate it," he declares of Saratoga in 1907) to the happy agreement with Gilbert that mural painting should "play a role in the establishing of a national art." Because the society also possesses the Blashfield Papers, a researcher may see the letters Blashfield, in turn, received from Gilbert—at least those that he saved. The collection is diminutive compared with Gilbert's; Blashfield was evidently not Gilbert's match as a keeper of papers. It must have pleased him to see his Essex County Courthouse murals described by the architect as "my plea for the advancement of the art of mural decoration in our public buildings. . . . Nothing will give such a building greater distinction" (see chap. 1, fig. 1.7, plate 2)."[6]

Gilbert's personal files demonstrate his unflagging interest in promoting American fine arts as a distinct cultural category. A supreme networker (to use a current locution that he would likely disdain), he was sought out as an advocate for governmental support of the arts. His files include a 1919 invitation from Walter Damrosch to join a dinner for "about a dozen members of the Academy and Institute of Arts and Letters in order that we may discuss informally the advisability of urging the establishment of a Department of Fine Arts as one of the branches of our Government in Washington, with a Secretary of Fine Arts as a member of the President's Cabinet."[7]

Any person's accumulated papers, preserved and made accessible for later generations, will raise as many questions as they answer. Some items will perplex. To Blashfield in 1909, Gilbert offered heated disapproval of competitions: "I earnestly hope you great painters will not let the competition idea obtain a foot hold, for it will be the most disastrous thing to your art. It has been a curse to Architecture—and I a winner of many competitions say this in all sincerity." Yet Gilbert continued to engage in competitions to obtain commissions throughout his career.[8]

Some items provoke amused curiosity: a bill from Acker, Merrall, and Condit, liquor purveyors, in February 1919 enumerates Gilbert's purchase of almost six hundred bottles of spirits. Was he anticipating passage of the Volstead Act? Nearby in the files is a flyer for "Regenerated Beverages," concoctions made "without a still," offering "guaranteed fullbodied production" and "shipment made immediately in an absolutely discreet way." How long did all the wine, whiskey, gin, port, sherry, and champagne last? Was Gilbert compelled to resort to the regenerated alternative?[9]

Around this same time, Gilbert considered a possible diplomatic appointment. His files show that George Pratt Ingersoll and he conferred after Thomas Nelson Page resigned as ambassador to Italy. The question of an alternative posting to Denmark came up and Gilbert wired Ingersoll that he would "prefer the southern location." The paper trail dwindles away. No appointment was forthcoming. One wonders why, and also what effect such an ambassadorship would have had on Gilbert's career.[10]

Other items can raise an eyebrow even as they inform. In 1924, in a long reply to a *New York Evening Post* columnist who had asked, "What may be the ultimate result of the present type of high buildings now being erected in New York?" Gilbert wrote:

> The present tendency to create a peculiar type of buildings *[sic]* is practically the direct result of the Zoning Law or Setback Ordinance passed a few years ago. . . . The direct result appears in the type of high buildings which are now being erected all over the city and it will produce a very curious and interesting, not to say picturesque, aspect. It has already produced some structures that might have found their prototype in the Zikkurat architecture of the Babylonians or Assyrians. Perhaps there is a certain propriety in this unconscious and enforced reversion to type in a city which has been called "the modern Babylon" and where so many of our people are descended from the races that once inhabited the Assyrian plains.[11]

His files, a reflection of their era, include many cablegrams. Those that are business-related often drop into code. Gilbert, however, rarely kept a copy of the applicable key with the telegram. A key clipped to one cabled message in 1905 clarifies that "is overleap" means "is office work proceeding satisfactorily?" and "fascinador" means "if nothing requires my attention, will not return until. . . ." But can we figure out, unaided, what "ex fallanza" means or "important ligenous Paris loach?" A fundamental understanding of the culture of Gilbert's office can start to recede from our grasp.[12]

Within these files, we see pencil sketches deftly executed on pieces of club and hotel stationery, scribbled in the margins of the many loving letters he received from his wife, Julia, and grown children, or undertaken on scraps of card stock. They all show a swift, sure hand, but we cannot easily determine what projects they relate to or what purpose each may have served.

In the summer of 1912, Blashfield received a letter from Gilbert in which the architect, while at work on the Woolworth Building project, grew nostalgic: "Will we ever again have just such a group of artists and such a client as in the old Minnesota Capitol enterprise—with you and La Farge, Millet,

Simmons, Pyle, Walker, Cox, French and Ramsey. What a group! Is our American Renaissance passing? All too short lived? Or are we going on to yet greater things." Many would say that Gilbert, in 1912, was at the summit of his career, with only the U.S. Army Supply Base in Brooklyn as a subsequent project that demonstrated innovation.[13]

World War I dislodged Gilbert from an isolationist position. Initially believing that Germany was behaving honorably, he was quite rapidly disillusioned and offered full support to the U.S. war effort. "You and I have not met very often lately for some reason or other and I wonder how you are prospering. I trust, however, that you are getting through these terrible war times without very much serious trouble, but we all have our troubles and no doubt you have yours." So wrote F.W. Woolworth to Gilbert in 1918. Although Gilbert and his family ultimately came through the war without "serious trouble" (Gilbert's son, Cass Jr., had served on the front), Gilbert's personal files indicate the intensity of his feelings in support of England and France and against Germany. There are, for example, two lengthy letters, one to Sir Aston Webb in 1915 and one in reply to Albert Jaegers, the German-born sculptor, in 1916. In each he outlines his sense of betrayal by the Germans and the course of events that led him to cast aside his neutrality. It is as if he needed to put the words down on paper to properly dismiss his long-held feelings of trust and honor. He directs his anger not only at Germany but also at those he calls "hyphenated Americans," who he felt were not supporting the Allies. He did not mail either letter. The one to Webb remains in his files, with "found in a suit pressed March 15" noted by him at the top. He annotated the letter to Jaegers "not sent."[14]

In the years after World War I, Gilbert no longer wanted to reside in New York City, and he moved his family from East Sixty-fourth Street to Ridgefield, Connecticut, where he had a summer home. "Cass dear, Just a modern typewritten love letter with a wobbly January at the top." So begins one of Julia Finch Gilbert's letters from this time. Gilbert was in West Virginia, at work on what would be the last neoclassical state capitol built in the country. Public architectural design, along with the typography of his wife's letters, was moving on to a new era of modernism that was leaving Gilbert behind.[15]

He classified himself as a "loyal Republican," and his papers make evident his support for the successive administrations of Harding, Coolidge, and Hoover, with notes and invitations coming to him from the White House. Although a great admirer of Theodore Roosevelt, he was no fan of FDR and actively supported Hoover in the 1932 election.

To his brother Samuel, he wrote in 1933: "I wish America would leave Europe to run its own affairs. . . . I like Mussolini's way. . . . He looks out for *Italy!* and you know there is no nonsense about him."[16] At this time, of course, many people admired the efficiency Benito Mussolini seemed to be bringing to Italy. Had Gilbert lived longer he might well have changed his views of the man and again shifted from his isolationist stance. In any case, Gilbert's warm relations with Mussolini, whom he met more than once when in Europe, helped to secure the Siena marble used in interior columns of the U.S. Supreme Court building, his last commission, a project that his Republican connections to William Howard Taft may have helped him obtain. The final project of the man who had been called "the prophet of the skyscraper age" was one that looked backward.[17]

"New schools of design," said Gilbert, "come with intervals of centuries between, by slow evolution, and can no more be created out of whole cloth than new social orders or systems of government."[18] In this pronouncement, he was mistaken, both as an architectural and as a social critic. The *New York Times* for May 18, 1934, carrying the news of his death, showed headlines that made abundantly clear the rapid formation of new social orders and programs: "20,000 Nazi Friends at a Rally Here"; "President to Ask Congress for Far-Reaching Reforms, Both Social and Economic."[19]

Cass Gilbert's miscalculations were slight compared with his overall eloquence as a designer, communicator, and craftsman. The essays in this volume, and the exhibit they accompany, testify to his prodigious gifts. His papers at the New-York Historical Society, like all his works, embody the spirit and enterprise that characterized his life. In a letter to Blashfield, he provided an appropriate adieu when he wrote: "Let us hope, and work on. Yours affectionately, Gilbert."[20]

Margaret Heilbrun
Library Director
New-York Historical Society

Notes

1. C. S. Woolworth to Cass Gilbert, January 14, 1924, Personal Papers, 1923–9, folder 2, Cass Gilbert Collection, New-York Historical Society.
2. Cass Gilbert to Hubert T. Parson, January 17, 1924, Personal Papers,

1923–9, folder 2, Cass Gilbert Collection, New-York Historical Society. I am grateful to Gail Fenske for providing me with additional information and for correcting my details.

3. Emily Gilbert to R. W. G. Vail, director of the New-York Historical Society, June 3, 1957, Gilbert File, Legal Records, New-York Historical Society Archives. Permission to quote graciously granted by Julia Gilbert Post (Mrs. Walter A.) Bastedo.
4. Sarah Bradford Landau, *George B. Post, Architect: Picturesque Designer and Determined Realist* (New York: Monacelli Press, 1998).
5. Typescript of poem beginning "Oh, the Architect bold," December 20, 1901, Personal Papers, 1923–9, folder 6, Cass Gilbert Collection, New-York Historical Society.
6. Invitation from Charles Dana Gibson to Cass Gilbert, n.d., and letters from Edwin Howland Blashfield to Cass Gilbert, including those quoted of August 17, 1907, and January 26, 1909, Personal Papers, 1923–9, folder 4, Cass Gilbert Collection, New-York Historical Society. Cass Gilbert to Edwin Howland Blashfield, January 18, 1908, Gilbert File, Edwin Howland Blashfield Papers, New-York Historical Society.
7. Walter Damrosch to Cass Gilbert, March 13, 1919, Personal Papers, 1923–9, folder 6, Cass Gilbert Collection, New-York Historical Society.
8. Cass Gilbert to Edwin Howland Blashfield, March 2, 1909, Gilbert File, Edwin Howland Blashfield Papers, New-York Historical Society.
9. Acker, Merrall, and Condit, Statement, February 1919; "Regenerated Beverages" flyer, dated as "Rec'd Dec 1922," Personal Papers, 1915–33, folder 1, Cass Gilbert Collection, New-York Historical Society.
10. Draft of telegram message from Cass Gilbert to George Pratt Ingersoll, February 13, 1919. Other communications referred to include George Pratt Ingersoll to Cass Gilbert, January 10, 1919, January 16, 1919, and February 14, 1919; Cass Gilbert to George Pratt Ingersoll, February 21, 1919, Personal Papers, 1915–33, folders 1, 4, and 5, Cass Gilbert Collection, New-York Historical Society.
11. Typed memo, April 2, 1924, Personal Papers, 1923–9, folder 1, Cass Gilbert Collection, New-York Historical Society.
12. Cablegram from "Cabert" to Cass Gilbert, and accompanying key, July 8, 1905, Personal Papers, 1904–6, folder 1, Cass Gilbert Collection, New-York Historical Society.
13. Cass Gilbert to Edwin Howland Blashfield, July 9, 1912, Gilbert File, Edwin Howland Blashfield Papers, New-York Historical Society.
14. F. W. Woolworth to Cass Gilbert, June 22, 1918, Personal Papers, 1915–33, folder 1, Cass Gilbert Collection, New-York Historical Society; Cass Gilbert to Sir Aston Webb, March 10, 1915, Personal Papers, 1915–33, folder 1, Cass

Gilbert Collection, New-York Historical Society; Cass Gilbert to Albert Jaegers, August 31, 1916, Personal Papers, 1923–9, folder 4, Cass Gilbert Collection, New-York Historical Society.

15. Julia Finch Gilbert to Cass Gilbert, January 22, 1923, Personal Papers, 1915–33, folder 1, Cass Gilbert Collection, New-York Historical Society.
16. Cass Gilbert to Samuel Gilbert, June 24, 1933, Personal Papers, 1915–33, folder 5, Cass Gilbert Collection, New-York Historical Society.
17. *New York Times,* May 18, 1934. The *Times* is here quoting from a tribute to Cass Gilbert by the Society of Arts and Sciences in 1931.
18. Quoted in his obituary, *New York Times,* May 18, 1934.
19. *New York Times,* May 18, 1934.
20. Cass Gilbert to Edwin Howland Blashfield, July 9, 1912, Gilbert File, Edwin Howland Blashfield Papers, New-York Historical Society.

ACKNOWLEDGMENTS

Inventing the Skyline owes its existence to Betsy Gotbaum, president; Ed Norris, chief operating officer; Paul Gunther, director of development; and Stewart Desmond, director of public affairs, whose untiring work in support of the New-York Historical Society made this project possible.

I am profoundly grateful for the help of many people whose efforts contributed to the publication of this book. Pamela Dewey, head of the historical society's department of prints, photographs, and architectural drawings during the editorial process, brought her project management skills and her wondrously even temper to the task of coordinating all procedures relating to the original architectural drawings reproduced for this book. It is due to Grace Hernandez, scrupulous editorial consultant, and indeed the most graceful of colleagues and friends, that this book was completed within a tight schedule. Our work together was seasoned with many happy moments that I will long savor. Sarah Grossman joined collections assistant Holly Hinman in hours of checking caption copy against the original images, always with great care and good humor. Sarah's calm efficiency with the page proofs saw me through that phase of the project. Laird Ogden and Nicole Wells smoothly passed the materials through the department of rights and reproductions. Glenn Castellano undertook all photography of items from the historical society's collections. Many colleagues on the library staff kindly assisted with their own expertise: Alan Balicki, Richard Fraser, Borinquen Gallo, Megan Hahn, Melissa Haley, Nina Nazionale, and James Polchin.

I am indebted to Mary Beth Betts, Barbara Christen, Gail Fenske, and Sharon Irish, Cass Gilbert experts of national stature, whose scholarship is the essence of this book. They kindly reviewed and corrected my preface, but I am solely responsible for its content. From far afield (email and fax machines be praised), they stayed in close touch with me as *Inventing the Skyline* took shape. I became editor of this book and a curatorial contributor to the exhibit in my capacity as the historical society's library director and former curator of manuscripts, rather than as an architectural scholar, a circumstance about which Mary Beth, Barbara, Gail, and Sharon were unfailingly gracious.

Hugh Hardy was most generous to provide the book with an introduction. He enlarges our comprehension of the academic response to Gilbert as well as of Gilbert's current status in the field.

I thank Julia Gilbert Post (Mrs. Walter A.) Bastedo, for kindly allowing me to quote from Emily Gilbert's correspondence.

Henry Hope Reed offered very helpful advice about Cass Gilbert's role in supporting the work of muralists and sculptors. Andrew Berner, librarian of the University Club of New York, cordially answered many questions.

At Columbia University Press, my sincere thanks go to William B. Strachan, president and director; Kate Wittenberg, editor-in-chief and publisher for the social sciences; her assistant, James Burger; Ronald C. Harris, assistant managing editor; and Linda Secondari, creative director, without whom the book would not exist. I am grateful to Anne R. Gibbons, copy editor, for her keen eye.

As the historical society's curator of architectural collections, Mary Beth Betts devoted a decade to improving the conditions of the collections under her purview, first under the leadership of Barbara Knowles Debs, with Holly Hotchner as museum director and Jean Ashton as library director, and then under Betsy Gotbaum, with Jack Rutland overseeing museum collections. Her years of work with Cass Gilbert's papers and her key role as an interpreter of Gilbert's work have been crucial to this project.

Before turning these acknowledgments over to Mary Beth, I send loving thanks to my daughter, Penelope, my heart's joy, for tolerating my late hours and suggesting that I read her this book instead of Dr. Seuss.

Margaret Heilbrun

I am in debt to many people for their assistance, comments, and thoughts. In particular, I deeply appreciate the efforts of Pamela Dewey, Margaret Heilbrun, Grace Hernandez, and Holly Hinman at the New-York Historical Society. Their competence and commitment made it possible for me to leave the challenges of the historical society for the rigors of the New York City Landmarks Preservation Commission with the knowledge that this project would be responsibly and intelligently completed. Additionally, the past and present staff of the department of prints, photographs, and architectural drawings at N-YHS, including Lynn Bodnar, Borinquen Gallo, Diana Kane, Dale Neighbors, Laird Ogden, Pat Paladines, and Wendy Shadwell, has assisted in the access and preservation of the Cass Gilbert Collection. Many past and present staff members of N-YHS have also assisted in conserving, photographing, and supporting the Cass Gilbert Collection and this project, particularly Alan Balicki, Glenn Castellano, Mary Cropley, Barbara Knowles Debs, Stewart Desmond, Martin Duus, Reba Fishman Snyder, Betsy Gotbaum, Paul Gunther, Holly Hotchner, Andrea Morgan, Ed Norris, Jack Rutland, Juliana Sciolla, Rebecca Streeter, and Nicole Wells. The collection has been made accessible through the efforts of the following interns: Jeffrey Aviles, Kevin Connolly, Hansel Diaz, Charles Krekelberg, Gaylin Lynch, Diana Slavit, and Paul Tapogna.

Conservators Konstanze Bachmann, Mindy Horn, and T. K. McClintock have brought many Cass Gilbert drawings back to life. My colleagues Angela Giral, Janet Parks of Avery Architectural Library, Ford Peatross of the Library of Congress, Morrison Hecksher, Catherine Hoover Voorsanger and Amelia Peck of the Metropolitan Museum of Art, and Peter Simmons of the Museum of the City of New York have provided guidance, resources, and moral support. Scholars Rosemarie Haag Bletter, Geoffrey Blodgett, William Clark, Andrew S. Dolkart, Sarah Landau, Marjorie Pearson, the late Eugene A. Santomasso, Richard Stapleford, L. Bailey Van Hook, Carol Willis, and Mary Woods have inspired my work but should not be held responsible for any of my errors.

Gail Fenske and Sharon Irish have generously shared their knowledge of Cass Gilbert with me over several years and have been highly esteemed colleagues in this project. Barbara Christen has contributed to this project as a staff member at the New-York Historical Society, as an editor, and as a Cass Gilbert scholar. My essay and the entire book could not have happened without the generous support, meticulous scholarship, and intelligence of these three scholars.

Finally, for his insights into the architecture profession, his intellectual and moral support at all times, and his tolerance of and, at times, interest in Cass Gilbert, I thank my husband, the arch-modernist, Charles Ayes.

Mary Beth Betts

BIOGRAPHICAL TIME LINE

CASS GILBERT, 1859–1934

1859	Born, November 29, Zanesville, Ohio
1868	Family moves to St. Paul, Minnesota
1876	Begins architectural training in St. Paul office of Abraham Radcliffe
1878–9	Studies architecture at the Massachusetts Institute of Technology, Boston
1880	Enters McKim, Mead, and White's office in New York City
1881	Founding member of the Architectural League of New York
1882	Moves back to St. Paul, Minnesota
1885	Forms partnership with James Knox Taylor in St. Paul
1887	Marries Julia Tappen Finch
1891	Partnership with James Knox Taylor ends
1895	Wins design competition for Minnesota state capitol
1899	Moves architectural practice and family to New York City
	Wins competition for U.S. Custom House, New York City
1900	Broadway Chambers Building, New York City, completed

1902	Essex County Courthouse, Newark, New Jersey, completed
1904	Designs Festival Hall and Art Building (later the St. Louis Art Museum) for the Louisiana Purchase Exposition, St. Louis, Missouri
1905	Minnesota state capitol completed
1907	U.S. Custom House completed
	West Street Building, New York City, completed
	Keeler Tavern, Ridgefield, Connecticut, purchased as country home
1908	Finney Chapel, Oberlin College, Ohio, completed
	Elected president of the American Institute of Architects
1909	Closes St. Paul office permanently
1910	Appointed to National Commission of Fine Arts by President Taft
1911	Appointed architect for Oberlin College
	Ives Memorial Library (later New Haven Free Public Library) New Haven, Connecticut, completed
1913	F. W. Woolworth Company Building, New York City, completed
	Wins competition for Detroit Public Library
	Elected president of Architectural League of New York
1915	Cox Administration Building, Oberlin College, completed
1917	Allen Memorial Art Building, Oberlin College, completed
1918	Elected president of the National Institute of Arts and Letters
1919	U.S. Army Supply Base, Brooklyn, completed
1921	Detroit Public Library completed
1925	Allen Memorial Hospital, Oberlin College, completed
1926	George Washington [Hudson River] Bridge schemes proposed
	Elected president of the National Academy of Design
1928	New York Life Insurance Building, New York City, completed

1930	New York County Lawyers' Association Building, New York City, completed
1931	Theological Group, Oberlin College, completed
	Receives Gold Medal for Architecture for the design of the Woolworth Building from the Society of Arts and Sciences
1934	Dies, May 17, in England
1935	U.S. Supreme Court Building, Washington, D.C., completed

INTRODUCTION

Hugh Hardy, FAIA

In the 1950s a whole generation of professionals was taught that only modernism could offer the true path to good design. Any association with traditional architecture was abhorrent. Ornament was ridiculed, and each design had to be an exercise in "pure form." Reference to historical style was denounced as a misguided embrace of the past. This modernist revisionism rendered many American architects invisible to students. Cass Gilbert was one of them. Though he designed some of America's most significant buildings, by midcentury his structures were held up as proof of "where American architecture went wrong" and his name was seldom mentioned.

This breach in architectural thought is only now being healed, as the merits of traditional form have become apparent to an increasing audience, both public and professional. Fueled by pressure from citizens bored with faceless monotony, the preservation movement has resurrected the reputation and restored the work of an entire period of American architecture, with Cass Gilbert in its forefront. Because my firm (Hardy Holzman Pfeiffer Associates) has pursued restoration of two of his early buildings, the St. Louis Art Museum, built for the Louisiana Purchase Exposition of 1904, and the New Haven Free Public Library, 1908–11, we are familiar with the sophistication and authority of his designs, and I welcome this presentation of his work with particular interest.

FIGURE 1.1

The New Haven (Connecticut) Free Public Library building (formerly known as the Ives Memorial Library), with the recent addition (right) designed by Hardy Holzman Pfeiffer Associates (HHPA). HHPA also undertook renovation of Gilbert's original structure.

(Photograph by Cervin Robinson, courtesy Hardy Holzman Pfeiffer Associates)

It is a cautionary tale that someone so prominent in his profession could be completely lost to view. Two of his contemporaries, Charles McKim and Daniel Burnham, also made substantial contributions to architecture by word and deed. Both are better known. But Gilbert took greater risks, interpreting the past with designs that never imitated, never used the same combination of forms. McKim, uneasy with high-rise structures, went so far as to make direct copies of classical buildings, adapting them to new uses, such as the great ticket hall in Pennsylvania Station, which replicated the Baths of Caracalla. Burnham was not shy about designing commercial structures and used a classical vocabulary to horizontally layer his high-rises. But Gilbert, by employing Gothic to express verticality, produced a completely new skyline silhouette in lower Manhattan with the Woolworth Building.

Gilbert also made lasting contributions to architecture through the organizations he helped to launch and lead. Although he eventually became part of the core of professional life in the United States, he began work outside the eastern establishment, finding its existing institutions too exclusive. Instead, he championed more broadly based support of the profession, which included talent from across the country. He served as president of the national American Institute of Architects and advised the federal government on the arts through the Council of Fine Arts, appointed to its presidency first by Theodore Roosevelt, then William Howard Taft. In New York he was a founder of the Architectural League and the American Academy in Rome (with Charles McKim). He helped organize, and presided over, the Institute of Arts and Letters, and was president of the National Academy of Design. You can sense his influence when, in 1918, it was said about the Architectural League, "Its purpose is, and always has been, to establish more friendly relations between the architects, the decorative painters, the sculptors, and the landscape architects, and since its non-resident membership is large it will act as a focal point to which men from other cities will be drawn and from which they may gather much information of value to them."[1]

Aside from creating buildings with historical allusions, Gilbert was mindful of their physical surroundings, using ambitious master plans to position his structures. Sensitivity to context distinguishes his work and is reflected in the grand, landscaped boulevard that links the New Haven Green with his train station for the New York, New Haven, and Hartford Railroad. It enhanced the prominence of both structures, incorporating adjacent individual buildings into an urban vision. At Oberlin College he created similar links among existing and proposed buildings so the campus would become one coherent entity. The first, after L'Enfant, to participate in a developed, monumental vision for Washington, D.C. (before the McMillan Commission's efforts), Gilbert saw the plan as an opportunity to express a unified vision of democracy's symbolic place.

Gilbert believed it was possible to respond to market forces in human terms. Whatever the program, he immersed his buildings' occupants in sensory experience. He chose forms, materials, colors, landscape, sculpture, and murals to compose visual symphonies that conducted the observer through a grand progression of spaces. These were buildings to be used by everyone, buildings whose generosity of spirit and directness of expression immediately involved their inhabitants in the richness of their imagery and execution. Too often discussed only in relation to their style, Gilbert's buildings reveal more than the ornamental delights of surface manipulation; they use historical references to properly convey program ideas. He made the vertical vocabulary of Gothic into the apt expression of height for the Woolworth Building and was at the same time astute enough to give his client a distinctive identity in the landscape of downtown New York. In Washington, he consciously selected the visual language of ancient Rome to link the Supreme Court with the legacy of Roman law, maneuvering classical forms to house contemporary functions.

It was this ability to use traditional forms to impart meaning to present-day purposes that gave Gilbert's architecture its prominent place in public appreciation. More than a costume pageant, his work employs classical or medieval references to join America's ambitions with Europe's civic achievements. The history of Western civilization was used to help identify and ennoble our houses of government, courts of law, libraries, and train stations. The invention of totally new forms for this purpose would not have generated buildings an immigrant nation could call its own.

Now that modernism itself has acquired a history, the rejection of Cass Gilbert as an important part of America's cultural legacy holds a certain irony. Although modernism continues to deny direct association with the classical language, it is seeking ways to connect with its own past and to create more expressive, sculptural forms. Designers who adhere to the tenets of simplicity and abstraction do so pursuing a less rigid, more wide-ranging modernist design vocabulary. For these professionals, architecture is once again developing a common language with which each generation can build upon the work of those past.

Many options are open to a new generation of architects attempting to bridge the gap created by modernism. With a few exceptions, current practice does not suggest literally going back to the forms and associations of Gilbert's work. Construction techniques, the large scale of contemporary buildings, an expansion of the technology for creature comforts, our own sense of time and place—to say nothing of building-code issues or the accomplishments of modernism itself—permit no easy return to Gilbert's design ideas. Nonetheless, careful study of his buildings will disclose the clarity of their plans, an intimate relation between outside and inside, plus a fearless pursuit of the decorative arts: all achieved within a consciously chosen historical setting. Viewed in abstract, this approach offers indispensable instruction, even for modernists. Enjoy the work of this forgotten master in the pages that follow. See how his interpretation of tradition is again part of a larger view of architecture, one now embraced across America.

Notes

1. "Editorial and Other Comment," *Architecture* (February 1918): 40.

INVENTING THE SKYLINE

THE ARCHITECTURE OF CASS GILBERT

CHAPTER ONE

Sharon Irish

CASS GILBERT IN PRACTICE, 1882–1934

"Maxims for My Office Organization"

Remember that dignity of bearing commands respect—familiarity breeds contempt.

Remember that as long as you are in this office you are not acting for yourself alone. My interests are deeply involved in everything you say or do, or have [left] unsaid or undone.

In conducting business (especially for the office) never forget that the greatest danger arises from cocksure pride.

Beware of over-confidence; especially in matters of structure.

I don't expect you to know everything. In fact, I don't want you to know everything, for, if you did, you would not be working here and you would have that pride of opinion "that goeth before a fall" and that "haughty spirit that goeth before destruction" [*sic*].

It is only the young and callow and ignorant that admire rashness. Think before you speak. Know your subject.

I expect you to have *intelligent ignorance*. It is much safer, and in the end more successful. The kind of ignorance that is conscious of its own limitations and dangers, and the kind of intelligence that will cause you to seek to know all about the subject before you act, and to move forward always cautiously and only after having explored every line that a trained and active imagination can suggest and taken counsel with men who *do know.* Acquire knowledge, it is your capital. Use your own time for this purpose.

Be cautious. Do not be afraid.

Be slow to express an opinion as to anything—especially as to tangible things like material, cost, design, construction, and policy of procedure. Do not hurry. Do not delay.

Remember *always* that you do not act for yourself alone, and that a single false step may ruin the work of two lives—mine for the past and future—yours for the future. Your care for my interests should be equal to what you would expect if I represented you. Not alone because they are *my* interests, but because your interests and my interests are closely allied as long as you are here.

Cass Gilbert[1]

Cass Gilbert practiced architecture during a period of rapid change in the United States, a time when an individual architect could create buildings in growing urban areas and often with new technology that would fulfill new demands—functional, stylistic, or civic—with few guidelines from within or without the profession. No one, however, acts in isolation, particularly in architecture, and Cass Gilbert was no exception.[2] With contractors, engineers, and real estate agents, he worked in the practical, sometimes risky, realm of business and the sometimes frustrating arena of government, as well as for educational institutions. These groups required buildings, and to provide them Gilbert needed inventive solutions, flexible approaches, and good teamwork.

Gilbert's commission for the Minnesota state capitol (St. Paul, 1895–1905, fig. 1.1) serves as a good example of his take-charge approach. The Minnesota legislature decided in 1893 to build a new statehouse. Architects objected to the terms the legislature proposed for the competition for the capitol because, among other things, the winning architect was to receive compensation of only 2.5 percent of the building cost, which was not to exceed $2 million. The legislators also wanted to buy the design outright and avoid having the architect oversee the building construction. Gilbert was president of the Minnesota chapter of the American Institute of Architects (AIA) in 1894, when this controversy peaked.[3] Gilbert became the AIA spokesman and met with the Board of State Capitol Commissioners to object to the legislative limitations. While the AIA did not prevail in time for

FIGURE I.I

Cass Gilbert atop Minnesota state capitol during construction, May 9, 1901.

(Courtesy Minnesota Historical Society)

the first competition in 1894 (which some architects, including Gilbert, boycotted), it received a second chance. The board eventually rejected all the designs sent in the first round and prepared for a second competition in 1895, which accommodated most of the local AIA's wishes, including higher fees and superintendence.[4] Gilbert submitted what became his winning entry for the design of the Minnesota state capitol.

For the capitol commission, Gilbert pushed for guidelines favorable to architects, then he put forward a winning design, and finally, he convinced the state to build it, with all the embellishments that he had planned. In leading the battle over rules governing the competition for the design of the state capitol, Gilbert helped establish standards for professional practice in the state, gaining him personal attention, both positive and negative.[5] Not incidentally, Gilbert established his national reputation with Minnesota's marble monument.[6]

Gilbert sought to integrate efficient planning, economical construction, and artistic effect in every work. The integration of art and function and the coordination of artists, contractors, engineers, and clients required excellent organizational and communication skills. Gilbert exercised his leadership in several arenas: as an arts advocate, as a spokesman for the architectural profession, and as a business executive who managed his firm, often in conjunction with other large construction or real estate enterprises.

Gilbert's Early Office Team

Cass Gilbert had only one partner in his entire career: James Knox Taylor (1857–1929?), a boyhood schoolmate and a fellow student at the Massachusetts Institute of Technology (1878–9).[7] Their partnership in St. Paul lasted from 1885 until 1891. (Taylor moved to Philadelphia in 1892.) Gilbert viewed Taylor's business acumen as complementary to his own considerable drawing skills and charisma. After Taylor's departure, Gilbert remained in their offices on the fifth floor of the Endicott Building in downtown St. Paul, a building designed by the firm in 1889 and completed in 1891 (fig. 1.2).

When Gilbert began his practice in 1885 with Taylor, they hired boys to help with the many repetitive tasks and paperwork. As business increased, Gilbert and Taylor hired young men who probably had some drafting skills, but they were essentially apprentices. They acquired experience and polish in the firm. By 1895 Gilbert's office consisted of young men he had hired locally: George Carsley (dates unknown), Thomas Gannett Holyoke (1866–1925), and John R. Rachac (1873?–1951, known as

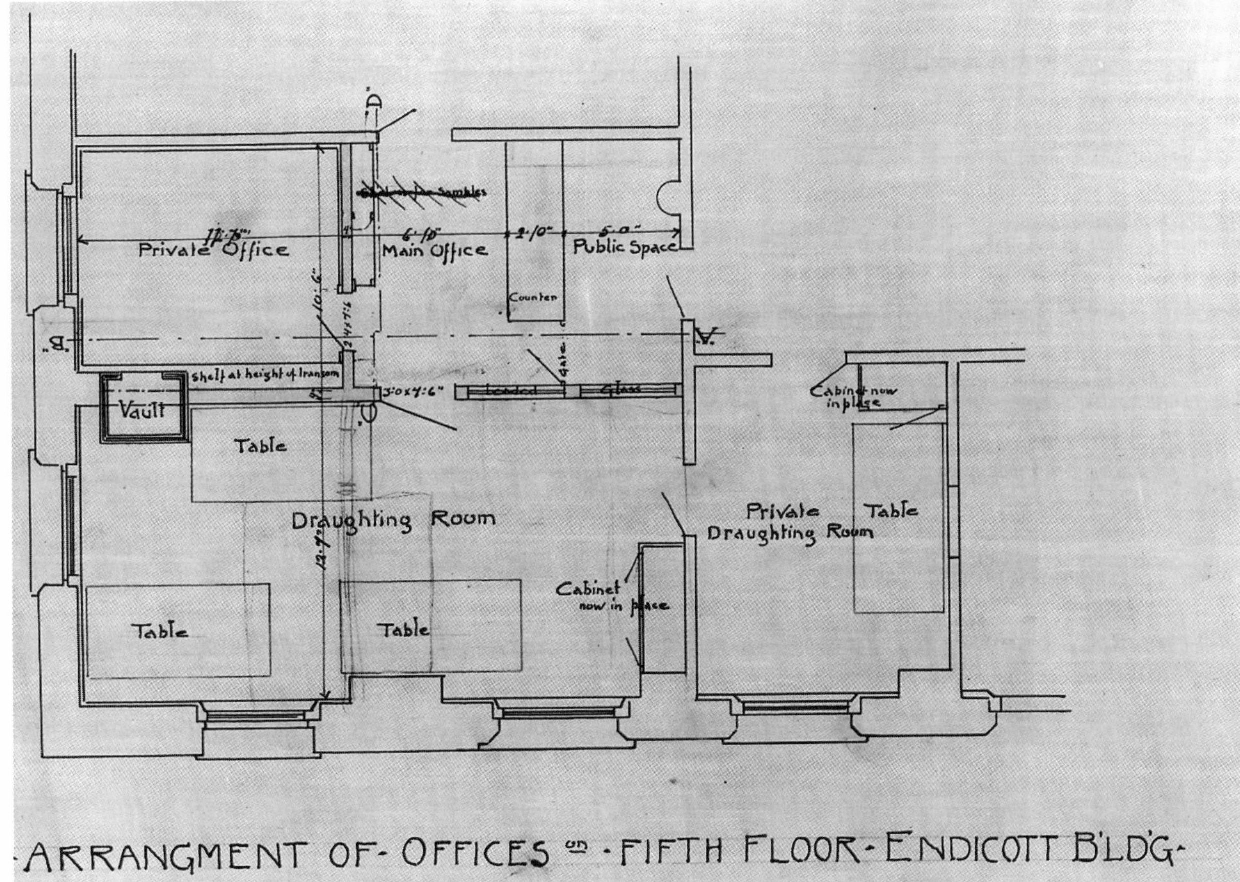

FIGURE I.2

Plan of Endicott Offices, December 3, 1891. Ink on linen, 29 in. × 20 in. *(Cass Gilbert Collection, courtesy New-York Historical Society, neg. no. 72888)*

FIGURE 1.3

Cass Gilbert (seated on stool) in Minnesota office with staff, ca. 1900. *(Courtesy Minnesota Historical Society)*

John Rockart after 1902).[8] Gilbert was a mentor for many of his employees, both in Minnesota and later in New York (fig. 1.3). Attending architecture school was not yet a necessity for getting work in an architect's office: many simply learned on the job, sometimes working without pay for the first few months. Scrapbooks, undated and haphazardly organized, that are now in Gilbert's office archives would have offered examples for study. Each page is crammed with clipped images of contemporary and historic architecture of the United States and Europe (fig. 1.4). Gilbert also maintained a library.[9]

If a particular employee had the talent and ambition, Cass Gilbert helped him travel to Europe and even attend the Parisian Ecole des Beaux-Arts, the revered center of architectural education for many Americans in the late nineteenth and early twentieth centuries. For example, Samuel-Stevens Haskell (1871–1913), who started in Gilbert's St. Paul office as a boy in about 1883 and enrolled in MIT for the academic year 1890–1, left for Paris in 1894 and attended the Ecole des Beaux-Arts for four years with Gilbert's help. Gilbert then hired him in 1899 to manage his New York office. Haskell moved into independent practice in 1903.

Haskell was not the only Gilbert employee to study abroad. Thomas Holyoke, only seven years younger than Gilbert, traveled to Europe with Gilbert's help between 1890 and 1892, having begun in the office in December 1889. Holyoke was back on Gilbert's payroll in 1895 (the year in which Gilbert won the Minnesota capitol commission). In 1900 he started an independent practice in St. Paul. He also conducted business for Gilbert until 1909, when Gilbert closed his St. Paul office. A third employee, John Rockart, left for Europe in 1899 and remained there for two years, returning to work for Gilbert in 1902.[10]

Gilbert's men who had studied in Paris provided contacts that led to other French-trained architects' being brought to New York, a tactic Gilbert sometimes used in competitions. Steve Haskell imported his friend Ernest Hébrard in 1899 to render the U.S. Custom House design; another employee, Thornton Carson, was the liaison between Léon Murier and Gilbert's office in 1904. At least four men who had been Ecole students worked on competitions in Gilbert's office: Hébrard, Murier, Georges-Eugène Thiré, and Donn Barber.[11]

To guide a team of men—many of whom were temporary, some quite inexperienced—through a design process under deadline required an overall vision of the final outcome, a clear division of labor, and some reward for those involved in the process. In Gilbert's office, Steve Haskell, Ernest Guilbert, George Wells, and then Thomas R. Johnson were likely the men who set the tone in the drafting room and cultivated a positive atmosphere.[12] At a staff banquet held to celebrate the holidays and the commissions of 1901, men posed in togalike costumes and laurel wreaths, fostering a camaraderie that may not often have thrived within Gilbert's earshot (fig. 1.5).[13]

Cass Gilbert's New York Office

Cass Gilbert opened an office in Manhattan when he received the commission for the Broadway Chambers office building on lower Broadway in 1899. While Gilbert enjoyed the allegiance of at least half a dozen men for most of his practice, he relied heavily on temporary personnel when business was brisk.[14] At the busiest times in his firm, during construction of the F. W. Woolworth Company Building between 1911 and 1913, for example, about twenty to twenty-five men were working. His ledger books are full of names of people who were paid for one or two months and then disappear from the payroll; the same names sometimes crop up again several years later. "Sometimes," Gilbert wrote, "I will confess the thought has been in my mind to call in some of the young fellows like Holyoke, Haskell, Rockart or [George] Wells who have been with me for so many years and make a regular partnership, but my temperament has always deterred me from doing so."[15] Instead, Gilbert hired men who were team players and followed his lead.

Thomas R. Johnson (1872–1915) was clearly a leader in Gilbert's office, and with his early death, Gilbert's practice lost his design skills and facility with drawing, as well as his ease with people, which endeared him both to his boss and those he supervised. Hired in April 1900 at a salary of $140 a month, Johnson rose quickly in the office, earning $160 a month by December 1900. By August 1909 he was earning $250 a month. At the time of Johnson's death, Gilbert noted that he had played a vital role in many of the firm's designs.[16]

When Samuel-Stevens Haskell left to set up his own practice in 1903 in Montreal, Gilbert wrote him at length about "the relations of the different fellows in the office. . . . Mr. Wells . . . will take charge of matters during my absence from New York. He will, of course, as heretofore, take charge of the supervision of construction." Gilbert went on to explain that Ernest Guilbert would be in charge of the Essex County Courthouse and the American Insurance Company Building, both in Newark, New Jersey, while Johnson gave his full attention to Festival Hall at the Louisiana Purchase Exposition. John Rockart would continue to conduct the firm's work in

THE GLOBE BUILDING, MINNEAPOLIS.
E. Townsend Mix, Architect.

irrelevant beauties

THE PORTLAND OPENED TO THE PUBLIC APRIL, 1890.

ENTRANCE TO NEW YORK LIFE BUILDING, ST. PAUL.

VESTIBULE OF NEW YORK LIFE BUILDING, MINNEAPOLIS.

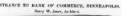

BANK OF MINNESOTA, ST. PAUL.—Wilcox and Johnston, Architects.

PORCH IN ST. PAUL.—A. H. Stem, Architect.

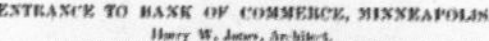

ENTRANCE TO BANK OF COMMERCE, MINNEAPOLIS.
Henry W. Jones, Architect.

Mannheimer's Store.

PORCH IN ST PAUL.—Mould and McNichol, Architects.

PORTE COCHÈRE, ST. PAUL.—Wilcox and Johnson, Architects.

A CHELSEA DOORWAY.

ENTRANCE TO TRINITY CHURCH RECTORY, BOSTON.
H. H. RICHARDSON, Architect.

HOTEL IMPERIAL,
BROADWAY AND 32d STREET, NEW YORK.
ABSOLUTELY FIRE-PROOF.
STAFFORD & WHITAKER.

AUPPEGARD, NORMANDIE BY CHARLES G. BACHMANN.

AN APARTMENT BUILDING OF ST. PAUL.

FIGURE 1.4

Pages from scrapbook assembled by Cass Gilbert.

(Cass Gilbert Collection, courtesy New-York Historical Society, neg. nos. 53122, 53120)

FIGURE 1.5

Cass Gilbert *(standing, with right hand resting on table)* at staff party, 1901.

(Courtesy Avery Architectural and Fine Arts Library, Columbia University)

the West. "Confidentially," Gilbert noted, "I will say to you that I feel there is no one man in the office whose temperament, training and experience fits *[sic]* him to handle the whole office alone. Wells comes nearer to it than the others. . . . I have not, however, given him full control of the draughting room or placed him in charge of the planning and design."[17] As it turned out, Ernest Guilbert headed the drafting room briefly after Haskell left. Guilbert had entered Gilbert's office in December 1900 with a recommendation from a Minneapolis architect.[18] From April to July 1904 he took leave to travel in Europe. By May 1905 Guilbert teamed up with another Gilbert staff member, James Oscar Betelle, and they left the office to start their own firm. Guilbert and Betelle became successful New Jersey architects, responsible for many schools and banks.[19]

Aymar Embury II (1880–1966) was another Gilbert employee who, after a short stint in the firm, became fairly well known by the next decade. Embury began in the office in January 1902 and worked on the Louisiana Purchase Exposition and the Essex County Courthouse. He left in May 1903. Embury, associated with Charles C. Haight at Yale and with Cope and Stewardson, became known for his renderings in Gothic styles. In the 1940s Embury was consulting architect for the New York City Parks Department and, upon the recommendation of Robert Moses (then the parks commissioner), he helped renovate and expand the Metropolitan Museum of Art.[20]

After World War I, Gilbert traveled for relaxation more frequently and his buildings were less a reflection of him than of the team with which he had been working to carry on his business. By 1925 his letterhead listed John Rockart, Eugene Ward, Samuel A. McGuire, Cass Gilbert Jr., Rex D. Read, Fred Stickel, and Joseph T. Mohn. Rockart and Ward had been with Gilbert off and on since 1891 and 1894, respectively. Gilbert's only son was in the unfortunate position of trying to follow in his father's footsteps. McGuire had worked with Gilbert since at least the Woolworth Building project (1911). Read was the office manager and Stickel was head of the drafting room. Most received some share of the firm's profits.[21] The work of this team included the New York Life Insurance Company Building (1925–8), the New York County Lawyers' Association (1930), the Federal Courthouse at Foley Square (1929–36), and the U.S. Supreme Court Building (1928–35).

Job Hustling

Getting work, even in prosperous building times, was a constant endeavor. Gilbert brought in enough jobs throughout his career to provide well for his family and, usually, to support his long-time staff members. He cultivated clients, joined real estate developers in their plans, and lobbied politicians. As much as he disliked them, he also entered and often won competitions. Between 1894 and 1905, for example, he entered eight competitions and won five of them: the Minnesota state capitol (St. Paul, 1895), the U.S. Custom House (New York City, 1899; plate 1), the Union Club (New York City, 1901; fig. 1.6), the Essex County Courthouse (Newark, N.J., 1901), and Madison High School (Wisconsin, 1905). He lost the Washington University (St. Louis, 1899), Carnegie Technical Schools (Pittsburgh, 1903), and Wisconsin state capitol (Madison, 1905) competitions.[22] He described the giddy exhaustion of the last-minute preparations for the Washington University scheme:

> We dusted the drawings with a rabbit's foot, laid upon them lucky coins, tossed a new quarter three times and got heads twice, put them in a huge tin tube and sent them forth. A procession marched all around them before the tube was filled, with one man pounding on the tube for a drum and another banging its cover for cymbals. The office was a pandemonium of French and jargon and songs and enthusiasm, while the typewriter clicked away at her machine and I finished the last carefully rounded phrases of the letter to the Board that went with the drawings. Such is the end of La charette.[23]

Despite the rabbit's foot and the lucky coins, Gilbert did not win.

The architect was frequently frustrated by the expenditure of time and money for no gain in competitions. "This whole competition system is wrong—and I'm sick of it," he wrote in 1899. "It is too much to ask a man to spend months of study and work and thousands of dollars all on chance then to have to work by political methods to hold what you may have won fairly by merit."[24] Nevertheless, competitions provided Gilbert with jobs, especially at the beginning of his career. In each case he incurred considerable expense, paying staff overtime for work into the night and on holidays.

Gilbert was always pleased to get work without having to enter a competition. He noted that about one commission emerged out of every seven leads.[25] Usually those commissions came to him through contacts made in previous jobs. Of the West Street Building job, received in 1905, he wrote: "I have just been commissioned as the architect of a great skyscraper here [in New York City] which will be on the river front near the Cortlandt Street ferry. . . . It was given to me without any competition and that is the

FIGURE 1.6
The Union Club (demolished), New York City, ca. 1903. Unidentified photographer.
(Cass Gilbert Collection, courtesy New-York Historical Society, neg. no. 59199)

way that work ought to come in." In the case of the West Street Building, Gilbert knew John Peirce, a contractor on the 1899 U.S. Custom House and a member of the West Street Improvement Company. Gilbert knew Howard Carroll, the West Street Building's owner, possibly through a mutual friend, Samuel Thomas.[26]

On occasion Gilbert only got a job if he agreed to work in association with another firm. He resisted this arrangement, wanting jobs on his own terms. His admonitions to John DuFais, the architect with whom he built New York City's Union Club (1901–3), are indicative of his attitudes. Initially he wanted to buy out DuFais, paying him for competition expenses and an additional five thousand dollars in cash. DuFais refused, however, and arranged to have an office adjoining Gilbert's. Then Gilbert explained: "I did not expect to do any manual work on the drawings, any more than in my other practice; . . . I was willing to give to [the Union Club] the same amount of time as I would proportionately for other work in the office, but not otherwise; and . . . there were times when I must be uninterrupted and free from intrusion in my own office, even though I were not doing other work."[27] DuFais was amenable to this arrangement. Gilbert's statement indicates that by 1901 a system was in place that he used throughout his practice: he did little "manual work" on the drawings; he divided his time among the various jobs in the office; and he kept himself aloof from the day-to-day activities, both to maintain perspective and keep a clear division between him and his staff.

On balance, Cass Gilbert did very well financially as an architect.[28] In 1901 Gilbert reported that he had $6 million worth of building under construction; at a 5 percent fee, or $300,000, Gilbert would have been able to run his business and be very comfortable. The most highly paid men in his office at that time earned less than $2,500 per year.[29] By 1932 Gilbert drew an annual salary of $36,000 from his firm, and that did not include income from his investments.[30]

Raising Standards

Throughout his career, Gilbert aimed to raise and uphold design standards. He looked to education as a means to improve design in America. In a letter to Andrew Carnegie about an endowment to fund lectures, traveling libraries, and scholarships for the AIA, he declared, "What America needs now is not *more architects* but *better ones* and it is only by the education of younger men that this result can be obtained." Gilbert did not limit his sights to future architects, arguing that training should be extended to em-

FIGURE 1.7
Essex County Courthouse interior showing *Mercy* and *Power* murals by Edwin Howland Blashfield, 1906. Unidentified photographer.
(Cass Gilbert Collection, courtesy New-York Historical Society, neg. 72889)

ployees of manufacturers of building materials, such as ornamental iron and terra-cotta. "Draftsmen and designers in such establishments should have a knowledge of architectural style and precedent so that their work shall be properly designed."[31] As one who worked closely with artisans of ornamental iron and terra-cotta, Gilbert wrote from experience.

In a sense, Cass Gilbert's office bridged the two worlds of theory and practice. The compositional methods of the Ecole des Beaux-Arts stressed precedent and theory, while in the United States, theory was often ignored in the headlong rush to build, and build quickly.[32] Still, Gilbert wanted those buildings to be of the highest quality, so he made sure he had reliable and well-paid superintendents on site to oversee the construction of his designs. To George Wells, who helped supervise the Custom House construction with John H. Sheridan, he advised: "Hold them [the contractor] strictly to the contract, and no matter how many times you have a thing done over insist upon it until it is right. Do this no matter how much they protest."[33]

Outstanding designs came off the drafting boards of Gilbert's office, among them, the Minnesota state capitol, the U.S. Custom House, the Woolworth Building, and the St. Louis Public Library. Each of these works was distinguished by sculpture, tilework, and other artistry, inspired by both the American beaux arts style and the Arts and Crafts movement. The beaux arts style originated from the Ecole des Beaux-Arts, where designs were based on historical precedents within a hierarchy of building types. By the end of the nineteenth century many beaux arts designers were also concerned with urbanism, the way in which individual buildings fit into the city.[34] The Arts and Crafts movement was a diffuse but determined effort to preserve handcrafted design and elevate the taste of the general public.[35] Gilbert's efforts primarily contributed to the beaux arts style, but his designs benefited from the Arts and Crafts approach as well. He teamed up with decorative ironworkers, mosaicists, carvers, sculptors, and muralists to embellish his work. The artists who worked with Gilbert benefited from their association with him and in turn gave his designs an elegance and distinction through careful detailing and hands-on techniques (fig. 1.7, plate 2).

While committed to raising standards, Gilbert was ambivalent about beaux arts design methods. He himself had attended the beaux arts-influenced MIT for just a year (1878–9), had traveled for a few months in Europe, and then had taken a job as a draftsman in 1880 in McKim, Mead, and White's New York office. When it seemed expedient, he hired highly skilled French draftsmen; otherwise he wanted American architecture to grow out of American needs. To Francis Swales, Gilbert explained: "I believe hearti-

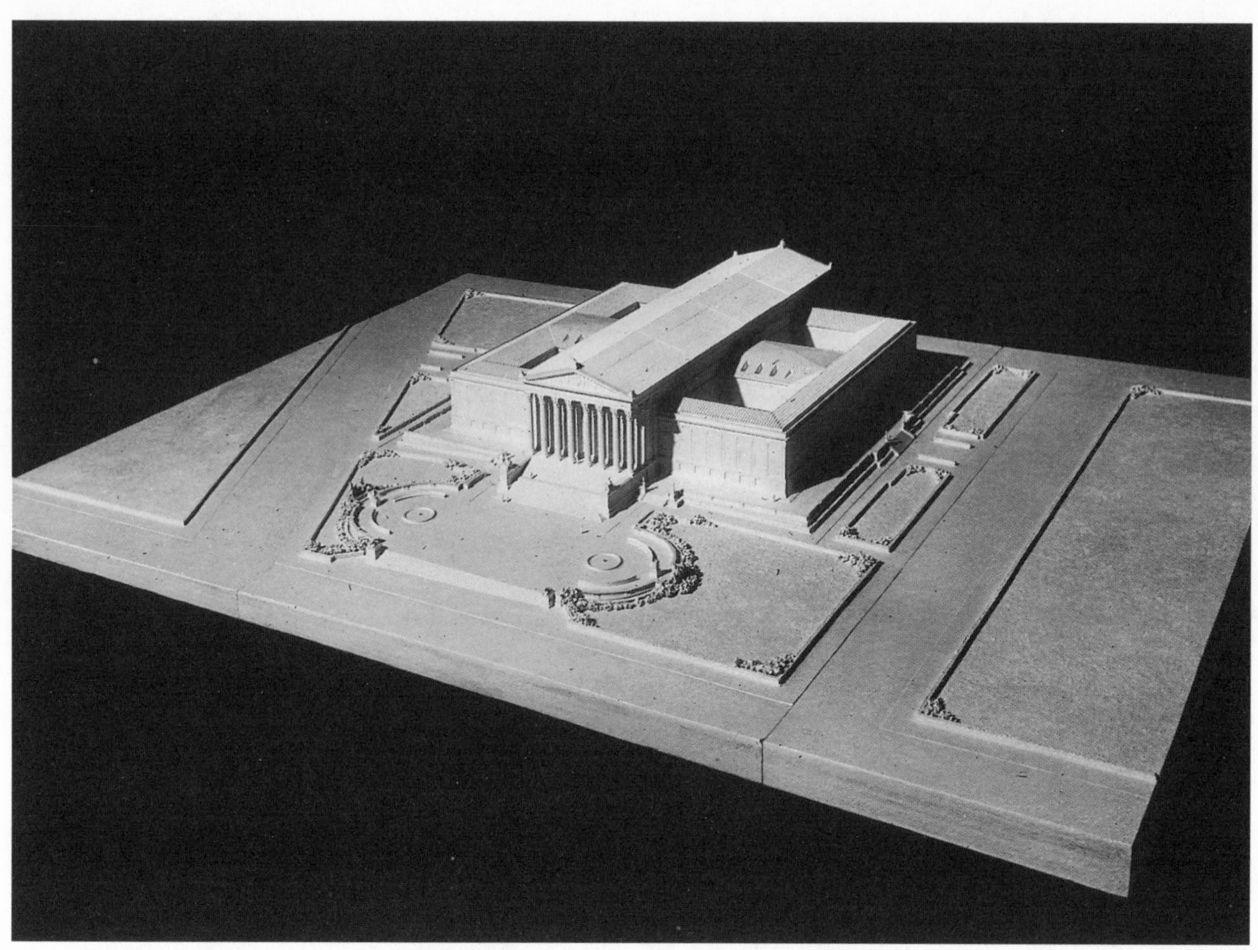

FIGURE 1.8

Photograph of model of the U.S. Supreme Court building, ca. 1928.

(Cass Gilbert Collection, courtesy New-York Historical Society, neg. no. 72890)

ly in the general training of the Ecole des Beaux-Arts which Mr. [Eugene] Letang [of MIT] so admirably represented, but I think the training that is desirable for France is not always usable in America. . . . I believe that our modern problems such as the skyscraper and the railroad building should be wrought out in harmony with the needs and the structural materials and that out of this will grow the vital and beautiful architecture."[36]

To ensure that the results of his busy architectural practice were indeed beautiful, Gilbert used a number of strategies. Building, of course, involved more than translating drawings into finished products.[37] One technique Gilbert used to test his ideas was to build models. For the Custom House commission, Gilbert had a full-scale plaster model made of the elevation to check the proportions of the ornament in relation to the mass of the building.[38] Models were also used for the Austin, Nichols and Company Warehouse to help the clients understand the design and persuade them of the efficacy of Gilbert's solution.[39] Gilbert's office had a model of the Supreme Court made as well, probably as a means of public education, allowing people to visualize their Court by viewing the model on display (fig. 1.8).

Beyond the confines of his office, Gilbert continued to pursue the goal of raising professional standards and directed many organizations. He was an organizer of the Architectural League in New York in 1881, serving as its president in 1913–4. Gilbert helped incorporate the American Academy in Rome in 1905.[40] As president of the national American Institute of Architects from 1908 to 1909, Gilbert sought to increase membership during his tenure from eight hundred to one thousand.[41] National leadership positions allowed Gilbert to press for improvement in the profession, by working within the organization and forming alliances with related groups.

As an initial member of the Council of Fine Arts, he advised the federal government on the arts. In 1909 President Theodore Roosevelt appointed him council president; he was reappointed in 1910 by President William Taft and served until 1916. Gilbert's national stature helped him maintain contacts with the Royal Institute of British Architects and with the International Congress of Architects. Toward the end of his life he worked on behalf of the restoration of the Parthenon and advocated banning tall buildings from Athens.[42] Further, Gilbert was the first architect elected to serve as president of the National Academy of Design (1926–32; fig. 1.9). In that role, he laid the foundation for the Edwin A. Abbey Fund to support professorships in mural painting. As a leader in organizations and in his own practice, Gilbert fostered the careers of artists and artisans, as well as advocating internationally on behalf of quality architecture.

"Practical Economy with Architectural Beauty"

No matter how restricted by budgets and other practicalities, Gilbert aimed for beauty in his own work. His most notable early commission, one that brought many artists into collaboration, was the Minnesota state capitol. He pushed for artistic treatments in his other building projects as well, even when they were erected as speculative real estate investments, because he believed that architectural embellishment brought financial rewards.[43] Quality materials and quality workmanship made good business sense in addition to the intangible benefits of beauty. His advocacy for all the arts, from mural painting and sculpture to iron and ceramic work, raised his profile among artists and gave him additional prestige as he hired and coordinated the efforts of painters, decorators, and sculptors.

By 1905, when Gilbert received the commission for the West Street Building, his firm was busy enough to hire another firm to carry out the West Street Building's interior design. Gilbert chose Paris and Wiley, who would work with him until the end of his career. For the West Street Building, W. Francklyn Paris (1876–1954) created light fixtures, Gothic-inspired elevator screens, and stencil work in the plaster vaults (fig. 1.10). Rookwood Pottery provided enameled clay panels for the building, and the Atlantic Terra Cotta Company sprayed the terra-cotta cladding with color to vary the beige.

Atlantic received the contract for the Woolworth Building in 1911. This was a huge undertaking, and Atlantic draftsmen started work right in Gilbert's office in June 1911. By November they had moved to the tenth floor of the same building (the Metropolitan Life Building) because they needed more space.[44] In the terra-cotta business most work was made especially for a building, using the architect's drawings, with no stock material on hand. Once the details for the Woolworth Building were worked out, the sculptors hired by Cass Gilbert to execute the terra-cotta ornament, John Donnelly and Eliseo Ricci, moved into Atlantic's modeling area for the duration of the project.[45]

An article in the *New York Times* praised terra-cotta for being "the only building material that combines practical economy with architectural beauty." Tall office buildings "erected as investments rather than monumentally . . . must be thoroughly high class and dignified in appearance." Gilbert stressed to the public that the Woolworth Building "must be as economical in construction and operating expenses as possible and in that respect is necessarily different from a monumental structure in which those factors can be to some extent subordinated." To be simultaneously

FIGURE 1.9
Portrait of Cass Gilbert, 1907. Kenyon Cox, artist. Oil on canvas. *(Photograph courtesy National Academy of Design)*

CASS GILBERT·A·N·A·
BY KENYON COX, 1907·

FIGURE 1.10

Paris and Wiley rendering of West Street Building interior showing elevator screens and globe lamps, ca. 1905. Watercolor.

(Photograph courtesy Avery Architectural and Fine Arts Library, Columbia University)

high-class and economical then, Gilbert chose terra-cotta. Several colors of glazes on the upper reaches of the tower increased the readability of the details in contrast to the generally light gray tone. The hues (blues, yellows, greens) did not carry to the street level, but rather heightened and enriched the shadows. Samuel Howe declared in 1912, it takes experience "to lay out a scheme [with] colors that shall sing as jewels in the distance."[46] Gilbert gained experience in urban embellishment not only on commercial structures but also on civic ones.

At the Detroit Public Library Gilbert worked again with Paris and Wiley, as well as with the metalsmith Samuel Yellin (1885–1940) and a local ceramic firm, Pewabic Pottery. According to Peter Federman, Gilbert sent Frederick Wiley to the American Academy in Rome in 1920–1 to study Italian Renaissance ceiling treatments for adaptation in Detroit.[47] The Pewabic Pottery firm installed a Wiley-designed mosaic ceiling in the loggia of the main facade.[48] Yellin was a leader in ornamental ironwork, with studios in Philadelphia.[49] In Detroit, he designed a wrought-iron gate for the Fine Arts Room of the Detroit Public Library.[50] Gilbert often designed furniture for his public buildings, in addition to wall sconces, grates, gates, and lamp standards. Executing these elaborate designs required a level of skill among craftsmen that is rare and prohibitively expensive today.

Coordinating Experts

When Gilbert first started out in practice, he hired engineering help as the need arose. On the Endicott Building in St. Paul, for example, Gilbert consulted Louis E. Ritter, a Chicago engineer and a sometime-employee of William Le Baron Jenney, to help design the foundation work.[51] On Gilbert's first New York job, the Broadway Chambers Building, Corydon Purdy and Lightner Henderson were the engineers.[52] By 1900 Gilbert had found steady engineering associates. Norwegian-born engineer Gunvald Aus (1861?–1950) at first worked out of Gilbert's office. In 1902 Aus launched his own firm.[53] After Aus retired in 1915, his partner, Kort Berle, continued the association with Gilbert. Aus time and again effectively communicated structural requirements and engineering judgments to Gilbert and his clients, as exemplified in a letter about the pile foundations of the West Street Building (fig. 1.11). Burt Harrison (1870–?) was Gilbert's mechanical and electrical engineer from 1899 through the first decade of the twentieth century; he went into business for himself in 1901 but continued to work with Gilbert. Each man had his bailiwick, with several assistants assigned to him to help with the drafting.[54] Gilbert coordinated the whole process.

Gilbert saw this coordination of expertise as part of his role as an architect: "The architect performs his professional services in reviewing and correlating the work of such experts and in supervising their work, and also in the necessary conferences in bringing such work into harmony with the working drawings and design of the building and in adapting his own drawings to the necessities of such equipment, handling contracts, administration and general supervision of the work."[55]

Gilbert's talent was as much organizational as it was aesthetic. Gilbert had learned efficient business methods from other businessmen. Early in his career, he was able to profit from the pioneering management practices of the George Fuller Company, a construction firm that led the way in coordinating the various aspects of large building jobs. The architect encouraged his clients to hire experienced, large firms, like the Fuller Company (on the Broadway Chambers Building) or the Thompson-Starrett Company (on the Woolworth Building). Gilbert did not wholeheartedly endorse bigness but viewed these construction management firms as suited to some projects. Andrew Saint has pointed out that it was common practice to use separate contracts well into the twentieth century. The Fuller Company rejected this cumbersome process, however, coordinating the contractors, acting as a "general contractor." To Gilbert, the Fuller Company represented experience, and he could assure clients "that they have probably built more important office and business buildings than any other firm in the United States."[56] Yet Gilbert was not exclusively associated with them.

John Peirce did the superstructure of the U.S. Custom House (New York, 1899–1907) as well as that of the West Street Building (New York, 1905–7). Peirce received the contract for the Custom House superstructure late in 1901. He held major interest in the Bodwell Granite Company that supplied the pink and gray stone from Maine. While Peirce controlled the stone cutting and setting, steel work and interior finishing were completed by other contractors. Gilbert sometimes preferred this work with multiple contractors. He explained in 1907: "This setting up of the general contractor has resulted in the great building corporations of the present time. They have been able to force the sub-contractor to a lower price, consequently, they have introduced a lower grade of work, and have succeeded in keeping the architect at arm's length from the man who does the work. . . . As a rule it should be the sentiment of the architects of the country *to deal with the men that do the work*."[57] This sentiment was fostered by

GUNVALD AUS.
M. AM. SOC. C. E.
CONSULTING ENGINEER.

ORIENT BUILDING,
79-85 WALL STREET.

NEW YORK. January 16th, 1906.

Copy.

Mr. Emil Diebitsch,

Vice President John Peirce Company,

277 Broadway, New York.

Dear Sir:-

Referring to the question of pile-foundations for the West Street Building, I believe it proper to make you a statement of my position in the matter, which you may use in referring the question for further expert decision.

You will remember, that originally your intention was to place this building on rock-foundation, sunk by pneumatic caisons, as it was not thought possible to reach the rock by open pits, owing to the great amount of water that would be encountered.

The borings indicated that the sub-soil consisted of mud and sand to a depth of from 48-50 feet below curb. At this depth rock was encountered, forming practically a level surface, covered with 2-3 feet of hard-pan. Under these conditions the distance from the bottom of the foundations to the solid rock would be about 18-20 feet in the boiler-room, and about 25-27 feet under the rest of the building. In other words, a condition existed, that would indicate a pile-foundation as a natural, safe and economical manner of supporting the superimposed load.

This we discussed, and you requested me to prepare a plan of the required pile-foundations, so that you might obtain comparative estimates between such a foundation and a caison-foundation.

After having obtained such comparative estimates, you decided upon the use of piles and made a preliminary contract for the execution of the work to be superintended under your own directions.

While my connection with the work ceased by the preparation of the drawing above referred to, and a specification which you requested me to prepare after the contract was already let, and embodying the features of said contract, I have still paid frequent visits to the building and have seen a number of piles driven.

These piles have usually passed through soft material for a distance of about 8-10 feet, then through a stratum of sand, which I would judge to have been 3-4 feet thick and thence through harder mud to the hard-pan, overlying the rock and into this to absolute refusal.

Last Saturday I met you by request, to see piles driven at a particularly soft spot, as it had been suggested that the ground in places was so soft as not to furnish sufficient lateral resistance to prevent any horizontal deflection of the piles.

While the ground was very much softer than I had anticipated, and consequently the penetration of the piles several times greater than any I had formerly observed, the piles, nevertheless,

the necessary close cooperation between architect and contractor to get a quality job done.

Ultimately, Gilbert saw one of his most important roles as an architect to be that of purveyor of traditions to a clientele that needed his expertise. He not only knew the business and art necessary to design a particular building on a particular site but could also insert that design into a tradition, a tradition he and most of his clients valued. While he never wrote much about this viewpoint, it translates into an approach that could create variety within an urban setting unified by historic traditions.[58] In that sense, Gilbert had an urban viewpoint; he did not approach his building designs in isolation but saw them in the context of a growing metropolis or town. While many of his planning schemes remained on paper, never executed to any great extent, he thought of his designs as part of a larger work. Given his commitment to a whole, then, it is not surprising that he declared to his staff: "My plans are instruments of service not merchandise to be bought and sold."[59] His designs were to be built under his supervision; whenever possible, Gilbert worked out the landscaping design and proposed connections to other buildings.

Gilbert linked his clients with the systems needed to build buildings, much as a lawyer is an intermediary between a client and the legal system. To a prospective client, he wrote: "You will get better results by selecting some one architect of known standing to give serious and definite study to the design. . . . It is after all very much like employing a lawyer or a doctor, or any other professional man."[60] He helped his clients and building users by making design decisions for them. His buildings guided people through and into spaces that were derived from historical models and adapted for modern uses.

Gilbert was an "art architect," though a conservative one. He especially relished monumental commissions because they provided the opportunity for him to develop artistic ideas more fully than commercial structures did. Despite his dislike of competitions, he continued to enter them in order to gain commissions for these large civic buildings. Once a commission was obtained, his organization provided an array of design services, developed over the years, that included artists and craftsmen as well as engineers. He successfully appealed to the many clients who wanted traditionally styled and crafted architecture. To architectural critic Montgomery Schuyler, Gilbert wrote in 1902: "You must not make . . . too obviously a criticism on what Sullivan calls 'retrospective architecture.' Some day we may speak

FIGURE 1.11
First two pages of letter from Gunvald Aus to Emil Diebitsch explaining pile foundations for West Street Building, January 16, 1906.
(Cass Gilbert Collection, courtesy New-York Historical Society, neg. nos. 72891, 72892)

a new language of creative art, but until then let us speak a language that we all can understand."[61]

Finding a common language in architecture seems ever more elusive, yet many of Gilbert's buildings survive and are being renovated and reclaimed for new uses. While the buildings may not appeal to us in the same ways they did in the past, they have an an urbanistic sense and an integrity that make them welcome in an ever-changing world.

Notes

Margaret Heilbrun, of the New-York Historical Society, and Mary Beth Betts, now of the New York City Landmarks Preservation Commission, were indispensable to this project. Both of them, together with Pam Dewey, also of the New-York Historical Society, went to considerable trouble to arrange illustrations for my essay while I was out of the country. Also, the staff of the Minnesota Historical Society in St. Paul was very helpful, responding promptly to my queries from India. Mary Beth Betts, Barbara Christen, Gail Fenske, and Margaret Heilbrun each read a version of my essay and made useful comments, although the faults remain mine alone. Sarah Bradford Landau, in many conversations with me over the years, has prompted me to think more clearly about Gilbert and architectural practice at the beginning of the twentieth century.

1. Cass Gilbert, 1899 File, Box 6, Cass Gilbert Collection, Manuscripts Division, Library of Congress, Washington, D.C.
2. For an overview of Gilbert's career, see Sharon Irish, *Cass Gilbert, Architect: Modern Traditionalist* (New York: Monacelli Press, 1999).
3. The Minnesota chapter of the American Institute of Architects was organized in 1892; Steven Buetow, "The Founding Fathers," *Architecture Minnesota* 18 (November–December, 1992): 32–53.
4. Paul Clifford Larson gives a detailed account of the competition in *Minnesota Architect: The Life and Work of Clarence H. Johnston* (Afton, Minn.: Afton Historical Society Press, 1996), pp. 86–90. Thomas O'Sullivan, *North Star Statehouse: An Armchair Guide to the Minnesota State Capitol* (St. Paul: Pogo Press, 1994) and Neil B. Thompson, *Minnesota's State Capitol: The Art and Politics of a Public Building* (St. Paul: Minnesota Historical Society, 1974) provide further background.
5. Sharon Irish, "West Hails East: Cass Gilbert in Minnesota," *Minnesota History* 53, no. 5 (spring 1993): 206.

6. Gilbert's capitol received nationwide coverage, including: Kenyon Cox, "The New State Capitol of Minnesota," *Architectural Record* 18 (1905): 94–113; "Heating and Ventilating the Minnesota State Capitol," *Engineering Record* 49 (May 21, 1904): 652–5; "The Mechanical Plant of the Minnesota State Capitol," *Engineering Record* 49 (April 16, 1904): 474–8; and Russell Sturgis, "The Minnesota State Capitol," *Architectural Record* 19 (1908): 31–36.

7. James Knox Taylor and Cass Gilbert both attended Winslow House, a preparatory school in Minneapolis. They then worked in the office of Abraham Radcliffe in 1876–7. In 1878 they started the two-year architectural drafting program at MIT. Taylor apparently stayed two years. James Knox Taylor to Jeremiah O'Rourke, Supervising Architect, September 5, 1893, Treasury Department Personnel Records, Record Group 56, National Archives and Records Administration, Washington, D.C. See also Larson, *Minnesota Architect,* pp. 6–10.

8. For more information on Gilbert's employees, see Sharon Irish, "Cass Gilbert's Career in New York, 1899–1905," Ph.D. diss., Northwestern University, 1985. The women who worked for Gilbert, to the best of my knowledge, were either stenographers or telephone operators.

9. Gilbert's library was donated to the University of Maine at Orono. That institution sold the collection but did make a list of the titles Gilbert had assembled. Gail Fenske graciously supplied this information.

10 "Thomas Holyoke Dead," *St. Paul Pioneer Press,* March 30, 1925; "John Rockart Dies; Noted Architect," *New York Times,* October 14, 1951.

11. People who came into an office temporarily were called "floaters." Hébrard (1875–1933), who also worked on the Washington University competition and a proposed annex for the Broadway Chambers Building, remained in touch with Gilbert for the rest of his life. See Irish, "Cass Gilbert's Career in New York," pp. 646–8. Murier (1870–?) was well paid for his work on the Carnegie competition (about two hundred dollars a month); William P. Foulds to Cass Gilbert, June 26, 1904, Cass Gilbert Collection, Minnesota Historical Society, St. Paul. Georges-Eugène Thiré (1872–?) worked on the U.S. Custom House competition prior to receiving his diploma from the Ecole in 1900; Samuel-Stevens Haskell to Cass Gilbert, August 30, 1899, New York Custom House Letter Book, Cass Gilbert Collection, New-York Historical Society, New York City). Donn Barber (1871–1925) had studied at Yale, Columbia, and the Ecole before he entered Gilbert's office in 1899 to assist on the Custom House competition; "Donn Barber Dies in His Sleep at 53," *New York Times,* May 30, 1925.

12. Gilbert was viewed as pompous and formal by many but he also inspired a certain fondness among some of the employees. Charles Loring referred to Gilbert as "The Large One" in a letter to Thomas R. Johnson, January 12,

1914; William J. Smith wrote to Johnson: "Guess I'll always be a CGite, even with all the growls"; April 25, 1914, Thomas Robert Johnson Papers, Avery Architectural and Fine Arts Library, Columbia University. Paul Starrett, the construction contractor recalled: "My experience with [Cass Gilbert] had been that he was difficult to get along with, very exacting and unreasonable"; Webb Waldron with Paul Starrett, *Changing the Skyline* (New York: McGraw-Hill, 1938), p. 265.

13. "Don't permit unseemly levity or familiarity to exist in the office"; Cass Gilbert to Cass Gilbert Jr., June 21, 1929, Personal Letters, Cass Gilbert Collection, New-York Historical Society. Still Gilbert's office baseball team won the championship of the Architectural Baseball League in 1907 (the only year the league existed); Charles A. Johnson, "Silhouettes of American Designers and Draftsmen: 4. Frederick G. Stickel," *Pencil Points* 8 (October 1927): 595.

14. Gilbert's first office location was on the tenth floor of 111 Fifth Avenue, where he remained until 1903, at which time he moved his firm to 79 Wall Street; Memo, May 2, 1903, Box 401, Record Group 121, National Archives and Records Administration, Washington, D.C. By 1911 the firm was located at 11 East Twenty-fourth Street, and by 1916 the Gilbert firm occupied the sixteenth floor of the Heckscher Building at 244 Madison Avenue (at Thirty-eighth Street), where it remained until dissolving in 1940.

    Gilbert's office staff was never large. Forty was considered a medium-size office. For comparison, at its greatest extent in 1912, D. H. Burnham and Company had 180 employees, with branch offices in New York and San Francisco; Bernard Michael Boyle, "Architectural Practice in America, 1865–1965: Ideal and Reality," in Spiro Kostof, ed., *The Architect* (New York: Oxford University Press, 1977), p. 315.

15. Gilbert to Henry Rutgers Marshall, n.d., General Correspondence, Box 7, 1905 file, Cass Gilbert Collection, Manuscripts Division, Library of Congress, Washington, D.C. Later he noted: "I can never do my best work when I have to consider what an associate wants me to do or say"; Cass Gilbert to Cass Gilbert Jr., June 28, 1925, Personal Letters, Cass Gilbert Collection, New-York Historical Society.

16. Cass Gilbert to city editor of the *New York Times,* April 3, 1915, Letter Book of December 1914 to December 1915, Cass Gilbert Collection, New-York Historical Society. Many thanks to Mary Beth Betts for showing me this letter.

17. Cass Gilbert to Samuel-Stevens Haskell, January 10, 1903, Miscellaneous Letter Book, Cass Gilbert Collection, New-York Historical Society. I am grateful to Mary Beth Betts for showing this letter to me during her tenure at the New-York Historical Society.

18. Frederick Kees to Cass Gilbert, November 10, 1899, New York Custom House Letters, Cass Gilbert Collection, New-York Historical Society.
19. Ernest Guilbert's work was published in professional periodicals, for example, "Essentials of High School Planning," *American Architect* 108 (September 15, 1915): 161–9. By 1927 Betelle was an officer of the New Jersey chapter of the American Institute of Architects.
20. A. M. Githens, "Monographs on Architectural Renderers . . . of Today," *Brickbuilder* 23 (1914): 7–9; Morrison H. Heckscher, "The Metropolitan Museum of Art: An Architectural History," *Metropolitan Museum of Art Bulletin* 53 (summer 1995): 59–63.
21. For example, the office journal of October 1926 to May 1934 indicates that the following men received $1,000 extra in 1926: Ward; McGuire; Cass Jr.; Read; Stickel; and Mohn. Bonuses were also given to R. W. Weirick ($300), Z. N. Matteosian ($750), and McGuire ($1,500). In the same year, Rockart received $8,215.25 in special compensation; in 1927 he received $11,916.49. Cass Gilbert Jr. received $12,000 as special compensation in 1927; Journal, Cass Gilbert Collection, New-York Historical Society.
22. For a useful history of competitions, see Sarah Bradford Landau, "Coming to Terms: Architecture Competitions in America and the Emerging Profession, 1789 to 1922," in Hélène Lipstadt, ed., *The Experimental Tradition: Essays on Competitions in Architecture* (New York: Architectural League of New York, Princeton Architectural Press, 1989), pp. 53–78.

    Gilbert initially won the Wisconsin capitol commission in the 1905 competition but it was taken away from him. He did not enter the 1906 competition. See Henry-Russell Hitchcock and William Seale, *Temples of Democracy: The State Capitols of the USA* (New York: Harcourt Brace Jovanovich, 1976), pp. 240–2.
23. Cass Gilbert to Julia Finch Gilbert, October 15, 1899, Box 6, Cass Gilbert Collection, Manuscripts Division, Library of Congress.
24. Cass Gilbert to Julia Finch Gilbert, September 20, 1899, Box 6, Cass Gilbert Collection, Manuscripts Division, Library of Congress. In this letter he is complaining about the New York Custom House award, which set off a bitter dispute among architects and politicians.
25. Cass Gilbert to Cass Gilbert Jr., June 24, 1927, Cass Gilbert Collection, New-York Historical Society.
26. Cass Gilbert to E. E. Corliss, May 31, 1905, Box 20, Cass Gilbert Collection, Minnesota Historical Society. Samuel Thomas was a family friend from Ohio and a member of the Ohio Society of New York, as were Gilbert and Carroll; Cass Gilbert to Samuel Thomas, February 21, 1901, Box 19, Cass Gilbert Collection, Minnesota Historical Society. See also Sharon Irish, "A 'Machine That Makes the Land Pay': The West Street

Building in New York," *Technology and Culture* 30 (April 1989): 378–80, and Irish, "Cass Gilbert's Career in New York," pp. 543–4.

27. Daily Memo, Cass Gilbert dictating, July 8 to July 12, 1900, Cass Gilbert Collection, New-York Historical Society.
28. For example, Gilbert was paid $227,992 for the Custom House (over about seven years); this sum was $100,000 more than his colleagues were paid for twenty-seven more-modest government buildings constructed in the first decade of the twentieth century; "An Extract from a Public Document (House of Representatives Report 1029) Public Buildings and the Administration of the Supervising Architect's Office," *American Architect* 106 (August 14, 1912): 54.
29. John Sheridan was paid $151 a month in 1902 to supervise the Custom House construction. Rockart and Johnson each made $160 a month in 1902; George Wells made $200 a month in that year. Their salaries, of course, came out of Gilbert's earnings.
30. In 1911 Gilbert bought two insurance policies (at $2,500 each) with Union Central of Cincinnati, the firm for which he designed a skyscraper in that year. He also bought New Haven Railway stock, another client, and U.S. Steel stock from Seligman and Meyer. Seligman was also a client. In 1914 he purchased three hundred shares of Woolworth common stock on a tip from Mr. Woolworth. See 1911 and 1914 diaries, November 29 and January 22, respectively, Cass Gilbert Collection, New-York Historical Society.
31. Cass Gilbert to Andrew Carnegie, April 15, 1908, AIA Letter Book, Cass Gilbert Collection, New-York Historical Society.
32. Clare Cardinal-Petit describes the contrast: "Most architectural drawing conventions used at this time [ca. 1890], specifically the heavy emphasis on orthographic projection, were derivative of the more formal and theoretical practices of continental Europeans, especially those drawing techniques taught at the Ecole des Beaux-Arts. . . . The continental methods privileged formal composition over building craftsmanship—drawing construction over building construction, image over matter"; Cardinal-Petit, "Necessary Excess," *Journal of Architectural Education* 51 (September 1997): 53.
33. Cass Gilbert to George Wells, October 5, 1901, New York Custom House Letter Book, Cass Gilbert Collection, New-York Historical Society.
34. See Arthur Drexler, ed., *The Architecture of the Ecole des Beaux-Arts* (New York: Museum of Modern Art, 1977).
35. See Robert Judson Clark, *The Arts and Craft Movement in America, 1876–1916* (Princeton: Princeton University Press, 1972) and Wendy Kaplan, ed., *"The Art That Is Life": The Arts and Crafts Movement in America, 1875–1920* (Boston: Museum of Fine Arts, 1987). Clark dated the American Arts and Crafts movement from 1876 to 1916.

36. Cass Gilbert to Francis Swales, September 24, 1909, Box 8, Cass Gilbert Papers, Manuscript Division, Library of Congress.
37. See Robin Evans, "Translations from Drawing to Building," *AA Files* 12 (summer 1986).
38. John Peirce to H. A. Taylor, October 5, 1903, Box 401, Record Group 121, Washington National Records Center, Suitland, Maryland.
39. Mary Beth Betts provided the information on the Austin, Nichols model.
40. On the Architectural League, see Larson, *Minnesota Architect,* pp. 17–18. On the American Academy in Rome, see Lucia and Alan Valentine, *The American Academy in Rome, 1894–1969* (Charlottesville: University of Virginia Press, 1973).
41. Cass Gilbert to D. Knickerbocker Boyd, March 19, 1908, AIA Letter Book, Cass Gilbert Collection, New-York Historical Society.
42. Sue Kohler, *The Commission of Fine Arts: A Brief History, 1910–1976* (Washington, D.C.: U.S. Commission of Fine Arts, 1976); "North Side of Parthenon," *New York Times,* June 15, 1930, and Personal Letters, 1923–33, Cass Gilbert Collection, New-York Historical Society.
43. Cass Gilbert, "The Financial Importance of Rapid Building," *Engineering Record* 41 (June 30, 1900): 624.
44. Office Diary, 1911, Cass Gilbert Collection, New-York Historical Society. For more on the Atlantic Terra Cotta Company, see "Architectural Terracotta a Big Factor in New Building," *New York Times,* May 14, 1911; "A Fifty-two-Story Facade of Atlantic Terra Cotta," *Atlantic Terra Cotta* 2 (April 1915); and Susan Tunick, *Terra-Cotta Skyline: New York's Architectural Ornament* (New York: Princeton Architectural Press, 1997), p. 138.
45. Tunick, *Terra-Cotta Skyline,* p. 36.
46. "Architectural Terracotta a Big Factor"; Gilbert to Mailloux and Knox, n.d., Woolworth Building Letter Book, Cass Gilbert Collection, New-York Historical Society; Samuel Howe, "Polychrome Terra Cotta," *American Architect* 101 (February 28, 1912): 105.
47. Peter Federman, "The Detroit Public Library," *Classical America* 4 (1977): 94.
48. Federman, "Detroit Public Library," p. 89. See also Lillian Myers Pear, *The Pewabic Pottery: A History of Its Products and Its People* (Des Moines: Wallace-Homestead Book, 1976).
49. On Yellin, see Richard Wattenmaker, *Samuel Yellin in Context* (Flint, Mich.: Flint Institute of Arts, 1985) and Edward S. Cooke's entry on Yellin in Kaplan, ed., *"The Art That Is Life,"* pp. 137–8. Gilbert also hired Yellin as well as Pewabic Pottery to do decorative work on the Allen Memorial Art Building (1914–7) at Oberlin College in Ohio.
50. This gate was made by the John Polachek Bronze Company in 1920; Federman, "Detroit Public Library," p. 106.

51. Irish, "West Hails East," p. 202.
52. Harry S. Black of the Fuller Company had recommended Purdy and Henderson to Gilbert; Daily Memo, March 3, 1899, Box 3, Cass Gilbert Collection, Minnesota Historical Society.
53. Kenneth Bjork, *Saga in Steel and Concrete: Norwegian Engineers in America* (Northfield, Minn.: Norwegian-American Historical Association, 1947); "Gunvald Aus," *New York Times,* June 7, 1950.
54. John Van Vlanderen, for example, worked as an engineering draftsman under Burt Harrison from 1901. He stayed on Gilbert's payroll until at least 1911. See Ledgers, January 1897 to December 1902; January 1901 to June 1905; and Cashbooks, January 1903 to April 1907; April 1907 to 1910; July 1905 to September 1911; and Journal, p. 187, Cass Gilbert Collection, New-York Historical Society.
55. Cass Gilbert to Adam Strohm, August 7, 1914, Detroit Public Library Letter Book, Cass Gilbert Collection, New-York Historical Society.
56. Andrew Saint, *The Image of the Architect* (New Haven: Yale University Press, 1983), p. 73. For more on the Fuller Company, see Sarah Bradford Landau and Carl Condit, *Rise of the New York Skyscraper, 1865–1913* (New Haven: Yale University Press, 1996), p. 179; and Robert Bruegmann, *The Architects and the City: Holabird and Roche of Chicago, 1880–1918* (Chicago: University of Chicago Press, 1997), p. 81. Cass Gilbert to Edward Andrews, February 8, 1899, Box 18, Cass Gilbert Collection, Minnesota Historical Society.
57. "Report of the Committee on the Relations between Architects and the Various Contracting Systems," *Proceedings of the Fortieth Annual Convention of the American Institute of Architects* (1906–7): 90–1.
58. William R. Taylor wrote compellingly about the "progressive side of Beaux-Arts tradition. . . . This New York neoclassicism sought to monumentalize and unify the late nineteenth-century city. It moved from the architecture of individual buildings to the urbanism of comprehensive planning. It stressed the street perspective, the uniform cornice, the nineteenth-century tradition of the five-story street wall"; Taylor, *In Pursuit of Gotham: Culture and Commerce in New York* (New York: Oxford University Press, 1992), pp. 36–7.
59. Cass Gilbert to F. C. Gibbs, December 27, 1897, Box 18, Cass Gilbert Collection, Minnesota Historical Society.
60. Cass Gilbert to W. T. Starr, May 11, 1902, Box 19, Cass Gilbert Collection, Minnesota Historical Society.
61. Cass Gilbert to Montgomery Schuyler, October 2, 1902, Louisiana Purchase Letter Book, July 1901 to January 1904, Cass Gilbert Collection, New-York Historical Society.

CHAPTER TWO

Mary Beth Betts

FROM SKETCH TO ARCHITECTURE: DRAWINGS IN THE CASS GILBERT OFFICE

The architectural drawings produced by the Cass Gilbert office reflect changes in American architectural practice in the latter half of the nineteenth century. During that time, the structural and mechanical systems of buildings had became more complex. At the same time, architects no longer supervised a team of on-site craftsmen but instead coordinated the efforts of an array of specialists, laborers, and craftsmen working in different locales. Large project budgets and the need to maintain public accountability for civic projects in the late nineteenth century meant that clients were less willing to tolerate the expense of changing designs during construction. For all these reasons the need for drawings to study and document design ideas increased.[1] For example, 2,168 drawings survive from the design and construction of Cass Gilbert's U.S. Custom House (1899–1907). In contrast, approximately 150 drawings document the construction in New York City of John McComb Jr. and Joseph François Mangin's city hall (1803–12).

Gilbert's and other architects' offices were awash in a sea of drawings. His continual use of drawings confirms their importance.[2] Potential office employees were asked to submit a sample of their work, including watercolors, pencil sketches, and architectural drawings.[3] Gilbert's mentor, architect Stanford White, summarized the significance of drawing in his advice to a potential architect: "Of one thing tell him, he may be certain, and that

FIGURE 2.1

Sienna, Italy, 1880. Cass Gilbert, from European Sketchbook, 1880. Graphite on drawing paper, 10 in. × 7 in. *(Cass Gilbert Collection, courtesy New-York Historical Society, neg. no. 72852)*

is that architecture depends on draftsmanship more than anything else, because it is in this way only that ideas can be expressed, and that he should give as much of his time as possible to the study of free hand and mechanical drawing."[4]

Architects working in Gilbert's office produced three basic types of drawings: sketches that developed a design, working drawings that detailed how a design should be built, and presentation drawings that depicted designs for clients and the public. These drawings offer invaluable information about the design process within an architect's practice in general and Gilbert's office in particular.

Sketches

The term "sketch" refers to heterogeneous images, including conceptual drawings of designs, rendered perspectives complete with a building's context, and drafted preliminary plans and elevations. Sketches were essential tools of communication in Gilbert's office. They served as the vehicles through which design ideas were conveyed and discussed. For Gilbert, sketching showed how an architect thought about design. Gilbert emphasized the importance of sketching in a 1921 letter to architect A. Lawrence Kocher:

> Sketch everything in sight. Sketch from pictures, from published designs, from buildings and monuments. No matter how badly you draw, continue to draw. Study and sketch the patterns of fabrics, wallpaper, tapestries, and note the practical application of more or less geometrical forms to artistic ornament.
>
> Sketch mouldings and shapes of things by handling them as well as by looking at them, so that by feeling the contours of the moulding with the fingers you can determine the shape as well as by looking at it. Sketch and draw everything, even down to candlesticks and old silver. Keep the pencil active and the mind will keep pace with it.[5]

Sketching, Gilbert suggested, directly connected vision to drawing, mind to hand. Gilbert followed his own advice in this regard. In his European sketchbook, Gilbert created several finished perspectives of buildings and a series of three steeples en route from Dresden to Vienna via Prague (drawn seemingly from his view out a train window). He recorded a wide variety of other subjects including urns, Pompeian frescoes, sailboats on the

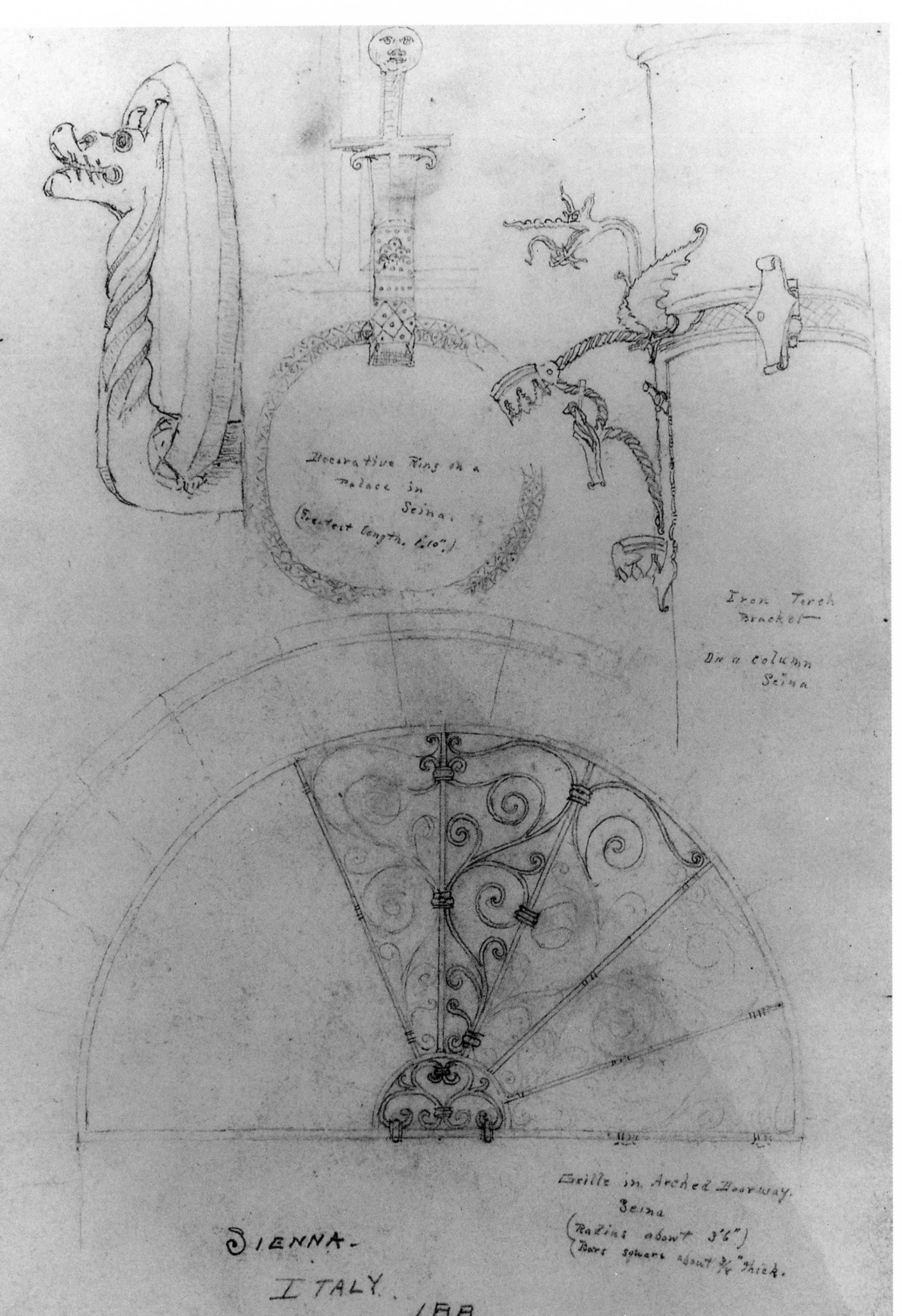

Decorative Ring on a
Palace in
Seina.
(Greatest Length, 1'10".)
Iron Torch
Bracket
On a column
Seina
Grille in Arched Doorway.
Seina
(Radius about 3'6")
(Bars square about 3/4" thick.
SIENNA.
ITALY.
188

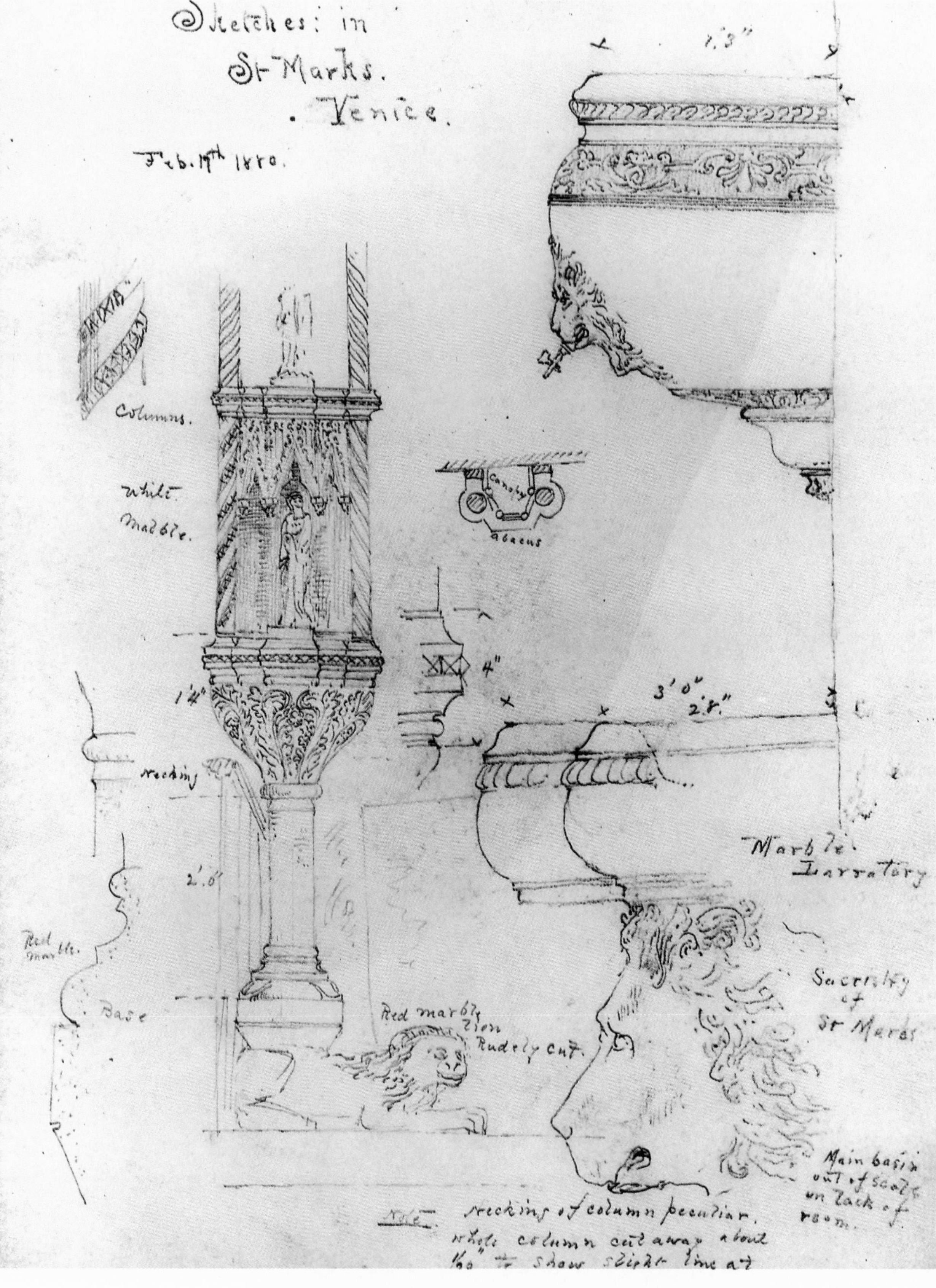

Sketches: in
St Marks.
. Venice.
Feb. 19th 1880.
1'3"
Columns.
White
Marble.
Canopy
abacus
4"
1'4"
3'0"
2'8"
Necking
2'0"
Red
marble.
Base
Red marble
lion
Rudely cut.
Marble
Lavatory
Sacristy
of
St Marks
Main basin
out of scale
on lack of
room.
Note— Necking of column peculiar.
Whole column cut away about
1/8" to show slight line at

Mediterranean, and even the silver candlestick at his Viennese pension. The majority of the sketches, however, depicted details. A page devoted to Sienna in Gilbert's 1880 European sketchbook includes an unlabeled dragon, a decorative ring on a palace, an iron torch bracket on a column, and a doorway grille, each taken from different buildings (fig. 2.1). Pages that were devoted to a single building were even broken down into a series of details. At Saint Mark's in Venice Gilbert recorded a marble lavatory and a shrine in elevation, together with profiles of the latter's moldings, details, a plan, and notes on finishes, dimensions, and carving (fig. 2.2).

FIGURE 2.2
Sketches in St. Mark's, Venice, February 17, 1880. Cass Gilbert, from European sketchbook, 1880. Graphite on drawing paper, 10 in. × 7 in. *(Cass Gilbert Collection, courtesy New-York Historical Society, neg. no. 72853)*

By fragmenting the visual recording of a structure's architecture, Gilbert broke it down into a working vocabulary he could employ. This technique explains Gilbert's use of history and historical precedents in his own designs. Unlike other architects who often based a design on a single historical source (for example, McKim, Mead, and White's modeling of Pennsylvania Station on the Roman baths of Caracalla), Gilbert wove the threads from diverse sources together. For instance, his proposal for the U.S. Custom House relied as much upon French Ecole des Beaux-Arts designs as it did upon those of the Italian Renaissance. Originality mattered less to Gilbert than providing forms appropriate to a building's function. If possible, his goal was to make these forms beautiful, as he wrote in 1909: "Where the designer chooses to work with entire freedom from traditional style to meet modern conditions he should do so but in doing it seek beauty rather than originality for if he achieves beauty originality will take care of itself."[6]

Drafting manuals of the period recommended that the first steps an architect designing a building should take were to read and study the program, quickly sketching ideas after the architect absorbed information.[7] Gilbert typically started design work on a building with a rough sketch. Noted renderer Hugh Ferriss once asked Gilbert to give him such a sketch to illustrate an article on rendering he was writing for the *Encyclopedia Britannica:* "It would heighten interest if I could include one of the quick thumb-nail sketches which you sometimes make at your desk to outline to your assistants the fundamentals of your conception; this would give me a cue to mention the significance of this quick prevision [sic] on the part of the architect."[8]

A series of preliminary designs dated July 1899 may have been some of Gilbert's first attempts to grapple with both the plan and exterior of the U.S. Custom House. Gilbert wanted his design for the building to be monumental. Yet he believed that its function as a government building in a dense urban setting precluded traditional elements such as a dome or ped-

FIGURE 2.3

Thumbnail elevation, U.S. Custom House, ca. 1899. Cass Gilbert, delineator. Graphite on tracing paper. Image: 3 in. × 3¾ in.; support: 21 in. × 24¾ in.

(Cass Gilbert Collection, courtesy New-York Historical Society, neg. no. 72854)

FIGURE 2.4

Preliminary elevation, U.S. Custom House, ca. 1899. Cass Gilbert, delineator. Charcoal on tracing paper, 22 in. × 33 in.

(Cass Gilbert Collection, courtesy New-York Historical Society, neg. no. 72855)

FIGURE 2.5

Preliminary elevation, U.S. Custom House, ca. 1899. Unidentified draftsman. Graphite on tracing paper, 22¾ in. × 29 in.

(Cass Gilbert Collection, courtesy New-York Historical Society, neg. no. 71873)

iment. Gilbert drew a thumbnail sketch of the elevation with a steep mansard roof, strongly rusticated end bays, and projecting piers framing the entrance (fig. 2.3). Though the competition program called for a ground floor entry and rotunda space, Gilbert indicated his differences with this requirement by creating more elaborate fenestration on the second floor and treating it as the *piano nobile* above an elevated basement. He designed the main door as a huge round arch stretching into the second story. A series of lines below the door suggested that he was already considering stairs to lift the entrance off the ground. Gilbert drew an outline around the drawing, indicating it should be further developed and studied.

In the next drawing, an elevation of the Custom House in charcoal, Gilbert resolved some design issues while he retreated on others (fig. 2.4). He made the mansard roof smaller and retained the projecting end pavilions. Colossal piers provided Gilbert's desired monumentality, a motif he refined in subsequent schemes. Gilbert returned to the requirement of creating a ground floor entrance. The window treatment, however, was still more elaborate for the second floor, indicating that the major public spaces were on that level. Gilbert introduced sculpture in this scheme, placing statues above the entrance, atop the pavilions, and across the attic. His inclusion of sculpture was a feature that distinguished his proposal from that of the other competitors.

In a third, partially drafted elevation in pencil Gilbert delineated sculptures flanking the entrance, statues placed across the attic, a central seal surmounting the entire building, and relief figures above the main door (fig. 2.5). The entrance was elevated to the second floor and reached by a broad flight of steps. The office would refine the design several times, changing the order and arrangement of the columns, returning to a mansard roof, and adding ornamental elements. However, this sketch was close to the final design. Gilbert was clear as to the effect the elevation should have; he wrote to his New York office manager Steve Haskell, "I want the thing BIG and GRANDIOSE."[9]

Gilbert followed standard office practice, as detailed in drafting manuals, by preparing several different designs to study a problem.[10] While plans for office buildings were usually generated by the size of the site and the desire to create as much rentable office space as possible, designs for institutions were often more complex and several layouts would be developed and studied. The exterior style of the building was usually decided fairly early in the design process, based on sketches depicting different materials, massing, fenestration, and ornamentation. The office drew plans first, then elevations, and finally a perspective. After the overall appearance and plan of the building had been determined, the office would study exterior details, major interior spaces, subsidiary spaces, and interior details.

During the early years of his practice, Gilbert and other members of the staff would work on designs at the same time. For instance, Gilbert, Haskell, and Ernest Hébrard all worked on the design for the U.S. Custom House. But when the quick and skillful Thomas R. Johnson joined the practice in 1900 much of the preliminary design work shifted to him.[11] After Johnson's death in 1915 the office continued to assign one architect to the development of a design for a project. A March 13, 1920, report from office staff member John Rockart to Cass Gilbert on office activities detailed that Frederick Stickel was "making studies of exterior and will have something to show you when you return" for the "Big Building" [an unidentified project] and that "E.W. is making studies of different schemes for the plan with light from the outside, and I hope will have some interesting solutions to show you" for the Federal Reserve Bank in Minneapolis.[12] Initial sketches were drawn freehand, and the office tended to use media such as charcoal, soft graphite, or conté crayon that encouraged sketching with simple, broad lines.

Sketches for the Woolworth Building offer an excellent example of how the office developed a design. Gilbert produced at least thirty different plans (an unusually large number for an office building) as he, Woolworth, and the realty company debated the size of the site and height of the building.[13] A number of exterior perspectives by Johnson explored designs of varying sizes, configurations, and styles. Three perspectives document different schemes for a building (figs. 2.6, 2.7, 2.8). In the first two drawings, Johnson illustrated a Gothic-style building, while in the third he created a classically derived exterior. Johnson depicted different tower heights and studied the relationship of the vertical plane to the horizontal in the elevation. He examined different window arrangements and versions of the transition from tower to roof. Color schemes were also explored. Figure 2.6 was drawn with a pale exterior and touches of color in the body of the building; figure 2.7 was rendered in a tawny shade; figure 2.8 was colored in pure white. In figures 2.6 and 2.7 Johnson used a blur of vertical lines to suggest the side elevations and obscured the bases by depicting the building at dusk or nighttime. The loose style of these perspectives indicates that they were design ideas quickly rendered and then rejected. Johnson drew figure 2.8 with far more detail and a greater sense of finish, as if it was the solution

FIGURE 2.6

Study for the F. W. Woolworth Company Building, July 6, 1910. T. R. Johnson, delineator. Graphite on tracing paper, 20 in. × 10 in.

(Cass Gilbert Collection, courtesy New-York Historical Society, neg. no. 45871)

FIGURE 2.7

F. W. Woolworth Company Building, October 1910. T. R. Johnson, delineator. Watercolor, graphite, pastel, and gouache on illustration board, 22 in. × 9 in.

(Cass Gilbert Collection, courtesy New-York Historical Society, neg. no. 63313)

FIGURE 2.8

Study for the F. W. Woolworth Company Building, 1910. T. R. Johnson, delineator. Graphite, conté crayon, and watercolor mounted on board, 29 in. × 12 in. *(Cass Gilbert Collection, courtesy New-York Historical Society, neg. no. 32068)*

most in favor at that point and would have figured seriously in design discussions with Woolworth.

The ability of the office to produce a large number of different studies for a building was aided by Johnson's celebrated speed. Each of the three Woolworth perspectives was drawn, mounted, and rendered in six hours. Johnson's speed and dexterity with perspective allowed the office the unusual opportunity to employ it in design: "So accurate is Mr. Johnson's knowledge of perspective that faults not apparent in direct elevation become surely visible in his perspectives, and much of the work from Mr. Gilbert's office is now designed in perspective aided by Mr. Gilbert's criticism and suggestions."[14]

Numerous sketches were created to develop a single design. In three versions of a design for the Atlantic Refining Company, drawn by George Koyl, dated October 11, 1919, one can follow the development of a particular design. Koyl's first drawing was a very rough sketch that laid out the basic mass of the building and suggested the groupings of windows (fig. 2.9 *[a]*). The base was vaguely sketched out and the fenestration of the crown of the buildings was crudely drawn in. Koyl firmly delineated the fenestration and started to suggest ornamental details in the second sketch (fig. 2.9 *[b]*). In the third drawing he began to define the location and type of ornament and suggest the urban context in which the building would have stood (fig. 2.9 *[c]*). These three drawings belong to a series of thirteen designs for the building, all drawn by Koyl on the same day.

After the overall design of a building was settled upon, details would receive the same painstaking study and refinement. On April 20, 1901, Haskell wrote Gilbert that it was important to determine the courtyard elevations for the Custom House and suggested that Thornton Carson work on them under Johnson's supervision. Carson studied one bay of the Custom House courtyard elevation in a series of drawings, beginning with a very rough freehand sketch in which he illustrated the arrangement of windows and suggested their ornamental articulation (fig. 2.10 *[a]*). This was followed by a drafted version of the elevation with cast shadows and suggestions of ornament drawn in freehand (fig. 2.10 *[b]*). The inclusion of ornament and shadows allowed the office to study the sculptural effects of the proposed design. A hard-line-drafted version of the image followed with all the ornament blocked out but not detailed (fig. 2.10 *[c]*). This proposal probably formed the basis for the final study, which was drafted with more defined details and then rendered in ink wash and watercolor to create shadows and suggest materials (fig. 2.10 *[d]*). Media and grade of tracing paper often in-

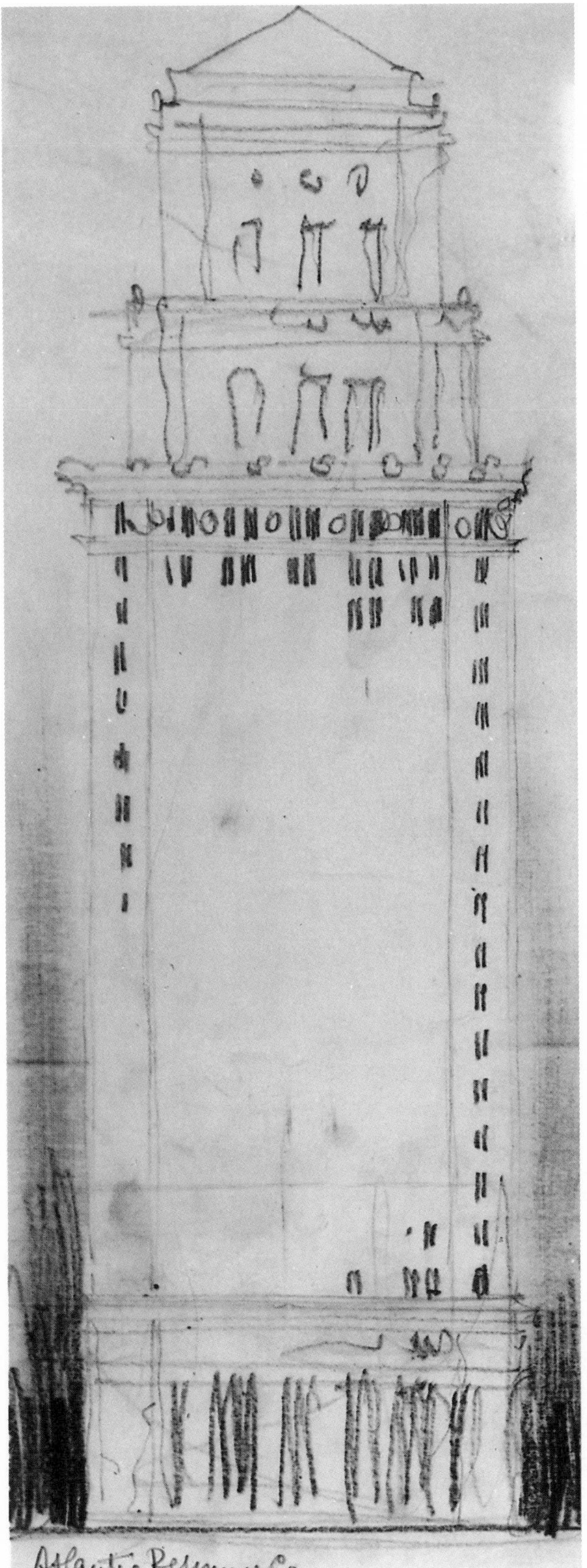

FIGURE 2.9

Atlantic Refining Company Building, three elevations, October 11, 1919. George Koyl, draftsman. Graphite on tracing paper, *(a)* 18 in. × $6\frac{3}{4}$ in.; *(b)* $19\frac{3}{4}$ in. × $7\frac{3}{4}$ in.; and *(c)* $20\frac{3}{4}$ in. × $9\frac{3}{4}$ in.

(Cass Gilbert Collection, courtesy New-York Historical Society, neg. nos. 72856, 72857, 72858)

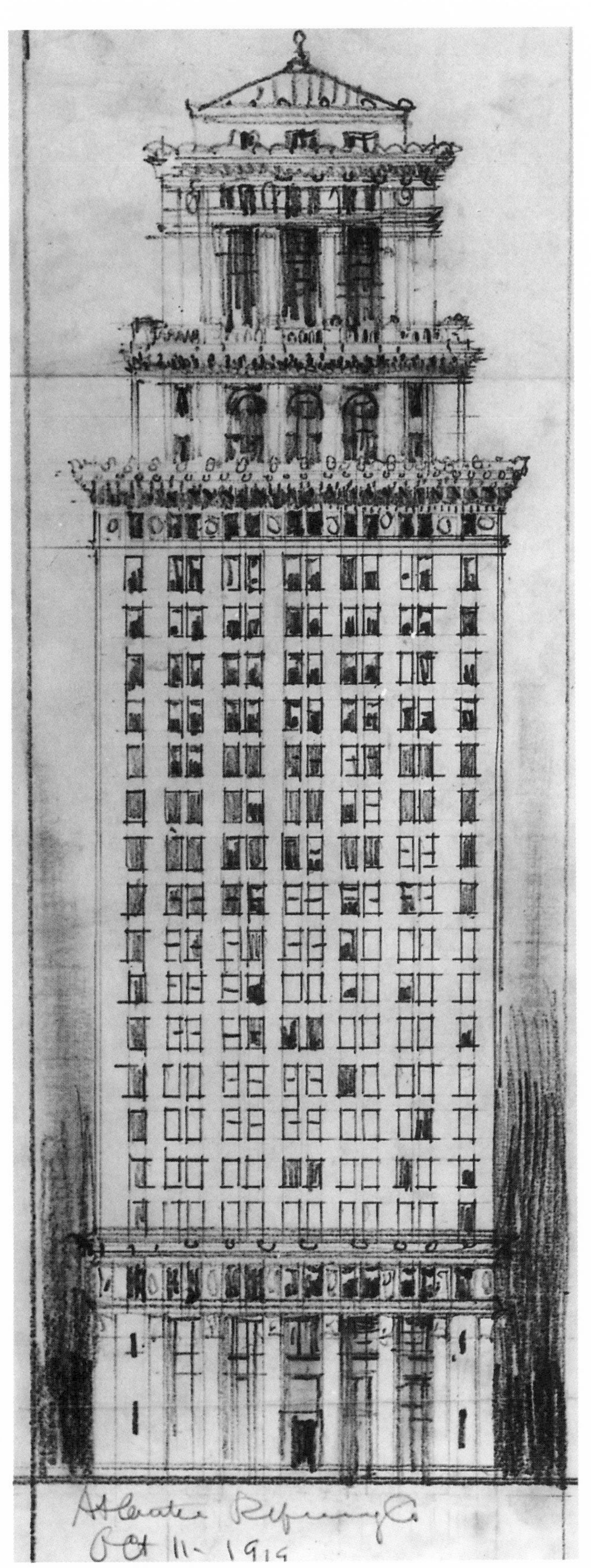
Atlantic Refining Co.
Oct 11- 1919

FIGURE 2.10

U.S. Custom House Courtyard, four elevations, April 1901. Thornton Carson, draftsman. *(a)* Graphite on tracing paper, 16 in. × 9¾ in.; *(b)* graphite, ink wash, watercolor on tracing paper, 19 in. × 8¾ in.; *(c)* graphite on tracing paper, 18¾ in. × 9 in.; *(d)* graphite and colored crayon on tracing paper, 19 in. × 10 in.

(Cass Gilbert Collection, courtesy New-York Historical Society, neg. nos. 72859, 72860, 72861, 72862)

dicated the level of design. A heavier white tracing paper and ink wash were used for more-finished studies; flimsy yellow tracing paper and graphite were used for preliminary work. Such preliminary studies were often shown to the client as a basis for discussing the design. Gilbert always stressed the provisional nature of these designs, stating that owners should not regard these sketches as the completed design. Gilbert described how the office produced and used sketches in a September 23, 1919, memorandum about the Atlantic Refining Company. He predicted it would take two weeks to make preliminary sketches: "these sketches would probably not be what they wanted at first but would be a basis for discussion and be remodeled in the course of study and that when completed would form the general basis of the future design."[15]

He also stressed the time-consuming and laborious quality of these preliminary studies. In 1903 he wrote to his friend and colleague Glenn Brown that "development of an architectural design is in many respects similar to the painting or the modeling of a statue. Parts of it are done over and over again; completed work is practically thrown aside and started afresh, and in short it cannot be judged until it is developed sufficiently to consider from all standpoints."[16] Sketches, in other words, were a frustrating, wasteful, and yet essential component of the design process.

Gilbert often used perspective sketches to study the proportions of a design. Such sketches could end up serving more than one purpose. In describing a perspective of the Broadway Chambers Building he noted that

> this drawing was laid out on a piece of common detail paper, as a trial, with the intention of transferring it to white paper for the rendering. It was used for studying the design over and over again, and laid around the office about six weeks, being grimed all over with dust and dirt. In the meanwhile, this scheme was abandoned, and we worked up the larger scheme. One day a telegram came requesting a water color of this scheme, and it was necessary to take it East immediately. I worked up the old brown paper into a watercolor that afternoon, and started East the next day.[17]

This explains, in part, why the Gilbert office retained such a large number of sketches. Design ideas could be revived with a current project or be reused for others.

Gilbert had an aversion to exhibiting this type of work. He was quite blunt about the matter in a letter he wrote to Harry Carlson about the

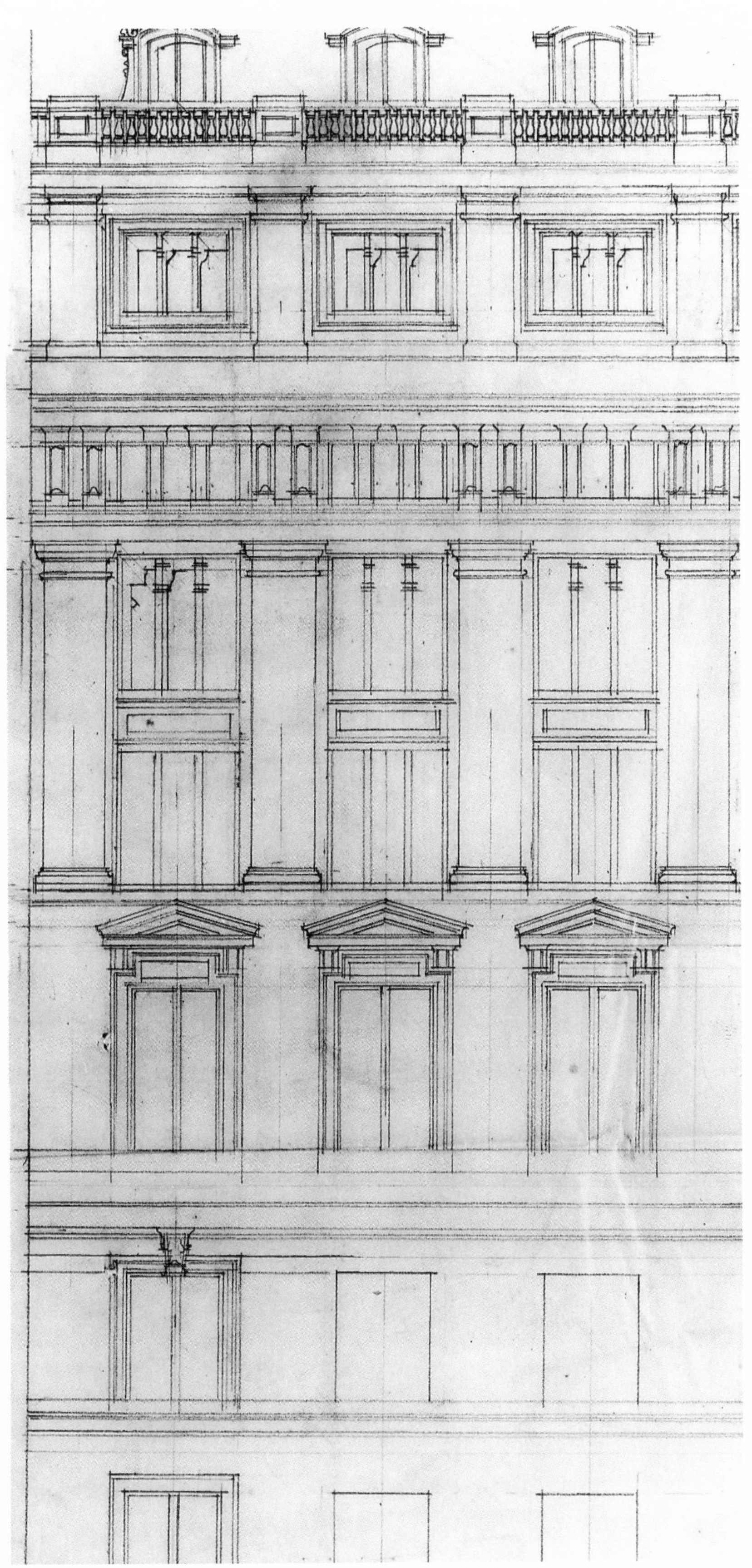

Broadway Chambers sketch: "The fact that the committee chose my water color of the Broadway Chambers, and that you evidently approve the choice is another evidence to me that you do not any of you know how to judge an architectural sketch. That drawing of mine was full of fake and trick, and was never intended for exhibition, while Holyoke's drawing was very straightforward and [a] sincere piece of work and he had ample time to make it."[18]

What did Gilbert mean by saying the drawing was full of fake and trick? From Gilbert's point of view, the cheaper grade of paper (evident in large portions of the sketch of the building), together with the very loose handling of the watercolor, made it a rough study, rather than a finished perspective. So-called tricks were used to make the drawing more attractive. For instance, the electric blue of the sky and flocks of birds created visual interest without telling very much about the design. Bits of color in the building were also used to catch the eye, particularly the colors of the terra-cotta used in the top stories, and the green metalwork of the cornice and balcony. Gilbert did not even consider Johnson's perspective studies of various designs of the Woolworth Building to be worthy of exhibition. He wrote Carlson that "no really good drawings suitable for exhibition purposes were made, except a perspective drawing [by Hughson Hawley] which is now in the possession of the owner and on permanent exhibition."[19]

But Gilbert did sometimes display "sketches." His entry to the Architectural League exhibition of 1906 included a "perspective" sketch of the West Street building, and he included two sketches of the Austin, Nichols and Company Warehouse and a pencil sketch of the Oberlin Art Gallery in a 1916 exhibition. These, however, were design sketches that had been subsequently finished with sophisticated graphite or watercolor rendering.

Working Drawings

Working drawings instructed contractors how to build a design and formed the basis of cost estimates. The drawings consisted of plans, elevations, sections, and details. They were drawn to scale and embellished with detailed dimensions and notes on materials and finishes. Delays in the completion of working drawings could have serious consequences, resulting in postponements in issuing contracts and completing the building and financial losses for the client. If the Gilbert office spent a considerable amount of time creating and studying sketches, they produced working drawings on a tighter schedule. For instance, the working drawings for the Woolworth

Building were made in eighty-six days.[20] His office typically spent more time creating working drawings for monumental public buildings with elaborate stone exteriors than for office buildings. Gilbert's staff produced the drawings for the Broadway Chambers Building in approximately fourteen months, while they created those for the Essex County Courthouse between 1902 and 1905. Gilbert wrote to Glenn Brown: "In my own experience I have found that drawings for the public buildings in my charge have cost very much more proportionately than any other class of work, excepting small residential buildings. I should say that such drawings to produce, cost from 30 to 50 percent more than the ordinary office work."[21]

Working drawings were produced in a prescribed sequence. First, the office drew general plans, elevations, and sections, then exterior details, followed by interior details. Engineers working with the office provided structural and mechanical drawings. Finally, the office would create full-size details. George Wells's report to Gilbert on the activities of the office in 1903 conveys a sense of the office at work, drawing:

> At present Messrs. Johnson and Foulds are engaged on Custom House details and will so continue until these full sizes are all out for the exterior of the building, unless otherwise instructed by you. On the Essex County details Messrs. Betelle, Dentz, Peter Smith and Hammond are engaged, and it is understood that Mr. Boynton will take up interior details of the general staircase and main vestibule. These men will be needed for this job for some time to come. There are occasionally little jobs to be done on the American Insurance Building for which one of these will be needed. McLaughlin will be used here and there as his capacity permits. Van V is on Mr. Harrison's Custom House work. Al. Smith and Ward on St. Paul work; Brazer and Bodker on Louisiana Purchase.[22]

Working drawings were laborious to make.[23] A draftsman first constructed the drawing in pencil either on a heavy grade of tracing paper or on drawing paper. These drawings would then be "traced" by ink onto tracing cloth (translucent linen treated with starch sizing), using the standard drafting techniques and practices of the day. Sheets of paper or tracing cloth were tacked to a drafting board to prevent slippage. The draftsman used a compass for curved lines and drew straight lines with a T-square and triangles. Tracings were completely finished in pencil before they were inked. Draftsmen used a ruling pen with an adjustable nib to draw ink lines of various widths. The draftsman inked the finished drawings from left to right, and from bottom to top. When curves ran into straight lines, the curves were inked first. Ornamental details were usually drawn freehand. Lines indicating the parts of the building closest to the viewer were drawn with a greater thickness than lines indicating parts farther away, giving a sense of depth and three-dimensionality. After a drawing was inked in, the pencil lines were erased with a rubber eraser. Draftsmen were trained to avoid unnecessary elaboration; if a building were symmetrical or ornamentation repeated, draftsmen only drew what was needed to indicate the ornament, then left the rest blank.

The elevation of the Broadway Chambers Building, drawn by Thomas Holyoke, demonstrates the office's use and manipulation of these drafting techniques (fig. 2.11). Holyoke drafted all the straight lines and used a compass to draw some of the circular portions, particularly the circular disks labeled "colored T[erra]. C[otta]. glazed." He used a heavier-weight line to create the outline of the building, projecting ornament, and moldings. Lighter lines were employed for the windows and courses of terra-cotta and brick. Holyoke used standard techniques to create a sense of liveliness and vibration in drawings, stopping some lines short of their intersection with perpendicular lines and allowing others to slightly cross a perpendicular line. He drew large portions of the image in freehand, particularly the elaborate cheneau (the cresting at the top of the cornice), the lions and female heads at the cornice, and the elaborate metalwork of the balcony rail and electric light. When an ornament repeated, Holyoke drew it once or twice and then merely created an outline with the note "repeat ornament." He supplemented the drawing with information about dimensions and specifications of materials.[24]

Up until the early 1900s depictions of full-size details of ornamental work were artistically delineated. After the turn of the century artistic skill was balanced by the need to convey enough information to fabricate the item. Holyoke's drawing for a door handle and kick plate in the Brazer Building, Boston, combines skillful drafting, atmospheric cast shadows, and watercolor rendering (fig. 2.12). Holyoke superimposed sections onto various portions of the elevations to indicate their modeling and depth. He rendered the interior of the sections in watercolor to make them stand out. His notes indicate that there were intervening steps between the drawing and manufacture; a note in the title block ordered the manufacturer to submit full-scale models based on this drawing, as the last step before the piece's fabrication.

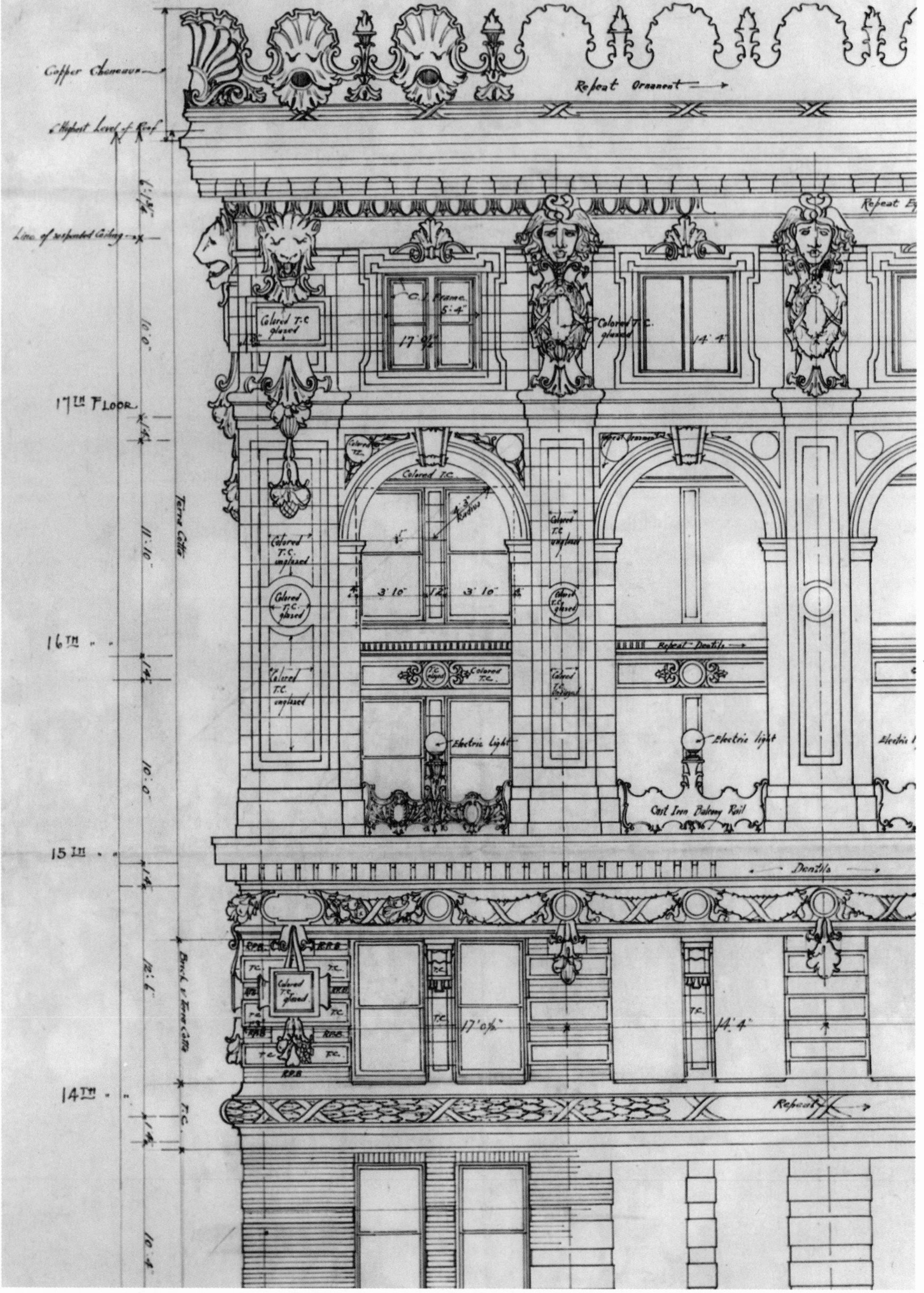
Copper Cheneaux
Highest Level of Roof
Line of suspended Ceiling
Repeat Ornament
17TH FLOOR
16TH
15TH
14TH
Terra Cotta
Brick & Terra Cotta
C.I. Frame
Colored T.C. glazed
Colored T.C. unglazed
Colored T.C.
Electric light
Cast Iron Balcony Rail
Repeat Dentils
Dentils
Repeat

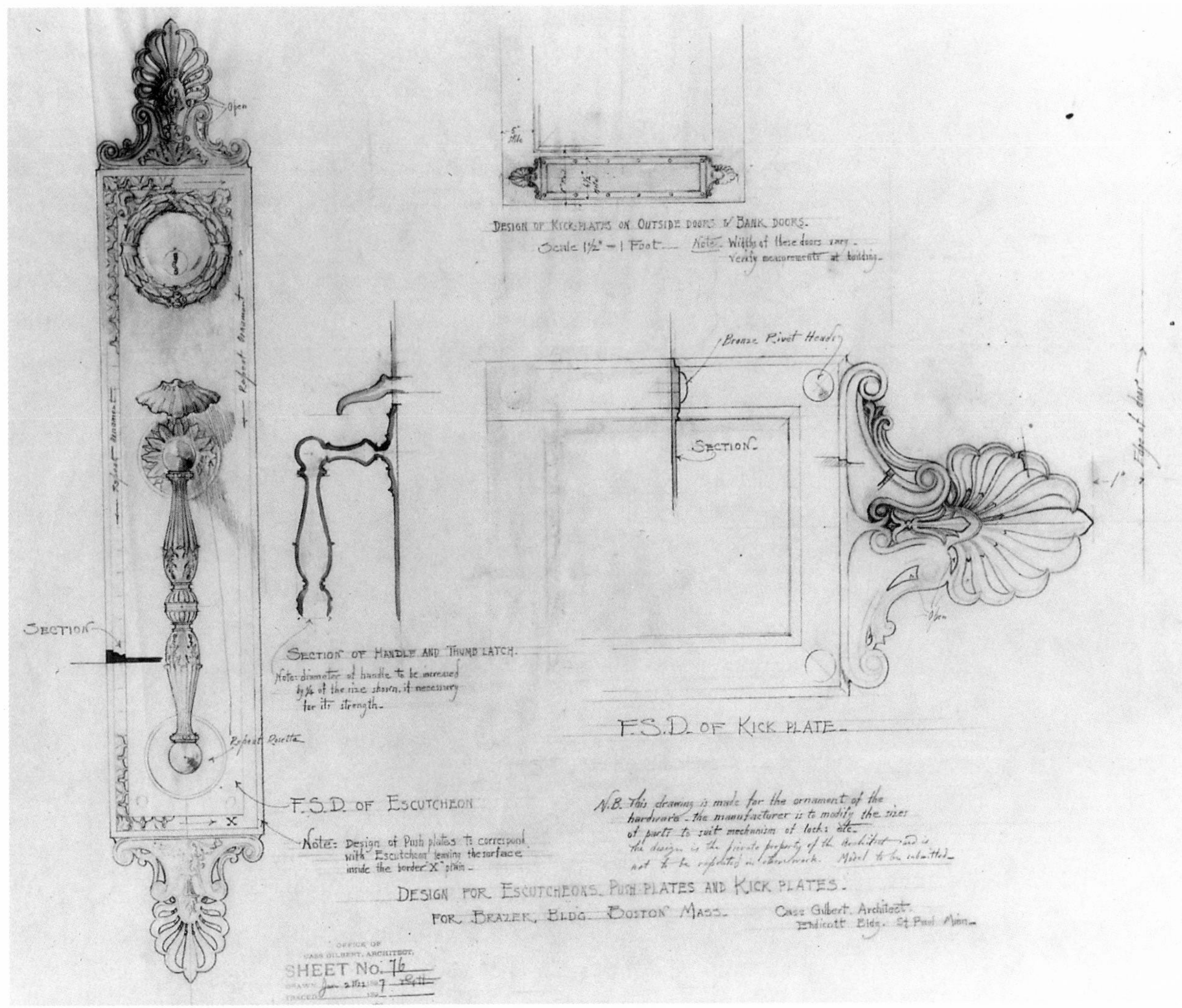

FIGURE 2.11

Broadway Chambers Building, Broadway elevation, May 28 and 29, 1899. T. G. Holyoke, draftsman. Ink and graphite on linen, 71 in. × 21¾ in.

(Cass Gilbert Collection, courtesy New-York Historical Society, neg. no. 72863)

FIGURE 2.12

Design for Escutcheons, Push-Plates, and Kick Plates for Brazer Building, Boston, Mass., June 21 and 22, 1897. T. G. Holyoke, draftsman. Watercolor, graphite on tracing paper, 23 in. × 28 in.

(Cass Gilbert Collection, courtesy New-York Historical Society, neg. no. 72864)

A subtle shift in how the office made working drawings occurred during the first decade of the 1900s. A series of drawings for the Essex County Courthouse in Newark, New Jersey, illustrates these changes. William P. Foulds drew the main elevation for the building, creating a border and using stylized lettering for the drawing title and title block (fig. 2.13). These items, together with the size of the sheet were standardized and repeated for all the Essex County Courthouse working drawings. In contrast, the earlier working drawings for the Broadway Chambers varied in size, had no border, and used randomly placed title blocks with a variety of lettering styles. The standardization of size, border, and lettering for a project became a typical practice in the Gilbert office but was not generally adopted by other offices until the 1910s. It gave the sets of drawings a more unified and professional appearance and freed the draftsman to focus on the drawings. Foulds's elevations for Essex, unlike Holyoke's for Broadway Chambers, did not detail the ornament of the building; instead he developed this on another sheet drawn with Johnson (fig. 2.14). On the left side of the drawing, Foulds and Johnson placed a portion of the entrance elevation complete with statue and Corinthian capital. In the middle of this elevation they intercut a plan of the columns and wall to indicate the precise depths and dimensions of these elements. To the right, they drew a section from the front of the column through the entrance door that provided the depths of the walls and depicted materials and methods of construction. Faint ink lines to the right of the section, and only visible on the original drawing, reveal that Johnson and Foulds shifted the section closer to the elevation, leaving only a 1/16-inch gap between the cornice of the elevation and section. The juxtaposition of elevation and section with details superimposed on both images gave the contractor most of the information needed to construct the building. The Gilbert office tended to use this layered, detailed technique for monumental stone buildings. The format was favored by the McKim, Mead, and White office, Gilbert's first employers, and can be traced back to the Ecole des Beaux-Arts, the French architectural school that Gilbert admired and some of his staff attended. Gilbert valued the presentation techniques of the Ecole and promoted them in the office. The architectural periodical *Brickbuilder* wrote of Johnson's working drawings: "The working drawings of some of Mr. Gilbert's work which have been from time to time published, that are signed T.R.J., will be found in every architect's office, and they are not only a delight to the eye in the arrangement of the sheets, in lettering, and in beautiful indication of ornament, but are also very complete and adequate construction details."[25]

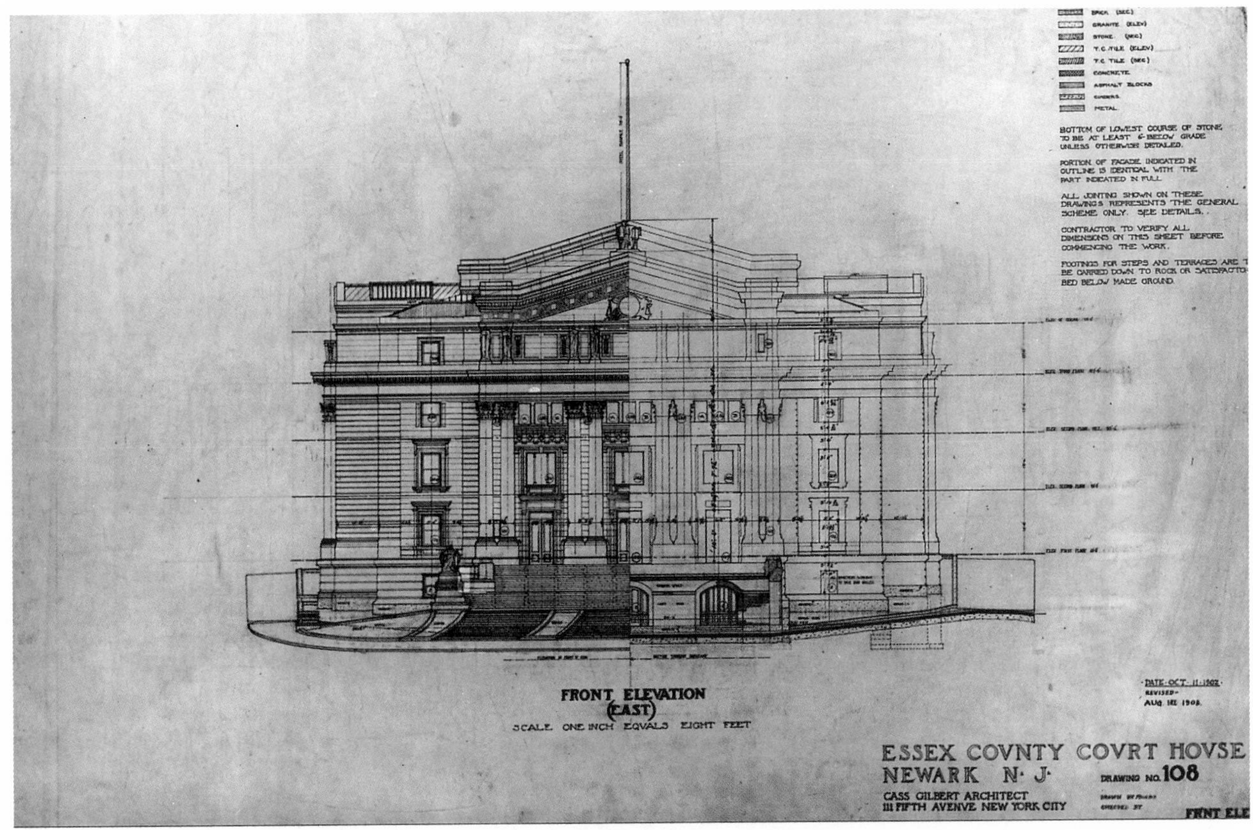

FIGURE 2.13

Essex County Courthouse, Front elevation, October 11, 1902, revised August 1, 1903. W. P. Foulds, draftsman. Ink on linen, 27 in. × 40 in.

(Cass Gilbert Collection, courtesy New-York Historical Society, neg. no. 72865)

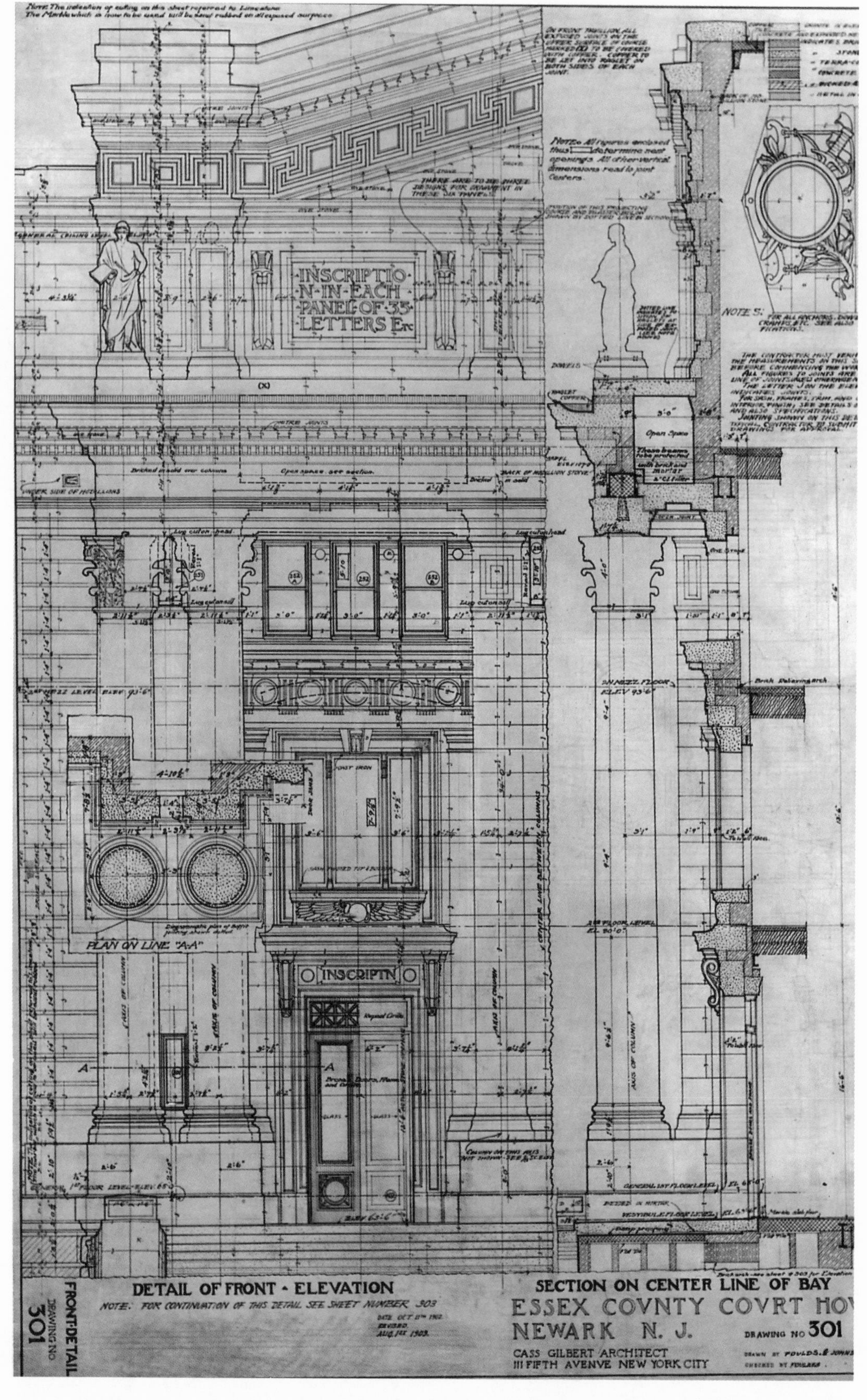
·INSCRIPTIO-
-N-IN-EACH-
-PANEL-OF-35-
-LETTERS Etc
PLAN ON LINE "A-A"
INSCRIPTN
DETAIL OF FRONT - ELEVATION
NOTE: FOR CONTINUATION OF THIS DETAIL SEE SHEET NUMBER 303
SECTION ON CENTER LINE OF BAY
ESSEX COVNTY COVRT HO
NEWARK N. J.
DRAWING NO 301
CASS GILBERT ARCHITECT
111 FIFTH AVENUE NEW YORK CITY
FRONT-DETAIL
DRAWING NO
301

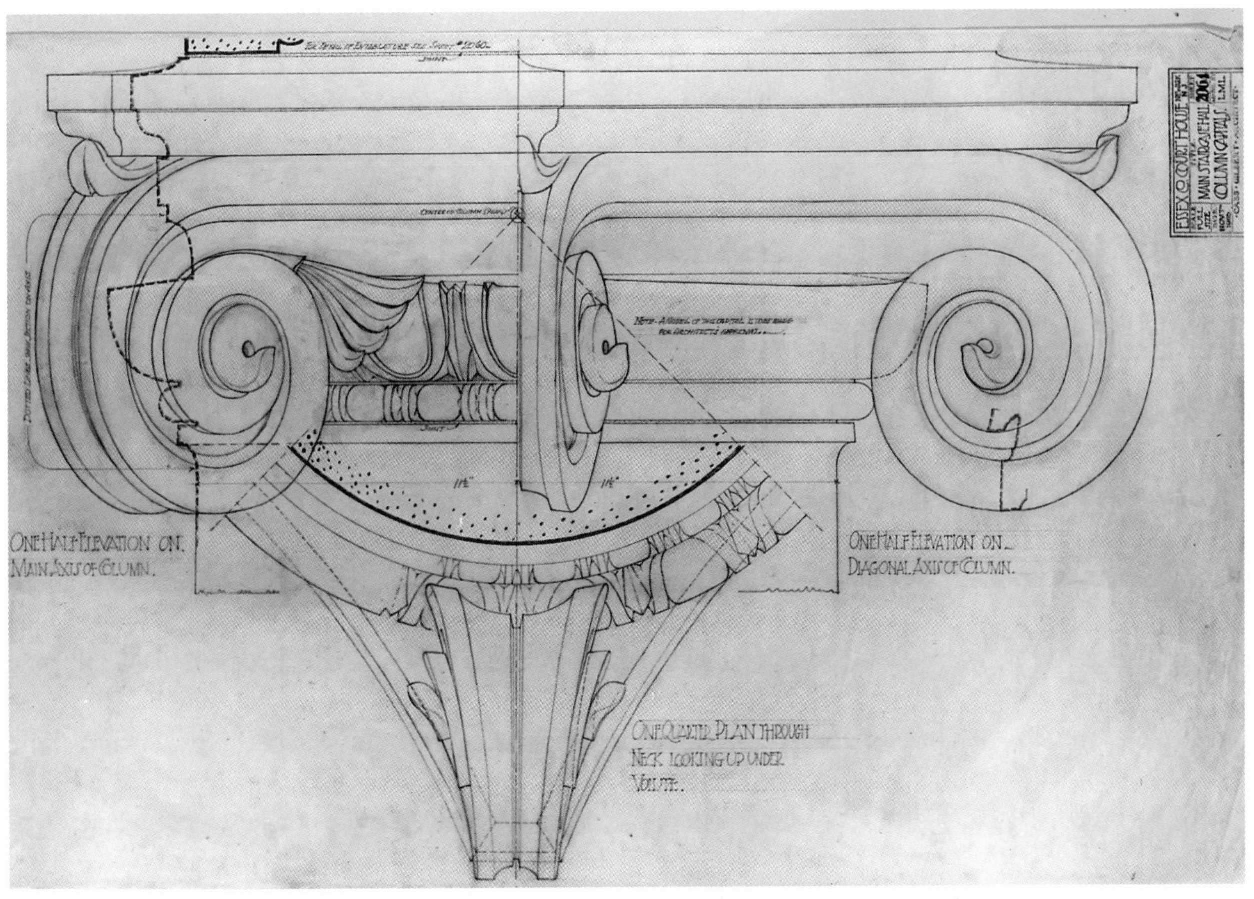

FIGURE 2.14

Essex County Courthouse, front details, October 11, 1902, revised August 1, 1903. W. P. Foulds and T. R. Johnson, draftsmen. Ink on linen, 27 in. × 40 in.

(Cass Gilbert Collection, courtesy New-York Historical Society, neg. no. 72866)

FIGURE 2.15

Essex County Courthouse, main staircase hall column capitals, November 7, 1903. L. M. L., draftsman. Graphite, ink wash on tracing paper. 30 in. × 48 in.

(Cass Gilbert Collection, courtesy New-York Historical Society, neg. no. 72867)

A shift in the office's treatment of full-size details also occurred at this time. Gilbert's friend the architect Francis Bacon had created many of the drawings published in the reports of the archeological excavations at the Hellenistic ruins of Assos in Turkey. Gilbert admired Bacon's drawings and decided the office would create full-size details in a manner similar to Bacon's.[26] The "Main Stair Case Hall Column Capitals Detail" for the Essex County Courthouse (fig. 2.15) is a far more analytical image than the earlier drawing for the Brazer Building. Similar to Foulds and Johnson's drawing of the entrance, the draftsman of this drawing juxtaposed visual information, placing different elevations of the capital side by side, intercutting sections through various portions, and putting a plan of the capital as the visual base of the image. Colored ink washes and cast shadows vanished from the full-size details created by the Gilbert office from this period on.

While working drawings were an essential component of the construction process, they were not the only documents that contributed to construction; specifications and models were also used to describe and refine work on a building.[27] Notes on a working drawing would frequently refer to a range of other drawings and specifications, creating a web of interconnections that revealed the complex nature of design and construction. Drawings could be revised during construction to reflect changes in designs, methods of construction, or materials. Contractors and engineers typically worked from prints made from the tracings. By 1900 a wide variety of printing methods existed, including traditional blueprints as well as whiteprint processes such as blue lines and sepia lines.

Although Gilbert employed a wide range of draftsmen, from college students working as unpaid apprentices to skilled long-time members of the office, the standards for drafting in the office were high. In looking for a draftsman Gilbert frequently noted that he needed someone "rapid and reliable." An article in the *Brickbuilder* commented on the high quality of working drawings in the Gilbert office: "Mr. Gilbert's office has always turned out extremely well finished working drawings, because Mr. Gilbert is himself a draftsman of superior grade and likes and appreciates technically good drawings."[28]

Gilbert did not believe the general public could easily understand and interpret working drawings, and in 1908 he refused to lend the working drawings for Oberlin College's Finney Memorial Chapel in Oberlin, Ohio, for an exhibition on campus.[29] Yet his working drawings did have a limited circulation within the architectural world. Gilbert sent copies of complete sets to architecture schools so students could study them; the office referred to drawings of previous projects for conventions and standards of representation in generating new sets of drawings; and working drawings were frequently published in architectural magazines. Given the circumscribed circulation of working drawings and their rather mundane function, the energy the Gilbert office invested in creating beautiful working drawings was greater than that called for by their intended audience and function. In part, the detail, precision, and beauty of the working drawings can be understood as an attempt to maintain control over an increasingly complex building process. But there was also a sense of pride in the skills that could produce such excellent work, as was shown by draftsmen creating an exhibition of their drawings in the office.[30]

Presentation Drawings

Presentation drawings were architects' tools of persuasion, created to interpret the architect's design intentions for the layperson, whether client, jury member, or general public. In Gilbert's office, presentation drawings could be sketches developed into more finished drawings, carefully rendered elevations and perspectives that were created for the client, or competition drawings. Competition drawings were the most abstract and formal of all presentation drawings, with plans and elevations rendered in monochrome ink washes and a perspective often created without rendering, because the organizers did not want a lay jury swayed by seductive watercolors. This technique was derived from the presentation drawings produced at the Ecole des Beaux-Arts and was highly esteemed by architects.[31] Gilbert called this type of drawing a "school" presentation, in reference to the Ecole. While Gilbert, along with other American architects, decried the competition system, throughout his career he entered competitions and frequently spared no labor or expense to make a compelling set of drawings. Of the Custom House competition drawings, he wrote that his aim was to "present the finest set of designs possible to produce."[32] Complaining about the expenses of the Wisconsin state capitol competition, Gilbert estimated that in another unnamed competition, other architects spent around $1,200 producing their drawings, while he spent $2,200.[33]

Gilbert would also employ the competition technique of monochrome washes on regular drawings. He instructed Johnson to render the Festival Hall drawings in graded tints "so as to make a regular school presentation of them."[34] Johnson's rendering of the Bowling Green elevation of the U.S. Custom House is an example of the use of competition techniques for a regular presentation drawing (fig. 2.16). The elevation was drafted and

FIGURE 2.16

U.S. Custom House, Bowling Green elevation, ca. 1900. T. R. Johnson, delineator. Ink wash, watercolor, gouache, ink, and graphite on board. 22 in. × 31 in.

(Cass Gilbert Collection, courtesy New-York Historical Society, neg. no. 48756)

the ornament was minutely and precisely drawn in freehand. Johnson used ink washes with thin underwashes of watercolors to create a subtle but richly colored image. He rendered cast shadows to create a sense of depth and emphasize the complexity of the ground level sculpture. Johnson highlighted the sculptural relief above the entrance door with gouache in order to give a sense of color, sculptural depth, and material. The rich but subtle opulence of this rendering was meant to mirror the ornateness of the building.

In order to create a perspective, the office researched and interpreted the building's setting to ensure that the context was accurate and the quality of the local traffic and life was captured. Gilbert gave detailed instructions to William Rotch Ware, editor of the *American Architect and Building News,* about rendering a perspective of the Bowlby Building, an office building in St. Paul, Minnesota. He called for horse carts and for railroad trains puffing smoke and steam to convey the character of that particular locale. Gilbert wanted to subtly manipulate certain aspects of the setting in order to give his building specific visual qualities. He asked Ware to have the adjacent building made as subdued as possible, while he hoped that his own building would be rendered "in quiet rich tones of warm buff brown mixed with gray or something like that. So as to look simple and strong and not too gay." Gilbert gave similarly detailed instructions to Hugh Ferriss for drawing the pier end at the U.S. Army Supply Base, calling for more detail on a building so as to give "a little added picturesqueness" and the addition of cranes for loading lighters and car ferry floats to emphasize the base's location on the New York waterfront.[35]

Renderings created for the Gilbert office were drawn by architects working in the firm as well as by freelance renderers. During his tenure with the Gilbert office, Johnson created most of the in-house perspectives. Johnson's 1901 rendering of the Minnesota state capitol used luscious bright greens, blues, and touches of red to surround the white and gold of the building (plate 3). He created a shimmering atmosphere with clouds casting pale blue shadows over parts of the facade while other parts gleam in the sunlight. He included a military parade and red banners in order to suggest a holiday. Promenaders, carriages, people walking dogs, and newsboys indicated an urbane and attractive civic center. Johnson's colorful, optimistic treatment of the building and its urban order was similar to the color and mood of drawings by other architectural renderers, particularly those by Hughson Hawley, F. L. V. Hoppin, and Jules Crow. Johnson's work changed around the time the office began to work on the Woolworth building. In the Woolworth perspectives Johnson emphasized the density and rush of traffic. He drew trolleys and cars, throngs of pedestrians, and in figure 2.7, two hovering airplanes. Before this, renderers depicted calm, well-dressed people with an automobile, cart, or carriage at a stately standstill. The Woolworth perspectives acknowledged the rush and speed of modern urban life. They suggested that the building originated in the modernity and speed swirling at its base, and that its solidity and scale provided an anchor and stabilizing agent amid this rush. His 1913 perspective of the Austin, Nichols and Company Warehouse, a food processing and storage factory in Brooklyn, also reflected this shift (fig. 2.17). He drew the building as a shadowy mass, rhythmically fenestrated and culminating in a curved cornice. He surrounded it with the bustle of laborers and smoke of industry billowing from railroad cars and smokestacks. Johnson depicted the building as both the receptacle and generator of these activities.

Frederick G. Stickel and John T. Cronin were the main renderers for the Gilbert office from the late 1910s until Gilbert's death in 1934. Stickel entered Gilbert's office in 1900 as a high school graduate, with drawing skills but no professional education.[36] Stickel became Johnson's protégé and excelled at formal India ink elevations and detailed hard line pencil perspectives. His perspective of the Detroit Public Library entrance hall of 1918 reflected the influence of Johnson's elastic, almost cartoonlike rendering of people (plate 4). But unlike Johnson's atmospheric and activity-filled drawings, Stickel's focused on the minute rendition of every architectural detail, the stone joints, marble veining, and ceiling coffers. The drawing is a tour de force of linear perspective and detail. Watercolor or any type of rendering would have only obscured the almost icy perfection of the image.

John T. Cronin joined the office in the early 1920s. In his 1926 perspective of the George Washington Bridge (at that time, the Hudson River Bridge), Cronin created a moody, atmospheric drawing in conté crayon that suggested the bridge would have the monolithic mass of an ancient monument (fig. 2.18). Cronin emphasized the bridge as civic gateway embellished with sculpture and lights, and as a place where people could gather to read, converse, or stroll. The cars on the bridge were drawn forming a stately procession with no hint of speed or exhaust fumes. Cronin's emphasis upon mass, light, and shadow probably reflected the influence of the noted renderer Hugh Ferriss but without the drama and energy of the latter's drawings. Although Cronin's work effectively suggested the bridge and its context, his treatment of sculpture, lights, and pedestrians was somewhat stilted, even clumsy.

FIGURE 2.17

Austin, Nichols and Company Warehouse, Brooklyn, 1913. T. R. Johnson, delineator. Graphite, conté crayon on illustration board, 15 in. × 28 in.

(Cass Gilbert Collection, courtesy New-York Historical Society, neg. no. 72868)

CRONIN

If the office was too busy, a draftsman would draw the perspective and then send it out to a freelance renderer. Gilbert commissioned work from all the major American renderers, including Hughson Hawley, Jules Guerin, Jules Crow, Birch Burdette Long, and Hugh Ferriss. Hawley was the favored renderer during the early years of the New York office, receiving commissions for the Minnesota state capitol, the Broadway Chambers Building, the U.S. Custom House, and the Union Club. Hawley's 1902 U.S. Custom House is a large drawing filled with precise detail concerning the building's architecture and context (plate 5). From the colorful mosaics of the entrance vault to the sculpture, Hawley delineated Gilbert's design intentions as they existed at that date. He indicated that pedestrian and vehicular traffic was crowded but not disorderly. He drew figures climbing up the grand entry staircase to suggest that the building was used by a number of people. While Hawley included an automobile in the scene, there was no sense of rush. Hawley and beaux arts–inspired architects and planners envisioned the city as a calm, prosperous environment.[37]

FIGURE 2.18
George Washington [Hudson River] Bridge, 1926. J. T. Cronin, delineator. Conté crayon on tracing paper, 24 in. × 17 in.
(Cass Gilbert Collection, courtesy New-York Historical Society, neg. no. 70324)

Gilbert began to commission renderings by Birch Burdette Long around 1907 and continued to use his services through the 1920s.[38] Long had worked for Frank Lloyd Wright, and his renderings were known for their use of artistic conventions found in Japanese prints. Long's drawing for the Beverly Public Library in Massachusetts has an overall warm tone, evocative of an autumn setting (fig. 2.19). He rendered the drawing in bright but delicate washes of green, orange, ocher, and beige watercolor. He used a conté crayon to draw in the foreground trees and applied a thin layer of crayon over the background trees to create texture and a sense of flickering light. Gilbert's office probably drew the building and its yard; Long added the trees, people, and background. While the drawing is a conventional perspective, Long's inclusion of asymmetrical framing trees and his use of unusual colors (particularly the small navy blue tree to the immediate left of the building) may be the result of some lingering influences of Japanese art. Gilbert was very taken with the drawing; he originally gave it to the library but later asked for it back. Apologizing for his inconsistency he wrote: "It is a very pretty drawing and if you would like to have it for the Library I will have a copy of it made and send it back to you with my apologies for having asked for it."[39]

Hawley and Long came from different professional backgrounds. Hawley worked as a set designer before he started to work as a renderer, while Long trained as an architect. These differences resulted in distinct drawing styles. In summarizing Hawley's and Long's artistic qualities for a colleague,

Gilbert said, "Mr. Hawley's drawing would be more vigorous and impressive for your purposes; Mr. Long's drawing would probably be more refined and artistic."[40] While Gilbert continued to use Hawley's services through the 1910s, the greater number of Long's drawings in the Gilbert archive indicate that he preferred Long's work.

Gilbert's office archive contains a number of drawings by Hugh Ferriss, who worked for Gilbert from 1912 (at first as an unpaid apprentice) through late 1914 when he left to open his own office as a renderer.[41] Renderings in the collection of the New York Life Insurance Building and the West Virginia state capitol represent Ferriss's mature drawing style of dramatically lit masses towering above the vantage point of the viewer. The largest number of drawings by Ferriss are the 1918 drawings of the U.S. Army Supply Base, created while Ferriss was still formulating his style (fig. 2.20). Using a soft pencil, Ferris emphasized the buildings' mass and created a dark smoke-filled sky. However, the drawings lack the dramatic lighting of his later images. In the view showing the two factory buildings and bridge connecting Building A to the powerhouse, Ferriss accurately delineated the details of the buildings, emphasizing their monolithic concrete construction, rhythmic organization of windows, and careful attention to proportions. He placed the buildings to either edge of the image in order to highlight the activity of marching troops, airplanes hurtling into the sunset, convoys of trucks and cars, and smoke spouting from trains and the powerhouse. Ferriss emphasized the function of the complex as a gathering point of men and goods for shipment overseas during World War I. Similar to Johnson's earlier drawings of the Woolworth Building, Ferriss's drawings depicted the U.S. Army Supply Base as a building engaged in its modern context.

As tools of persuasion, presentation drawings functioned in a variety of contexts. Hughson Hawley's rendering of the Broadway Chambers Building hung in the realtor's office, a luscious and large drawing made to convince potential tenants to lease office space in the building.[42] Gilbert displayed a series of perspectives of his plan for the Minnesota state capitol approaches in the St. Paul City Hall. He wanted the drawings placed in an area where they could be seen by the most people, hoping that the drawings would generate public support for his design.[43] The Ferriss drawings of the U.S. Army Supply Base were initially created to present Gilbert's designs to the clients, but they had an important second life in exhibitions mounted in a number of cities to document the war effort.[44] Exhibitions, the central means by which the public saw the office's presentation drawings,

FIGURE 2.19

Beverly (Massachusetts) Public Library, no date. Birch Burdette Long, delineator. Watercolor, graphite, crayon on paper, 18¾ in. × 34 in.

(Cass Gilbert Collection, courtesy New-York Historical Society, neg. no. 72869)

ranged from shows organized by local architectural clubs to international expositions. But exhibitions could also cause problems. In 1909 Gilbert wrote to a member of the Minneapolis Architectural Club, declining a request to exhibit the offices' drawings. "You must understand that I am called upon for the exhibition of drawings from all over the United States, literally from Massachusetts Bay to Puget Sound." In 1916 staff in the office complained of the demands of exhibitions: "The insistent demands of exhibitions in New York, Chicago, Philadelphia and many other cities during the past winter has made a constant draft in our time as nearly one hundred drawings, sketches, pictures, etc. have been shipped out of the office."[45]

In his letter to the Minneapolis Architectural Club, Gilbert downplayed the importance of exhibitions of presentation drawings for his career, claiming that they "are only valuable in cultivating public taste and developing draftsmanship and they do not increase one's practice."[46] Yet Gilbert's constant participation in exhibitions, and careful attention to what was displayed, suggests that he believed exhibitions played a significant role in shaping his reputation as an architect. In 1908 he refused to exhibit a hospital design because he had emphasized the building's functional needs over any architectural treatment. He felt this would not be apparent to a viewing public and would be injurious to his reputation.[47] When asked to contribute drawings of the Woolworth Building to a Boston architecture exhibit, the office responded sharply: "I would also like to say that I think Mr. Gilbert feels that in exhibitions of this character he would like to show other buildings than the Woolworth, such as the New York Custom House, Minnesota Capitol, St. Louis and Detroit Public Libraries, St. Louis Art Museum, etc. lest the impression become too firmly fixed that the Woolworth Building is his representative work."[48]

Gilbert's actual buildings, combined with photographs and drawings displayed at exhibitions, defined his office's reputation and brought in business. In a 1919 meeting Gilbert responded to a potential client's question as to how architects got business: "I told them I did not know; that I did not solicit business but I supposed it came to me because I was known to build certain classes of buildings well, and that people liked what I did. In short, it came from such general reputation as I might have."[49]

Like the office's working drawings, presentation drawings produced for the Gilbert office also underwent changes. These changes reveal subtle shifts in the office's architectural aesthetics as the drawings transformed over time. The office always produced sophisticated "school" drawings, ink wash elevations, sections, and plans influenced by the Ecole des Beaux-Arts.

FIGURE 2.20

U.S. Army Supply Base, Brooklyn, 1918. Hugh Ferriss, delineator. Graphite on drawing paper, 25¾ in. × 40 in.

(Cass Gilbert Collection, courtesy New-York Historical Society, neg. no. 69618)

Large, detailed, and vibrantly colored watercolors, however, grew increasingly rare by the 1920s, with the office favoring monochrome graphite, conté crayon, or charcoal perspectives. This followed a general trend in architectural rendering but also reflected a shift in the office's design preferences.[50] By the 1920s Gilbert had largely rejected the exuberantly colored and ornate style of his early work and favored the simplicity of colonial revival and Georgian revival styles. Monochrome renderings in ink wash, graphite, or conté crayon were more appropriate for the simplicity of Gilbert's later work. Renderings created from 1910 for the Woolworth Building through the 1918 U.S. Army Supply Base presented structures fully engaged with their modern and dynamic urban contexts. Later drawings, such as those for the George Washington Bridge or the New York Life Insurance Building, either generalized the context or idealized it, suggesting that Gilbert was no longer interested in representing the modern urban context or in taking part in modern design discourse.

By the 1920s Gilbert was increasingly uncomfortable with the designs and concerns of the younger generation of American architects. His remarks about Bertram Goodhue's designs for the Nebraska state capitol reveal Gilbert's lack of sympathy for both art deco architecture and changing public taste: "I do not find myself enthusiastic over this design as it looks to me more like a crematorium than a public building, though I am bound to say that it has certain artistic qualities, which are characteristic of all Goodhue's work. I have no doubt he will make a very interesting thing of it, though I greatly doubt if the state will ever build that tower or anything like it."[51] The state did build the tower.

Changes in the office's presentation techniques from watercolor to monochrome and from buildings grounded in the urban context to those set in an idealized context were symptomatic of larger shifts in Gilbert's aesthetic tastes and in his relationships with the architectural profession. Although the creation of drawings would remain an integral part of the office's design process, Gilbert's schooling and approaches were no longer as central to the field as they once were. The office continued to obtain commissions, however, and when Gilbert died in 1934 was one year away from completing the U.S. Supreme Court Building in Washington, D.C.

The drawings produced for the Gilbert office are important design documents that allow historians to follow the development of visual ideas as they were sketched, refined, and presented. Sketches offer us an opportunity to understand how Gilbert and his staff designed buildings; working drawings provide a glimpse into the complexity of the construction process; and presentation drawings reveal how Gilbert emphasized certain qualities of a design. A careful analysis of these images and their creation reveal other aspects, including the pride and enthusiasm of staff members and Gilbert's evolving aesthetic concerns. These drawings record the complexity of Gilbert's architectural practice and the multiplicity of voices within his office. The preservation of this vast archive by the Gilbert office, Gilbert's family, and now the New-York Historical Society provides more than a collection of documented images. By tracing the creative process, the drawings reveal how Gilbert and his office studied, looked at, and thought about architecture.

Notes

1. A number of publications about American architectural drawings were useful for this essay: Eve Blau and Edward Kaufman, eds., *Architecture and Its Image: Four Centuries of Architectural Representation Works from the Collection of the Canadian Centre for Architecture* (Montreal: Canadian Centre for Architecture, 1989); Charles E. Brownell, Calder Loth, William M. S. Rasmussen, and Richard Guy Wilson, *The Making of Virginia Architecture* (Richmond: Virginia Museum of Fine Arts, 1992); William Jordy and Christopher P. Monkhouse, *Buildings on Paper: Rhode Island Architectural Drawings, 1825–1945* (Providence, R.I.: Brown University, 1982); James F. O'Gorman, Jeffrey A. Cohen, George E. Thomas, and G. Holmes Perkins, *Drawing toward Building: Philadelphia Architectural Graphics, 1732–1986* (Philadelphia: Pennsylvania Academy of Fine Arts, 1986); Pauline Saliga, "The Types and Styles of Architectural Drawings," *Chicago Architects Design: A Century of Architectural Drawings from the Art Institute of Chicago* (New York: Rizzoli International Publications, 1982).
2. The best discussion of drawings in the Gilbert office is Sharon Irish, "Cass Gilbert's Career in New York, 1899–1905," Ph.D. diss., Northwestern University, 1985, pp. 118–45.
3. T. H. Anderson to Mr. J. Carroll Johnson, January 26, 1911, Misc. Letter Book 4/1910–1/1911, p. 669, New-York Historical Society (hereinafter N-YHS).
4. Stanford White to "Dear Charly," September 18, 1901, "Architects Education" M-15, 1968, McKim, Mead, and White Collection, N-YHS.
5. Cass Gilbert to A. Lawrence Kocher, December 30, 1921, [Cass Gilbert Personal] Letter Book 12/1920–2/1922, p. 636, N-YHS.

6. Cass Gilbert to Professor C. H. Reilly, April 23, 1909, "CGP" Letter Book, 2/1909–5/1910, p. 69, N-YHS.
7. A. Benton Greenberg with Charles B. Howe, *Architectural Drafting* (New York: John Wiley and Sons, 1913), p. 10.
8. Hugh Ferriss to Cass Gilbert, February 24, 1928, CGP Correspondence, N-YHS. Unlike most architectural offices, which did not retain design sketches because they took up space and were not useful for further work on a building, the Gilbert office preserved a large number of preliminary design drawings.
9. Cass Gilbert to Stevens Haskell, July 24, 1899, Broadway-Chambers Letter Book, 3/1899–1/1900, p. 351, N-YHS.
10. Greenberg, *Architectural Drafting,* 10; Frank A. Bourne, H.V. Von Holst, and Frank Chouteau Brown, *Architectural Drawing and Lettering* (Chicago: Technical World Magazine, 1908), p. 37.
11. Cass Gilbert to Stevens Haskell, October 5, 1901, Chronological Correspondence, 1901–2, N-YHS.
12. John Rockart to Cass Gilbert, March 13, 1920, "CGP" Letter Book, 10/1918–6/1920, p. 562, N-YHS.
13. Gail Fenske, "The 'Skyscraper Problem' and the City Beautiful: The Woolworth Building," Ph.D. diss., MIT, 1988, is the major work on the Woolworth Building.
14. "Monographs on Architectural Renderers: 5. The Work of Thomas R. Johnson," *Brickbuilder* 23 (1914): 110, 112.
15. Stevens Haskell to Cass Gilbert, April 20, 1901, Chronological Correspondence, 1901–2, N-YHS; Cass Gilbert, "Atlantic Refining Co. Building—Philadelphia, PA," memorandum, September 23, 1919, Atlantic Refining Correspondence, 3, N-YHS.
16. Cass Gilbert to Glenn Brown, November 9, 1903, Misc. Correspondence 1903, N-YHS.
17. Cass Gilbert to Harry Carlson, March 15, 1899, Misc. Letter Book 3/1899–9/1899, p. 32, N-YHS.
18. Cass Gilbert to Harry Carlson, June 2, 1899, Misc. Letter Book 3/1899–9/1899, p. 218, N-YHS.
19. Cass Gilbert to Harry Carlson, May 20, 1916, "CGP" Letter Book 7/1914–6/1916, p. 672, N-YHS.
20. Cass Gilbert to John Beverly Robinson, September 6, 1918, "CGP" Letter Book 8/1917–8/1918, p. 702, N-YHS.
21. Cass Gilbert to Glenn Brown, November 9, 1903, Misc. Correspondence 1903, N-YHS.
22. George Wells to Cass Gilbert, May 2, 1903, Misc. Correspondence 1903, N-YHS.

23. Bourne, Von Holst, and Brown, *Architectural Drawing and Lettering,* pp. 1–10; Greenberg, *Architectural Drafting,* pp. 7–17.
24. Carol Cardinal-Petit, "Necessary Excess," *Journal of Architectural Education* 51 (September 1997): 46–60. My thanks to Sharon Irish for giving me a copy of this article.
25. "Monographs on Architectural Renderers," p. 110.
26. Irish, "Cass Gilbert's Career in New York," p. 380.
27. Cardinal-Petit, "Necessary Excess," p. 47.
28. Cass Gilbert to James Taylor Knox, September 26, 1911, "CGP" Letter Book, 2/1911–6/1912, p. 394, N-YHS; "Monographs on Architectural Renderers," p. 110.
29. Cass Gilbert to President Sedge, September 29, 1908, Misc. Letter Book, 9/1908–7/1909, p. 23, N-YHS.
30. November 18, 1902, [Cass Gilbert Office] Journal 1899–1909, N-YHS.
31. H. Van Buren Magonigle, *Architectural Rendering in Wash* (New York: Charles Scribner's Sons, 1921), p. xiii.
32. Cass Gilbert to Senator Knute Nelson (R-Minn.), May 24, 1899, Misc. Letter Book 3/1899–9/1899, 186, N-YHS.
33. Memorandum to Commission for Wisconsin State Capitol, December 7, 1903, 1899–1903 Correspondence, Box 4, N-YHS.
34. Cass Gilbert to T. R. Johnson, March 2, 1903, Misc. Letter Book, 10/1902–5/1903, p. 407, N-YHS.
35. Cass Gilbert to William Rotch Ware, March 2, 1896, Office Book 10/1895–4/1898, p. 399, N-YHS; Cass Gilbert to Hugh Ferriss, August 16, 1918, Misc. Letter Book, 3/1917–10/1918, p. 620, N-YHS.
36. Charles A. Johnson, "Silhouettes of American Designers and Draftsmen: 4. Frederick G. Stickel," *Pencil Points* 8 (October 1927): 588–600.
37. The best work on Hawley is Janet Parks, "Hughson Hawley," in Kathy Benson, Jeanne Sullivan, and Nancy Ten Broeck eds., *New York on the Rise: Architectural Renderings by Hughson Hawley* (New York: Museum of the City of New York, 1999).
38. Harry C. Starr, "Birch Burdette Long: Architectural Delineator and Man," *Pencil Points* 10 (October 1929): 667–80.
39. Cass Gilbert to Miss Loring, May 18, 1915, "CGP" Letter Book, 12/1914–12/1915, p. 251, N-YHS.
40. Cass Gilbert to George Carsley, February 27, 1918, Misc. Letter Book, 3/1917–10/1918, p. 472, N-YHS.
41. Carol Willis, "Drawing towards Metropolis," in Hugh Ferriss, *The Metropolis of Tomorrow* (1929; reprint, New York: Princeton Architectural Press, 1986).
42. Stevens Haskell to Edward Andrews, June 8, 1899, Broadway Chambers Building Letter Book, 5/1899–3/1900, p. 67, N-YHS.

43. Cass Gilbert to George Carsley, August 30, 1909, Misc. Letter Book 6/1909–4/1910, p. 195, N-YHS.
44. R. C. Marshall Jr. to Cass Gilbert, September 21, 1918, U.S. Army Supply Base Correspondence, N-YHS, reported that the drawings on exhibition in Chicago were seen by 1.9 million people.
45. Cass Gilbert to A. A. Pollard, April 6, 1909, "CGP" Letter Book, 2/1909–5/1910, p. 42, N-YHS; Cass Gilbert Office to Harry Carlson, June 8, 1916, "CGP" Letter Book, 7/1914–6/1916, p. 688, N-YHS.
46. Cass Gilbert to A. A. Pollard, April 6, 1909, "CGP" Letter Book, 2/1909–5/1910, p. 42, N-YHS.
47. Cass Gilbert to J. Harleston Parker, December 3, 1908, Misc. Letter Book, 9/1908–7/1909, p. 198, N-YHS.
48. Cass Gilbert Office to Harry Carlson, June 8, 1916, "CGP" Letter Book, p. 688, N-YHS.
49. Cass Gilbert, "Atlantic Refining Co. Building—Philadelphia, PA," memorandum, September 23, 1919, Atlantic Refining Co. Correspondence, N-YHS.
50. Parks, "Hughson Hawley," p. 15.
51. Cass Gilbert to R. C. Colman, February 9, 1921, Letter Book, 8/1920–7/1922, p. 166, N-YHS.

CHAPTER THREE

Mary Beth Betts

CASS GILBERT: TWELVE PROJECTS

MINNESOTA STATE CAPITOL

BROADWAY CHAMBERS BUILDING

ESSEX COUNTY COURTHOUSE

U.S. CUSTOM HOUSE

WEST STREET BUILDING

THE F.W. WOOLWORTH COMPANY BUILDING

OBERLIN COLLEGE

U.S. ARMY SUPPLY BASE

DETROIT PUBLIC LIBRARY

NEW YORK LIFE INSURANCE COMPANY BUILDING

GEORGE WASHINGTON BRIDGE

NEW YORK COUNTY LAWYERS' ASSOCIATION BUILDING

The Minnesota state capitol commission gave Cass Gilbert prominence, experience constructing a large and complex building, and the opportunity to implement American Renaissance and City Beautiful ideals. These would be the themes upon which Gilbert would build his reputation.

Cass Gilbert was a child when his family moved from Zanesville, Ohio, to St. Paul, Minnesota, in 1868. In 1878 Gilbert went east to study architecture at the Massachusetts Institute of Technology, in Boston, Massachusetts, and then to New York City where he worked for McKim, Mead, and White. In December 1882 he returned to St. Paul as McKim, Mead, and White's western representative; however, the firm's western projects failed and Gilbert had to open his own architectural office. Gilbert formed a partnership with his boyhood friend James Knox Taylor in 1885, which lasted until 1891. The firm designed houses, churches, and commercial buildings.

In 1891 the Minnesota State Legislature began planning for a new state capitol. Two years later, the legislature approved the construction of the new building and created a Board of State Capitol Commissioners to oversee the project.[1] The governor, the nominal head of the board, appointed one man from each of Minnesota's seven congressional districts to the board. In turn, the board elected Channing Seabury, the representative from St. Paul, as the vice president and effective leader of the board. Despite the careful creation of board membership, initial plans for the building were controversial. The legislature had allocated what many believed to be a minuscule budget for construction and severely limited the role and fees of the architect. The Minnesota chapter of the American Institute of Architects (AIA) protested these actions and its president, Cass Gilbert, met with Seabury. While Gilbert and the AIA found Seabury and the board sympathetic, the legislature persisted in holding the competition under the original conditions. The results, all agreed, ranged from merely adequate to lackluster. The board persuaded the legislature to hold a second competition during 1895, and on October 30, 1895, the board awarded the design of the new state capitol to Cass Gilbert.

Gilbert's scheme called for a monumental, domed building resembling Saint Peter's in Rome. It would be fireproof, use the latest climate control systems, and have electricity. Gilbert's pairing of beauty with modern technology remained a constant theme of the project. He and members of the board studied precedents. At his own expense, Gilbert went to Europe during the winter of 1897–8 to look at monumental stone buildings. Upon his

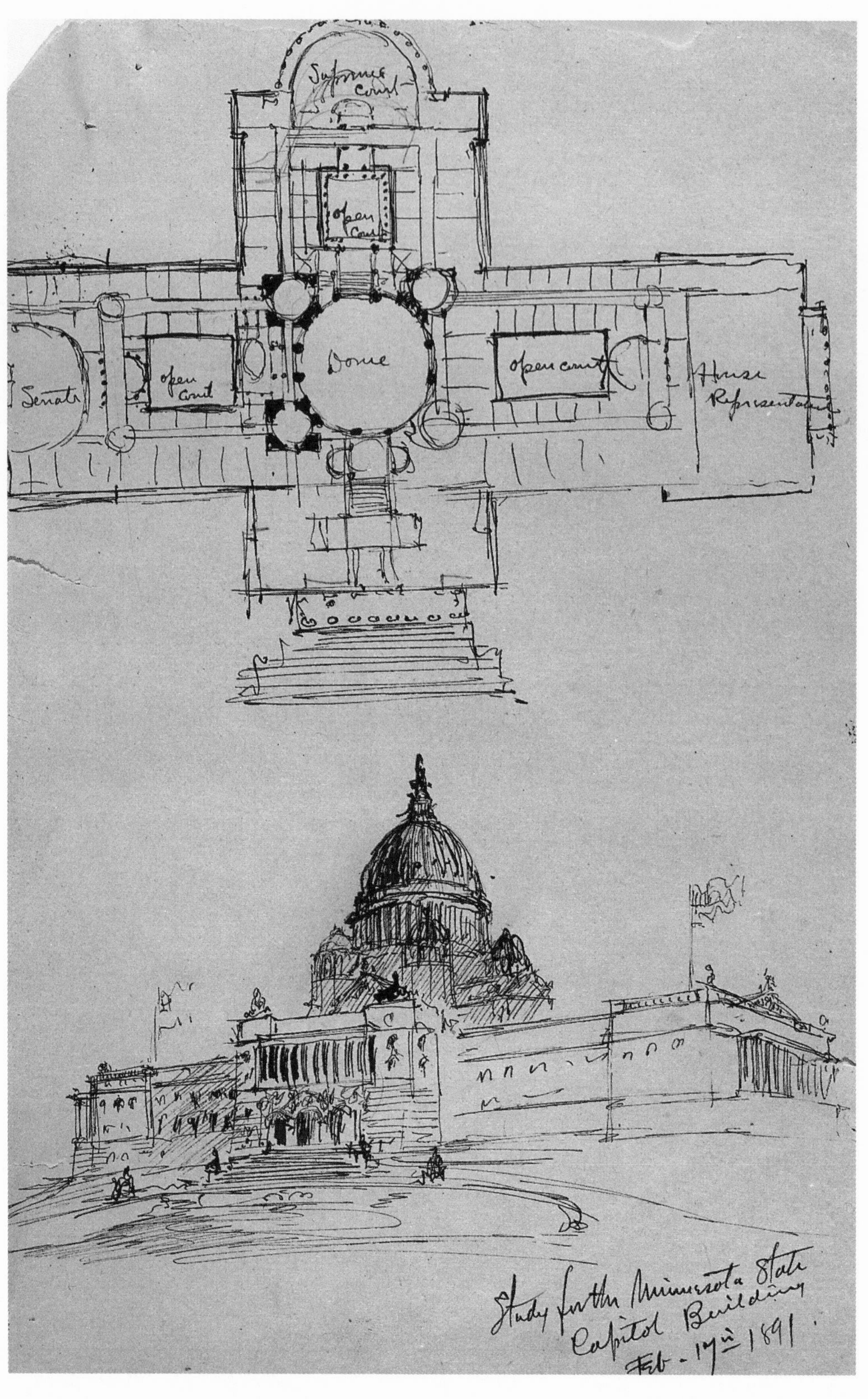
Supreme Court
open Court
Dome
Senate
open court
open court
House
Study for the Minnesota State
Capitol Building
Feb - 17th 1891

FIGURE 3.1
Study for the Minnesota state capitol building, February 17, 1891. Cass Gilbert, delineator. Ink on writing paper, 11 in. × 17 in.
(Cass Gilbert Collection, courtesy New-York Historical Society, neg. no. 72828)

FIGURE 3.2
Minnesota state capitol, no date. Unidentified photographer. Photograph mounted on board, 25 in. × 36 in.
(Cass Gilbert Collection, courtesy New-York Historical Society, neg. no. 72829)

FIGURE 3.3
Study for capitol environment, St. Paul, Minnesota, January 1908. Unidentified artist. Ink and ink wash on board, 29 in. × 35 in.

(Cass Gilbert Collection, courtesy New-York Historical Society, neg. no. 72830)

return he revised the design for the front entrance in order to give it a "more ample, massive and dignified character."[2] The board visited recently constructed public buildings in Boston, New York, and Providence, Rhode Island, in order to better understand the complexities and budgets of large projects.[3]

Gilbert described his design of the capitol as "in the Italian Renaissance style, in quiet, dignified character, expressing its purpose in its exterior appearance."[4] If the overall design was based on Saint Peter's, Gilbert synthesized sources from diverse periods and styles into the composition. Elevator grilles were based on examples of Spanish metalwork.[5] Gilbert wanted the color scheme of the main entrance vestibule to resemble that of the Byzantine tomb of Galla Placidia in Ravenna.[6] The Governor's Reception Room was Venetian in style.[7] Building the capitol was complicated by the volatile economics of the period, as well as the board's desire to use local materials and maintain a low budget yet create a capitol that rivaled those of other states. The legislation's original appropriation for the building never contained enough funds to finish the interiors in the manner Gilbert envisioned. Initial appropriations were passed in 1897 when the state had no money but prices for materials were very low. Because of the lack of funds, Gilbert parceled the job into separate contracts that were let at later dates when, unfortunately, prices were substantially higher.

The first major controversy Gilbert faced centered on the selection of the exterior stone. Both Gilbert and the board stated that the exterior would be of Minnesota stone. Local stone, however, presented two problems: most of it was too dark for Gilbert's taste, and it was difficult to quarry and carve, thus greatly increasing costs. In its stead, Gilbert proposed a Georgia marble as the "best material for funds and strong, durable and beautiful."[8] The board, torn between fiscal responsibility and local pride, voted four to three in favor of the marble. Every time Gilbert selected a non-Minnesota material for the building he was attacked by the local press.[9] In 1899 he decried the provincialism behind these attacks: "Minnesota sells her wheat, lumber, iron and other products all over the Union, and she is too great a state to surround herself with a Chinese wall which would exclude materials produced without her borders."[10]

Gilbert started to design the dome in late 1899.[11] Traditional domes, such as Saint Peter's in Rome and the Pantheon, had a double-shell construction consisting of an inner dome bonded to the outer dome. This construction, however, frequently resulted in leaks and extensive annual repairs. Gilbert preferred an all-masonry dome, believing this to be longer-lasting;

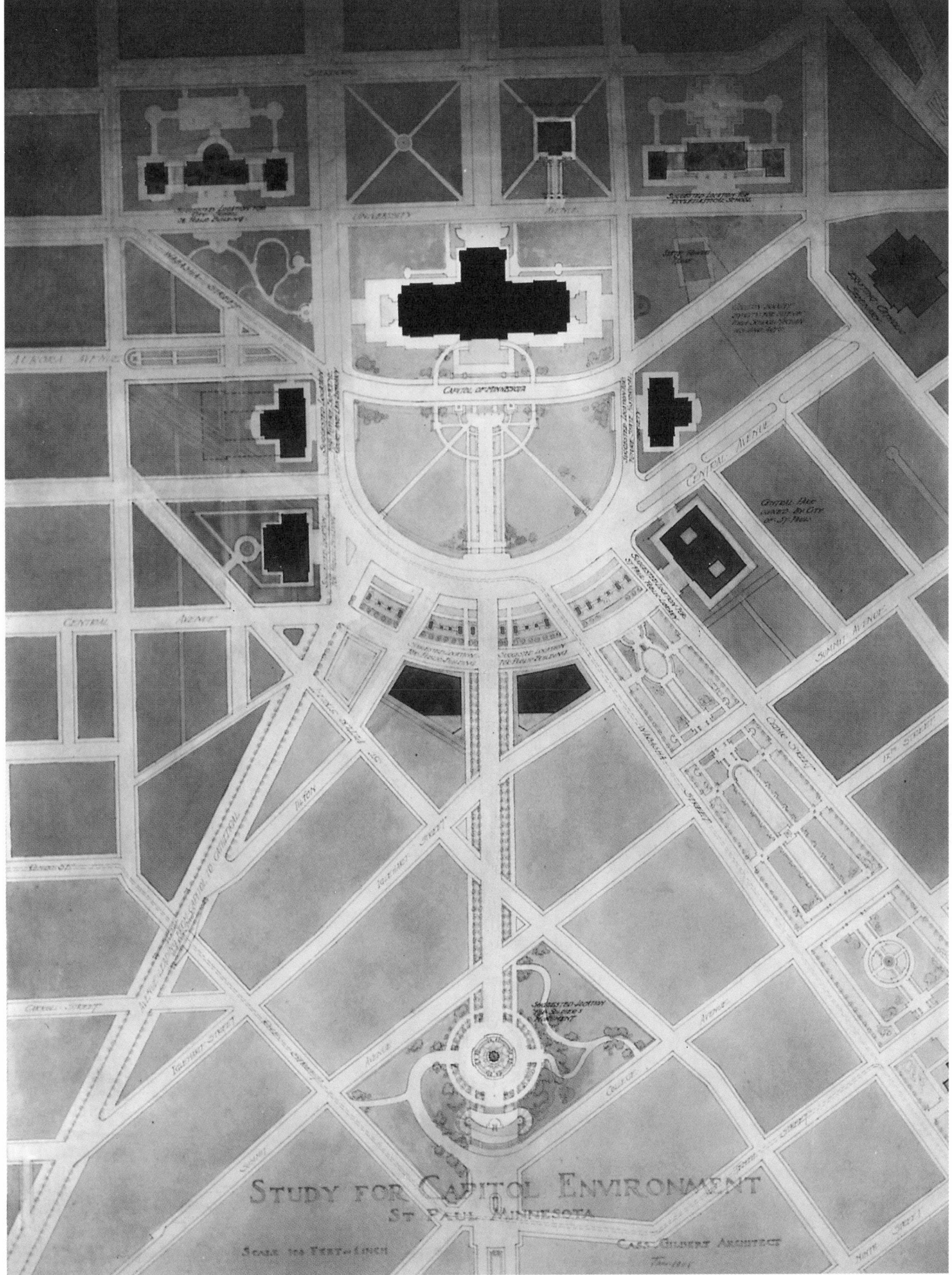

STUDY FOR CAPITOL ENVIRONMENT
ST PAUL MINNESOTA
SCALE 100 FEET = 1 INCH
CASS GILBERT ARCHITECT
CAPITOL OF MINNESOTA
AURORA AVENUE
CENTRAL AVENUE
SUMMIT AVENUE

FIGURE 3.4
Minnesota state capitol, main stairway leading to second level, ca. 1905. Edmund A. Bruch, photographer. Photograph, 9 in. × 7 in.
(Cass Gilbert Collection, courtesy New-York Historical Society, neg. no. 72831)

however, he was open to all materials and systems of construction. He studied domes of recently constructed buildings, including the Rhode Island state capitol; met with a variety of builders; and wrote to specialists. His solution was a triple dome, consisting of an inner masonry dome, a steel cage that would support the lantern, and a self-supporting exterior dome of marble. The Butler-Ryan Company, the main contractor of the building, and the R. Guastavino Company, specialists in vaulted masonry construction, guaranteed that this design was sound. By the spring of 1891, however, Gunvald Aus, Gilbert's trusted structural engineer, doubted the dome's stability, and Butler-Ryan suspected it could not construct the design. Gilbert, Butler-Ryan, and Aus finally devised a solution of backing the outer dome with brick, which was reinforced with steel rings.

Construction proceeded smoothly through 1901. Gilbert wanted an additional appropriation of $1.5 million to finish the interior. This included funds for murals and sculpture. In requesting the money Gilbert reminded the legislature of his fiscal responsibility: there had been very few "extras" or changes in design after the budget had been established; the budget in comparison with other public buildings was very low; and modern requirements of heating, ventilating, and lighting added to the complexity and cost of structures. Most important, the building needed murals and sculptures to give it "greater distinction, lend more to its educational value and to evidence of the advancement of civilization and intelligence of the State." Gilbert planned an elaborate exhibition to persuade the legislators to pass the appropriation. The request, however, was met with rumblings from the legislature and board. Early in 1902 Seabury had also expressed anxiety about the slow pace of work. Seabury wrote to Gilbert: "I want to impress on your mind the idea which I have, that we must *husband our resources,* (if this bill passes,) so as to absolutely *finish* the building properly; furnish it, buy the ground at the S.E. corner of the site, and grade the entire site, within the total of $4,500,000.00, for I have determined that *I* will never ask for any more."[12]

After the legislature approved the appropriation, a newspaper editorial ignited a new controversy. Suggesting that both the board and Gilbert had been fiscally irresponsible, the editorial called for an audit of accounts and the legislature complied.[13] Shortly into the process it was clear that although the board would be cleared, Gilbert might be sacrificed as a scapegoat. The committee criticized Gilbert on two accounts: his preliminary estimates were unreliable, and his fees were too high. Gilbert came to St. Paul in early March to answer the charges. The situation, he wrote to the New York of-

fice, had been stirred up by "disappointed bidders and unprincipled contractors," discontent because they had not profited from work on the capitol.[14] By the middle of March, Gilbert not only had his appropriation but also was totally vindicated of any wrongdoing.

With the new appropriation Gilbert obtained the finest materials and craftsmen, including a variety of local and foreign stones for the interior, furniture by Herter Brothers, and light fixtures by Edward Caldwell. Gilbert's plan to embellish the building with murals and sculpture dated back to 1896 when the National Society of Mural Painters approached him about including art in the building.[15] In 1898–9 Gilbert was able to commission sculptor Daniel Chester French to design six statues over the main south entrance. The new appropriation enabled him to commission a series of interior murals by Edwin Blashfield, Kenyon Cox, John LaFarge, Edward Simmons, and H. O. Walker, as well as decorative painting by Elmer Garnsey and the exterior sculptural quadriga by French. Gilbert firmly believed that the collaborative process enshrined by American Renaissance ideals was directed by the architect. He made detailed suggestions to artists in terms of their color schemes, composition, and subject matter.[16] The process was not without difficulties. Edward Simmons insisted on painting his mural in Paris, only to discover after he finished that the dimensions were incorrect and the mural had to be totally repainted.[17] John LaFarge aggravated both Gilbert and Seabury by his slow pace of work and constant demands for money.[18] With the murals under way, Gilbert then focused on the Governor's Reception Room. He wrote to Seabury: "It seems to me that if the Board does not cover the vacant spaces that somebody will get in their deadly political work later on and make that room a chamber of horrors in the name of patriotism."[19] Gilbert commissioned Howard Pyle, Francis D. Millet, Douglas Volk, and Rufus F. Zogbaum to paint historical scenes and Civil War battles for the room. By spring 1906 all the artwork was in place.

Gilbert was less successful in planning how the capitol would be connected to the rest of the city. By 1901 he was giving speeches, studying other cities, and lobbying for the establishment of a planning board.[20] While St. Paul offered a beautiful topography, the streets had been laid out with little thought of future development. Any plan, Gilbert believed, should also limit the heights of buildings near the capitol and prevent any structure from blocking the main axis to the capitol. Gilbert continued to lobby for a plan for St. Paul through the early 1930s without success.

Although Gilbert endured his share of controversies in constructing the Minnesota state capitol, he evidently enjoyed the challenges of such large and monumental structures. He competed, albeit unsuccessfully, for the Montana and Washington state capitols. He won the competition for the Wisconsin state capitol, only to have the competition overturned. He went on to design and build the Arkansas and West Virginia state capitols.

Cass Gilbert's first serious opportunity to establish a New York City practice occurred when he met Boston businessman Edward Andrews on November 22, 1896, to discuss a building for the corner of Broadway and Chambers Street in New York City.[21] Gilbert came to the meeting with sketches for a proposed office building; however, financial uncertainties would make Andrews postpone the project until early 1899. In the interim, Andrews pondered whether to increase the size of the lot by purchasing additional land, and Gilbert tried to keep Andrews's interest in the project alive. Gilbert signed the contract on March 1, 1899, and hired Samuel-Stevens Haskell as his office manager in April, thus launching his New York City practice.

Gilbert's designs alternated between a stone and red brick exterior, and a stone one with buff brick and terra-cotta. The red brick design was based on Venetian campaniles and Bruce Price's American Surety Building. Gilbert claimed that he could not rival Price's building because the size of his building precluded a square plan and the finances limited his ability "to use the finest material."[22] The buff scheme was modeled on the Brazer Building, a Boston office building Gilbert had just completed.

Andrews wanted a "first-class" office building, one that would attract the top rents. To ensure this, Andrews assembled a team of advisers, including Harry S. Black and Theodore Starrett of the George. S. Fuller Company and realtor Harry Southack. The Fuller Company, one of the largest construction companies in the country, helped to finance the building and arranged for a loan to Andrews. Fuller guaranteed Andrews $75,000 in rent for the first year, a promise the company would later regret.

Although Gilbert preferred a buff exterior, the greater economy and Andrews's preference for the red brick led him to develop that scheme.[23] He decided to use a paving brick manufactured by the Harris Brick Company of Zanesville, Ohio, for the shaft of the building. Gilbert liked the brick's varied color and rough texture; he also liked the large size of the brick, which would result in lower costs. He originally called for a base of limestone but decided that the brick demanded the color and texture of granite. The lower cost of the brick would offset the greater expense of the granite.[24] In April 1899 Harris Brick informed Gilbert that it could not manufacture the brick in the quantity or special forms he needed.[25] Gilbert began to restudy his entire scheme for the exterior, returning to using limestone for the base, with alternate bands of buff brick and terra-cotta for the

FIGURE 3.5

Top of Broadway Chambers Building, New York City, no date. Wurts Brothers, photographers. Photograph, 16 in. × 20 in.

(Cass Gilbert Collection, courtesy New-York Historical Society, neg. no. 72022)

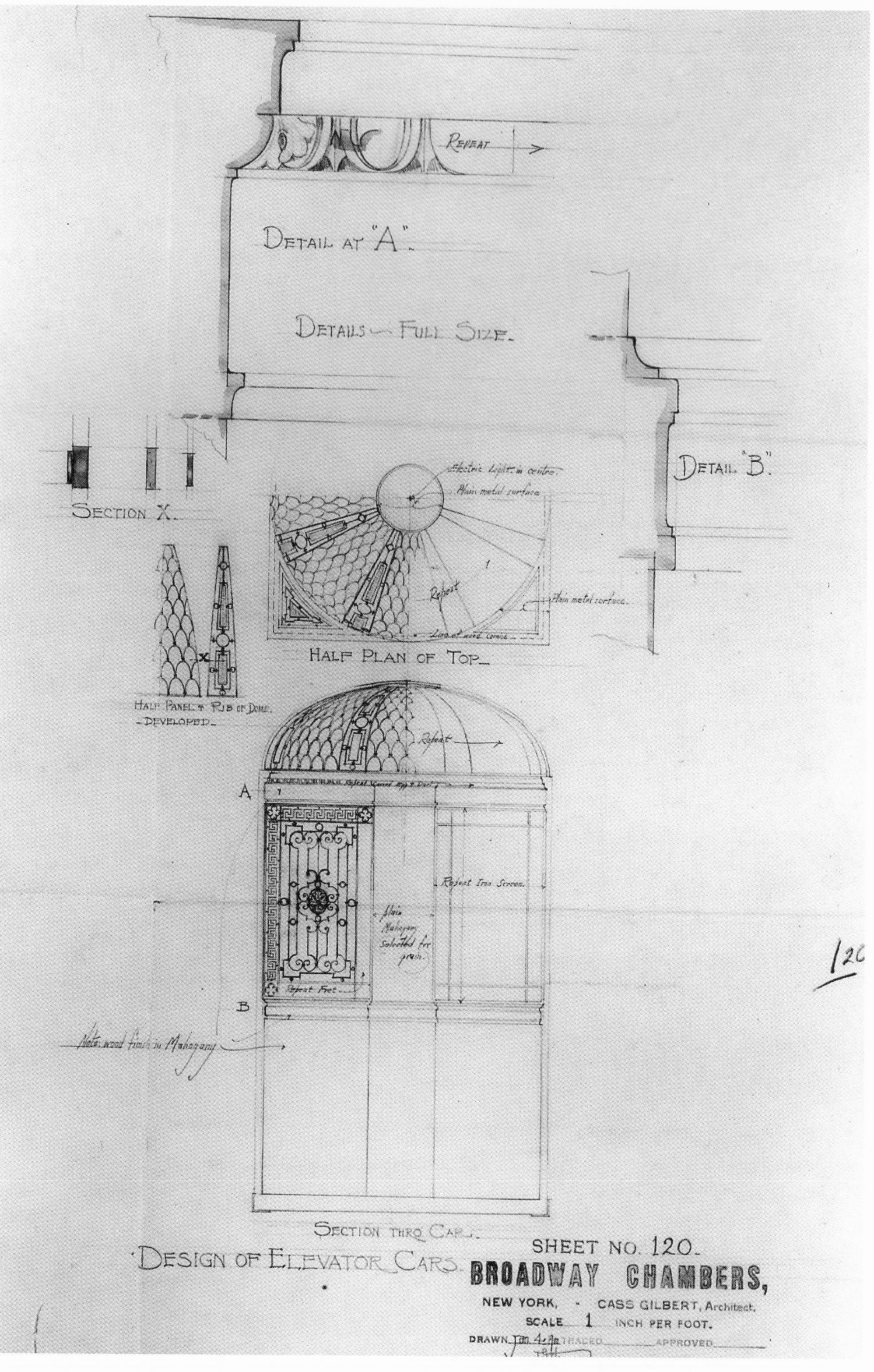

Repeat
Detail at "A".
Details — Full Size.
Detail "B".
Section X.
Electric Light in centre.
Plain metal surface
Repeat
Plain metal surface.
Line of wood cornice
Half Plan of Top.
Half Panel & Rib of Dome.
-Developed-
Repeat
A
Repeat Iron Screen.
Plain Mahogany Selected for grain.
Repeat Fret
B
Note: wood finish in Mahogany
Section thro Car.
Design of Elevator Cars.
Sheet No. 120.
BROADWAY CHAMBERS,
NEW YORK, - CASS GILBERT, Architect.
SCALE 1 INCH PER FOOT.
DRAWN TRACED APPROVED
120

main shaft. He studied the materials through April and asked Fuller to prepare estimates for three different schemes. By May he found another large paving brick, manufactured by the Townsend Brick Company of Zanesville. The company agreed to manufacture the bricks in the quantities and special shapes needed for the building.[26]

Haskell started to look at samples of granite for the base of the building. Fuller recommended Jonesboro granite because Fuller had a good working relationship with the company that used the granite, John Peirce. Haskell preferred Stony Creek granite for its greater variation in color.[27] Haskell and Fuller debated the choice of granite for more than a month before reaching a compromise; John Peirce would be the stone contractor, but he would use the Stony Creek granite. Andrews later wrote Gilbert about his delight in the granite, stating: "It has fine color, great vigor and the carving is beautifully done. It far surpasses any stone on Broadway."[28]

As with the Brazer Building, Gilbert wanted the Broadway Chambers to have a combination of glazed and unglazed terra-cotta "to emphasize certain panels and ornaments."[29] Gilbert commissioned the Perth Amboy Company to fabricate the terra-cotta using some of their recently developed colored glazes. The Broadway Chambers Building was one of the earliest buildings in Manhattan to use polychrome terra-cotta.[30] Gilbert was extremely pleased with Perth Amboy's work, particularly the slight variation of color in the main cornice and the general color scheme.[31] Gilbert's preliminary studies included an elaborate copper cheneau (a roof-top cresting). He considered eliminating this element because he feared it was too ornate. After studying the design, Haskell recommended retaining the cheneau in order to provide a sense of conclusion for the building.[32] Andrews's interest in an enlarged site continued during the design and construction process. Andrews had at first hoped to obtain more property on Broadway; however, the lots adjacent to the building on Chambers Street seemed a more likely possibility. Discussions continued into 1901, but a Broadway Chambers annex never went beyond the planning stage.[33]

As tenants began to rent space in the building, Gilbert's office had to revise plans to accommodate specific needs. When the Domestic National Bank rented the second floor in December 1899, Gilbert had to rapidly rethink bathrooms in the building. The bank employed more than thirty women, and Gilbert's scheme of placing women's toilets on every third story had to be reevaluated. After intense consultation with Southack, the office decided to place women's toilets on the second, eighth, and fourteenth floors. The office had the most difficulties with the tenants of the

FIGURE 3.6
Broadway Chambers, design of elevator cars. Sheet no. 120, January 4, 1900. T. G. Holyoke, draftsman. Graphite and watercolor on tracing paper, 25 in. × 17 in.

(Cass Gilbert Collection, courtesy New-York Historical Society, neg. no. 72895)

ground floor stores and basement restaurant. Morgan Marshall, the owner of the cigar store, almost came to blows with Haskell over Marshall's gilded signs and package of cigarettes hanging over the entrance of the store.[34] Of more serious concern were the claims made by the United States Life Insurance Company, the major tenant of the building. The company had been allowed to move in before the traditional May 1 moving date and had required special work to install large safes. This had disrupted construction during the final weeks. The company, however, complained that the elevators were not running properly and managed to get a concession of a free month's rent. These claims, together with low rents (Southack only collected $64,467 for the first year), caused Andrews to demand $10,000 from Fuller's $75,000 guarantee.[35] Fuller and Andrews bickered over rents through 1901; however, by April 1901 Andrews projected that with the building full for the coming season he would collect $100,000 per annum in rent.[36]

During the summer of 1899, the building's engineers, Purdy and Henderson, approached Gilbert about displaying the Broadway Chambers building in the 1900 Paris Exposition as an example of a typical tall office building. Gilbert, along with the engineers, the Fuller Company, and Andrews, paid for a plaster model of the building that was more than seven feet tall and an even larger model of the steel skeleton measuring around eleven feet, a model office, and a full-scale replica of the terra-cotta top. They supplemented the exhibition with elevations, sections, iron drawings, details, and Hughson Hawley's perspective. The exhibition garnered attention and undoubtedly helped attract tenants to the building.[37]

In late 1925 William T. Andrews, Edward's son, reported that two fragments of terra-cotta had fallen to the street. An inspection revealed that the problem was with the copper cheneau. Weak spots in the cheneau let in considerable amounts of water and caused the terra-cotta below to expand and contract. In light of these difficulties, Gilbert decided to have the cheneau removed, commenting "I think the cheneau is a little too large in scale."[38] In its stead a low brick parapet was erected.

FIGURE 3.7
Essex County Courthouse, front elevation, Newark, New Jersey, ca. 1906. Unidentified draftsman. Ink wash and graphite, 15 in. × 24 in. on 23 in. × 36 in. mount.
(Cass Gilbert Collection, courtesy New-York Historical Society, neg. no. 72832)

ESSEX COUNTY COURTHOUSE

In 1901 the Essex County Building Commission announced a closed competition to select an architect to design a new courthouse in Newark, New Jersey. Professor Warren P. Laird, a respected architect from the University of Pennsylvania, served as adviser to the commission. The invited architects were Babb, Cook, and Willard; Carrère and Hastings; Cass Gilbert; McKim, Mead, and White; and George B. Post. Although the omission of any New Jersey architects from the list initially caused a great deal of local controversy, the competition process proceeded smoothly. All the architects met with Laird and the building commission to review and revise the building program. These meetings persuaded the commission to reduce the space requirements and the number of stories from five to three, to establish a more accurate cost per cubic foot, and to allow six months for the architects to prepare their entries.[39] In December 1901 D. Leslie Ward, president of the commission, announced that Gilbert had won the competition.

Gilbert's relationships with Ward and the building commission were cordial. Early in the project, however, Gilbert and Ward had a major disagreement about the length of time needed to produce working drawings for the building. By July 1902 Ward was angrily threatening Gilbert with public denunciations if the office did not immediately complete the drawings. Steve Haskell, Gilbert's office manager, stated that the office was trying to complete the full set of drawings rather than issue small series of drawings. A full set, even though it took longer to complete, would enable them to obtain bids on the entire building and would save money in the long run. Haskell emphasized the complications of preparing drawings for a monumental building: "I told him that the design of such a building with every part different from the other, was a much more complicated proposition than any building used for commercial purposes."[40] Undoubtedly, the fact that Gilbert was on vacation during this encounter did not improve Ward's temper.

The commission's inability to settle on materials for the exterior also caused delays. Gilbert examined using granite, limestone, and marble for the exterior, but he preferred marble. Surprise support came from the stonecutters who petitioned that the courthouse be built of limestone or marble but not granite, because "the cutting would then be done in Newark by Newark men, and the money thus would pass through the hands of the merchants and banks of the city." Public support combined with the identification of marble as the most monumental of all building materials persuaded the commission to adopt marble for the exterior: "Dr. Ward said that as he remembered, Mr. Gilbert from the first had been highly in favor of a marble building, and the more he thought of it the better the idea appeared to him, and he told me he admitted to himself that he had worked up a lot of enthusiasm for marble and hoped that they would be able to carry it out in the finest kind of way."[41] Gilbert decided to use a pure white marble for the exterior, without veining or any discoloration. In October 1903 Gilbert made the last major modification of the exterior in order to improve interior lighting and create more space.

Construction of the exterior was hampered by strikes, bad weather, and poor workmanship, and exacerbated by a testy relationship between Gilbert and the general contractor V. J. Hedden and Sons. Gilbert's office continually complained about workers staining the marble, as well as breaking pieces then attempting clumsy patches. Poor workmanship finally caused Hedden to ask for the dismissal of two of the stone contractor's employees. The difficulty of hiring skilled labor, however, caused the contractor, George Brown and Company, to dismiss only one and to warn the other: "In regard to the setter (Telfer) we would say, it is very difficult to get setters of any kind at this time and we have therefore taken your suggestion and warned him."[42]

Strikes and general union unrest plagued the construction, causing Hedden to request numerous extensions of time. In a letter of October 1904, Hedden noted that the bricklayers and stonecutters were on strike,

FIGURE 3.8

Essex County Courthouse, front view, Newark, New Jersey, ca. 1906. Unidentified photographer. Photograph, 6 in. × 8 in.

(Cass Gilbert Collection, courtesy New-York Historical Society, neg. no. 72833)

FIGURE 3.9

Grand staircase, main hall, Essex County Court House, Newark, New Jersey, ca. 1906. Unidentified photographer. Photograph, 8 in. × 6 in.

(Cass Gilbert Collection, courtesy New-York Historical Society, neg. no. 72834)

FIGURE 3.10

Supreme Court room, Essex County Courthouse, Newark, New Jersey, 1906. Unidentified photographer. Photograph, 6 in. × 8 in.

(Cass Gilbert Collection, courtesy New-York Historical Society, neg. no. 72835)

while the electricians had just returned from strike. During the winter of 1903–4, work was delayed by extremely cold weather, which closed the Passaic River, stopped the shipment of marble, and kept the stone setters and masons from working.[43]

While the courthouse was not surrounded by extensive property, Gilbert was concerned with its setting. He urged Dr. Ward to develop the small triangular space in front of the building and proposed sidewalks surrounding a central grass-covered area or paving the entire space with Belgian blocks. The interior of the building was particularly elaborate. Gilbert's office supplied the designs for the finishes of the interior spaces, the furniture, and fixtures. As the Gilbert office raced to get the building ready for occupancy, the late delivery of some items of furniture caused serious concerns. Both the general furniture contractor, T. D. Wadelton, and the lighting contractor, Lloyd Garrett Company, received numerous letters of complaint from Gilbert. Gilbert wrote Wadelton: "WHERE is the bronze work for the Court rooms in the Essex Co. Ct. House, and WHEN will it be erected? Please get out your longest and sharpest prod and use it on the bronze-man."[44] Wadelton's failure to deliver hardware and furniture on time resulted in the occupancy of the courthouse being postponed. Gilbert set August 1, 1906, as a deadline only to discover that Wadelton was on vacation.[45] The building was slowly occupied during the fall of 1906.

Gilbert planned an elaborate series of artistic decorations for the courthouse building. The exterior was embellished by Andrew O'Connor's sculpture; the interior had decorative murals by a variety of companies and figural murals by Edwin Blashfield, George Maynard, Frank Millet, C. Y Turner, Howard Walker, Will Low, Kenyon Cox, and Howard Pyle. At times Gilbert had to mediate between the conservative tastes of the Essex County Building Commission and the vision of the artists. The commission found O'Connor's inclusion of female nudes in his relief inappropriate. While Gilbert felt that O'Connor should comply with the request to drape the figures, he soothed him by stating, "You or I or others should look upon these subjects differently."[46] Kenyon Cox's depiction of actress Ethel Barrymore as Justice caused even greater consternation. The building commission was appalled that a celebrity should be depicted in allegorical murals and Gilbert concurred, ordering Cox to repaint that section of the image.[47]

Rumors of corruption and poor workmanship have plagued the Essex County Courthouse since its completion. Gilbert believed the problems lay with poor maintenance, particularly of the mechanical equipment, and later difficulties with the disintegration of the exterior marble cladding due to air pollution. He complained: "I wish to add about the Court House at Newark that the building has never been properly operated excepting the first few weeks when we had a competent engineer and if you inquired there today you would be told that the ventilation of the criminal court is abominable. *It is* and will continue to be so long as unskilled engineers are employed." However, Gilbert concluded in the same letter about the building, "It is, however, I believe, one of the best court buildings of moderate size in the United States."[48]

FIGURE 3.11.

U.S. Custom House, New York, Bowling Green elevation, January 23, 1900. W. P. Foulds, draftsman. Watercolor, ink, graphite on drawing paper, 20⅛ in. × 31 in.

(Cass Gilbert Collection, courtesy New-York Historical Society, neg. no. 48755)

By the late 1890s New York City was one of the leading international ports and the largest national port. One-fifth of the U.S. Department of Treasury's revenues came from customs, and a large portion of that derived from goods being shipped into and out of New York City. The old Custom House at 55 Wall Street was cramped and out-of-date. Clearly the city needed a new and elaborate customs building.[49]

In 1899 the Department of Treasury held an invited competition for a new Custom House. Competitions had been a source of controversy in the U.S. architectural profession because architects who won a competition had no guarantee of actually receiving the commission for the building. Instead, a crony of the client would get the contract and use the winning entry as the basis of the design. Newly revised rules, approved by the AIA, stipulated that the jury be composed of professional architects and guaranteed that the winner would receive the commission. The federal government further reformed the competition process with the Tarnsey Act, which allowed private architects to compete for public appointments.

Cass Gilbert was determined to be on the list of invited architects for the Custom House competition. The commission would enable him to move from St. Paul to New York. He had two advantages: he was building the Minnesota state capitol, which demonstrated that he could manage a large public commission, and his former architectural partner, James Knox Taylor, was the supervising architect of the Department of Treasury, a man who could influence the composition of the list. Gilbert discretely but aggressively lobbied politicians and the secretary of the treasury. He speculated in a letter to Taylor that the list would probably be composed of George B. Post; Bruce Price; Howard and Cauldwell; McKim, Mead, and White; and two others, and closed with: "I most earnestly want to be one of the *two others*."[50] Gilbert's tactics succeeded; he received the invitation for the competition in early May. The list for the competition included Daniel Burnham of Chicago; Peabody and Stearns of Boston; Carrère and Hastings; George Post; McKim, Mead, and White; and Cass Gilbert of New York.

Gilbert put every effort into the design and drawings. He imported Ernest Hébrard from Paris to work on the drawings, figuring that an Ecole-trained architect could give him an edge over the other competitors. Gilbert, Hébrard, and Gilbert's New York office manager, Steve Haskell, who had also studied at the Ecole, spent the summer working on the project, studying how the old Custom House worked, looking at the new site on

FIGURE 3.12
U.S. Custom House, New York, preliminary perspective of rotunda, ca. 1902. Unidentified draftsman. Graphite on tracing paper, 17 in. × 29 in.

(Cass Gilbert Collection, courtesy New-York Historical Society, neg. no. 71870)

Bowling Green, and refining the design. Gilbert struggled to find an appropriately monumental form for the building's cramped site and government function, which, he believed, excluded traditional elements of significance such as domes and pediments. By late July Gilbert decided to ignore the competition stipulation of ground floor entrance and rotunda, and placed the entrance and rotunda on the second floor. A few days later he determined that colossal attached columns would provide an appropriate monumentality: "The idea of a great facade with attached columns (à la M. Duc's Palais de Justice, Paris) seems to me to give a great scale. We do not mean by this to copy Duc's design, but simply use it by way of illustration."[51] By the end of August the design was finalized and Haskell hired extra draftsmen to produce the competition drawings. On September 17, 1899, the office completed the drawings and sent off the entry. Gilbert wrote to Tom Holyoke describing the design and the strain of finishing the work:

FIGURE 3.13
U.S. Custom House, New York, detail of ornament of Whitehall and State Street entrances, 1902. T. R. Johnson, draftsman. Pencil, chalk and charcoal on drawing paper, 28 in. × 39 in.

(Cass Gilbert Collection, courtesy New-York Historical Society, neg. no. 58028)

> We finished and sent off the Custom House Competition drawings last night; the final touches being done by candle light, no other being available.
>
> I doubt whether there will be a better set of drawings in the competition. It is possible that Carrère & Hastings' drawings will be as good, but the fellows who have seen the drawings from other offices tell me we have nothing to fear on that account. The design as completed is a very strong one. I feel a little too rich in detail, but I am willing to take a chance on it.
>
> Hébrard fully met my expectations, and Steve was simply splendid. We had a dozen or fifteen men here working night and day for a week, and yet we were very much on-charette, and were all completely worn out when the thing was over.[52]

In September the jury narrowed the finalists down to Gilbert, and Carrère and Hastings. For more than a month the jury debated about what course to take. Should they hold a new competition, expand the number of jurors, or force the two firms to share the commission? Finally the jury decided; Gilbert's design had won the competition. Protests against the decision were widespread. Local politicians, led by New York collector of cus-

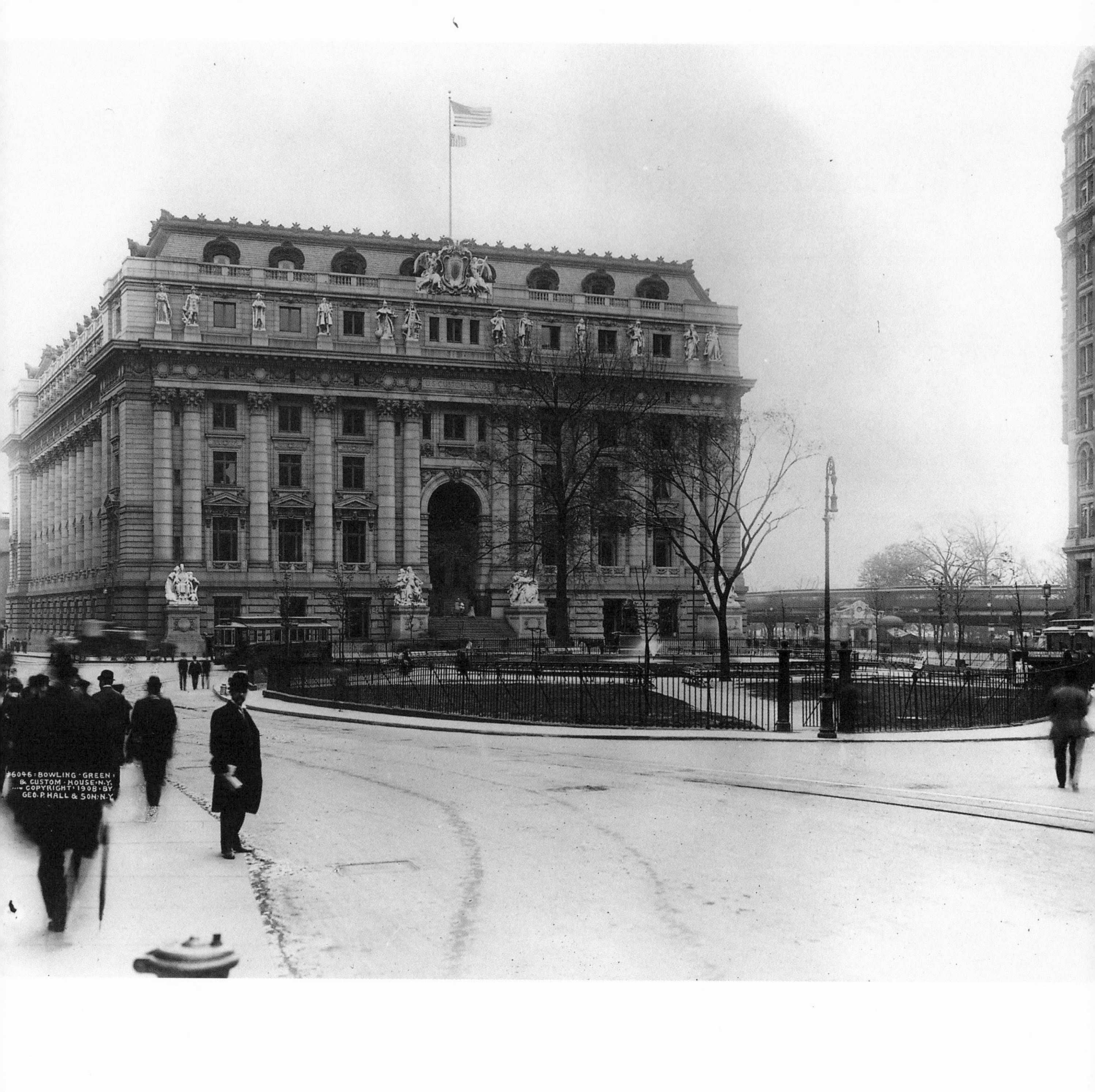
#6046: BOWLING · GREEN :
& CUSTOM · HOUSE · N.Y.
COPYRIGHT · 1908 · BY
GEO. P. HALL & SON: N.Y.

toms George Bidwell, Representative Lemuel Quigg, and Senator Thomas Platt opposed Gilbert's selection because he was not a New Yorker. They feared Gilbert would grant lucrative contracts to out-of-town firms, denying some of their key constituents fat contracts and themselves potential financial kickbacks.

Architects, particularly Carrère and Hastings, also protested the decision on more legitimate terms. The jury was composed of three architects, with Gilbert's former partner, Taylor, occupying one slot. Each competing architect had been asked to nominate potential jurors to fill the other two slots. Frank Miles Day was a popular choice nominated by many architects; however, Thomas Kimball was nominated only by Gilbert. Clearly, the jury was biased in Gilbert's favor.[53] Carrère and Hastings wrote a letter protesting the jury's decision and many in the New York architectural community supported their protest. The hostility of Gilbert's architectural colleagues so unnerved him that he considered not moving his office to New York. Finally the New York chapter of the American Institute of Architects, wanting to affirm the competition process and believing that Gilbert's design was a strong one, wrote a letter in support of Gilbert, which quelled the controversy.

Was Gilbert's design the strongest one? The jury made positive mention of Gilbert's decision to place the rotunda on the second story and provide major access to the space through a monumental stair. This raised the entrance above the traffic and noise of Broadway. The deliberate richness of Gilbert's design also seems to have been a point in his favor as well as his intent to include an allegorical sculptural program.

Next, Gilbert had to make peace with the politicians. First he met with Collector Bidwell who insisted that the design include a dome. Gilbert vehemently argued against this: "That the background of sky-scrapers did not admit of a satisfactory dome treatment on the Custom House, that the building was too small to carry a dome, and moreover, that a dome was not a consistent expression of the interior of the building, that there was no place of assemblage in the building such as is found in cathedrals, state and national capitols and other large buildings for which domes have been designed."[54] In February, at the insistence of the secretary of the treasury, Gilbert reluctantly met with Senator Platt as part of the peacemaking process.

Gilbert's designs for the Custom House fell into three phases: the competition, a revised design from 1900 through 1901, and the final design. In revising the scheme Gilbert refined proportions and clarified the relationship between various elements. He sought to simplify the design, making it

FIGURE 3.14
U.S. Custom House, New York City, 1908. George P. Hall and Son, photographers. Modern print from vintage negative, 11 in. × 14 in.
(Cass Gilbert Collection, courtesy New-York Historical Society, neg. no. 59216)

more Roman than French.[55] The final design, however, remained very ornate with symbols of commerce, the maritime, and the races and explorers of the world decorating the exterior.

Work on the building was divided into three contracts: Isaac Hopper was in charge of the excavation and foundations; John Peirce directed the construction of the superstructure; and J. C. Robinson oversaw the interiors. Each phase of work was plagued with difficulties. Irregular lot lines (the northern edge of the site was not parallel to the south) dictated a difficult and costly structural system. A change in lot lines, however, had to be approved by the board of aldermen, the Tammany politicians opposed to Gilbert's selection in the first place. Fortunately, Isaac Hopper had strong Tammany ties and managed to obtain approval of the changed lot lines without handing out bribes. John Peirce had substantial problems quarrying and transporting the granite for the exterior from Vinalhaven, Maine, to New York City. Two exceptionally cold winters and a series of labor disputes and strikes placed the completion of the building two years behind schedule. Despite Gilbert's complaints about Peirce's poor planning, the two managed to maintain a professional relationship and worked together on other projects. Gilbert's association with interior contractor J. C. Robinson, however, ended badly. Gilbert accused Robinson of encouraging subcontractors to pad their bids. In turn, subcontractors later complained that they were not paid for their work, suggesting that Robinson pocketed the difference. This resulted in several lawsuits in which Gilbert's office testified in favor of the subcontractors.

Gilbert had always envisioned an elaborate artistic program for the building. Sculptures on the exterior celebrated New York as the center of world commerce. Allegorical representations of the four continents framed the ground floor; a cartouche was placed over the main entrance; and twelve figures representing the important historical centers of maritime trade embellished the attic. Above this, Gilbert placed the Great Seal of the United States. Daniel Chester French received the commission for the four continents; Andrew O'Connor produced the cartouche; Karl Bitter designed the seal, while sculptors F. E. Elwell, F. W. Ruckstuhl, Augustus Lukeman, F. M. L. Tonetti, Louis Saint-Gaudens, Johannes Gelert, Albert Jaegers, and Charles Grafly created the attic figures.

Gilbert wanted to create an elaborate mural cycle within the building. In a letter to the secretary of the treasury Gilbert wrote: "I purposely omitted elaborate carving of marble work, mosaic, etc., customary in structures of this character with a view to using color decorations which in my judgement [are] more beautiful (if properly done) and less expensive." Gilbert had a list of artists he wanted to use on the interiors. But by the time the building was ready for occupancy in October 1907, delays and lawsuits had worn out the federal government's patience and budget. Finally, in 1911, the government hired Elmer Garnsey to create decorative paintings on maritime themes for the collector's suite, main hall, and stairs. The rotunda, the major interior space of the building, did not receive murals until the 1930s.[56]

Gilbert identified the Custom House as one the most significant buildings of his career, although he later came to feel that the building was a little too ornate. Gilbert reinterpreted the Custom House in several later buildings, including the American Insurance Company in Newark, New Jersey, the Detroit Public Library, and the U.S. Treasury Annex in Washington, D.C.[57]

FIGURE 3.15

West Street Building, New York City, rough sketch of elevation, May 7, 1905. Cass Gilbert, delineator. Graphite on board, 24 in. × 12⅛ in. on 26⅛ in. × 14⅜ in. mount.

(Cass Gilbert Collection, courtesy New-York Historical Society, neg. no. 57526)

Although the Broadway Chambers building established Cass Gilbert as a nationally known architect of office buildings at the turn of the century, he did not receive another commission for a New York City office building until 1905.[58] That year he was appointed architect for the West Street Building, to be located on the Hudson River waterfront in lower Manhattan. The owner of the property, Howard Carroll, assembled a team of building and real estate experts, including John Peirce and Walter Roberts of John Peirce Company contractors and Judge S. P. McConnell, a lawyer with extensive financial, legal, and real estate expertise, to form the West Street Improvement Company. Gilbert was hired after the West Street Improvement Company had completed the financing and initial planning for the building. In the Broadway Chambers project and later in the Woolworth Building project, Gilbert participated in arranging the financing for and planning the size of the building. For the West Street project Gilbert was more of a traditional designer, creating the exterior design, planning the offices, and coordinating the contractors.

The site, West Street facing the Hudson between Albany and Cedar Streets, was a major transportation hub for ships, passenger ferries, and lighters (boats that carried freight over from the railroad terminal in New Jersey to Manhattan). Before the completion of Pennsylvania Station, boats were the only vehicles that transported people and goods from New Jersey to New York. General Carroll was vice president of the Starin Transportation Company, which specialized in river transportation. The waterfront site created difficulties for the builders. The soil was so waterlogged that special designs had to be devised to ensure sound foundations and prevent leaks. Peirce and Gilbert's frequent collaborator, structural engineer Gunvald Aus, designed a pile foundation driven to meet the bedrock some forty-eight to fifty feet below ground, with concrete poured over the piles. The pile foundation was the first use of piles for such a large site. Engineering and architectural journals noted Aus and Gilbert's innovation and placed Gilbert in the forefront of skyscraper design as an architect employing the latest structural devices.

Gilbert's initial sketch called for a building with vaguely Gothic details and a tower. He then assigned several different designers in the office to work on the preliminary designs. While all the designs featured a blocklike building with a tower, styles varied from Gothic to classical. Gilbert eventually decided on a scheme close to his initial sketch, an ambiguous mix of

Belgian–French Gothic details on the exterior with exuberant ornament and a steep, pitched roof. The building was planned with a granite base and terra-cotta-clad shaft. The building became more spirited toward the top, with vivid animal forms and colored terra-cotta concluding in a roof punctuated by dormers and elaborate corner tourelles. The proposed tower would give the building a distinctive profile on the New York skyline and make it taller than the Flatiron Building.

Gilbert's design was notable for his emphasis on the building's verticality and the ambiguous style. Previous New York City skyscraper designers had tended to favor a tripartite elevation; Gilbert instead created a tower, which emphasized the building's height. Styles favored by architects for skyscraper construction came quickly into and out of fashion. A building designed in the Romanesque style could be stylistically obsolete and therefore less attractive to tenants in the course of two to three years. By creating a stylistically ambiguous building, Gilbert designed a structure that would remain distinctive. The building's exuberant and richly colored exterior added to its singular appearance on the Hudson River and as part of the New York City skyline and increased the building's significance and desirability.

Gilbert had originally called for a granite base and terra-cotta shaft. At John Peirce's insistence he reconsidered these materials, studying the possibility of an Indiana limestone base with a matching brick and terra-cotta shaft. He did, however, continue to insist on a certain amount of polychrome terra-cotta at the top of the building "to bring out the design."[59] By January 1906 Gilbert had reverted to his original scheme of the granite base and light beige terra-cotta-clad shaft with inserts of colored glazed terra-cotta and marble.

In April 1906 Carroll decided to omit the tower, probably as a cost-saving measure. Gilbert deeply regretted the decision, feeling that it diminished the building's visual significance: "I feel that while it will be a fine structure without the tower, still you are losing the opportunity to make a very distinctive and beautiful building which would be an important landmark."[60] In order to compensate for the loss of the tower, Carroll and Gilbert decided to enlarge the tourelles and raise them as high as possible to create a distinctive silhouette on the Manhattan skyline.[61] Gilbert designed an opulently decorated lobby as another way of giving the building distinction. Rookwood Pottery provided faience work; Frederick J. Wiley decorated the area with gilded stucco and stenciled designs on the vaults.[62]

The desired completion date of May 1, 1907, put pressure on Gilbert, Peirce, and all the subcontractors. Early in the process Peirce requested that Gilbert speed up producing the drawings. Gilbert responded that the magnitude and importance of the building created many time-consuming design problems. Gilbert, in turn, complained that Peirce ordered changes in the building without consulting with him.[63] The greatest difficulties occurred in the fabrication and construction of the steel frame. Gilbert accused the steel subcontractor, Milliken Brothers, of negligence on several occasions.[64] A strike by structural steel erectors in the spring of 1906 led Peirce to reconsider the method of floor construction, in order to comply with a labor law that mandated floor construction at the same pace as the frame. Milliken Brothers suggested replacing rivets with bolts in the floor beam connections. Gilbert and Aus rejected this suggestion. Gilbert wrote: "I know that such work is done, but not in the best class of buildings, and it is not considered by engineers good construction."[65]

By January 1907 it was apparent that the mechanical equipment was behind schedule. Gilbert wrote to the mechanical subcontractor, Boyd Equipment Company, imploring them to speed up their work. In February, Gilbert noted that delays in both the mechanical and elevator equipment had resulted in the rental agent not being able to show the building to prospective tenants; he threatened Boyd with nonconsideration for any future work: "Your record in connection with this work will be carefully noted and remembered in the future."[66] Despite these delays, tenants were able to move into the building ahead of schedule, in mid-April 1907. Rentals of the space proceeded smoothly. The Delaware, Lackawanna, and Western Railroad Company decided to rent the seventeenth through twentieth floors for offices in January 1907.[67] The company's presence made the building a magnet for other railroad interests, and although the developer initially intended to call the building the Railroad and Iron Exchange, by 1907 it was already being referred to as the West Street Building.[68] Also in January, Carroll decided to place a club-restaurant on the top floor of the building.[69]

In describing the West Street Building, Gilbert stressed its engineering innovations, terra-cotta skin, and elaborate ornament. He reported that "the building has been much admired and I have heard many compliments regarding it."[70] Gilbert's combination of engineering and artistry put him at the forefront of skyscraper design, and he would reinterpret the combination of tower, terra-cotta, and vague Gothic style for his next major New York City skyscraper, the Woolworth Building.

FIGURE 3.16

West Street Building, New York City, preliminary drawing, no date. Unidentified artist. Graphite on board, 29 in. × 19 in.

(Cass Gilbert Collection, courtesy New-York Historical Society, neg. no. 58103)

FIGURE 3.17

West Street Building, New York City, preliminary drawing, no date. Unidentified artist. Graphite on board, 27 in. × 13 in.

(Cass Gilbert Collection, courtesy New-York Historical Society, neg. no. 58105)

FIGURE 3.18

F. W. Woolworth Company Building, New York City, preliminary perspective, April 22, 1910. T. R. Johnson, draftsman. Watercolor, gouache, graphite on illustration board, 29⅞ in. × 17⅞ in.

(Cass Gilbert Collection, courtesy New-York Historical Society, neg. no. 57748)

By 1909 Cass Gilbert had achieved national recognition as an architect of large-scale institutional and commercial buildings.[71] That year he received a commission that forever altered his career: Frank Woolworth approached him to design an office building. The building was to be a speculative venture. While two floors would be occupied by Woolworth's corporation, the rest were to be rented out, providing Woolworth with substantial revenues. For at least two years Woolworth and Gilbert developed and studied thirty different proposals for a structure of varying sizes and heights. Gilbert's office drew a variety of exterior solutions as well, looking at different schemes for massing and ornamentation. The bulk of the designs were in a Gothic revival style, yet at least one perspective depicted a classically derived building.

News of the commission first circulated in 1910 and caused intense excitement in the building community, with many contractors hoping to receive the lucrative and prestigious commission. But plans for the building only took final form in 1911 when Woolworth purchased the block on Broadway between Barclay and Park Place, and drawings for the world's tallest building were completed in a rapid eighty-six days.[72] Construction of the building required excellent planning and engineering. Gilbert's team planned for bringing massive amounts of materials to the site, provided adequate foundations, and designed a steel frame that would take into account the effects of high winds. As impressive as these plans were, the public was more fascinated by the design of the high-speed elevators with air cushions, a feature meant to arrest the drop of a car should an accident occur.

Woolworth and Gilbert programmed the building to offer many amenities, including a restaurant, swimming pool, observation deck, and social club. The design of the ground floor entrance lobby was particularly ornate, using marble, bronze, and mosaics. The lobby had a Latin cross plan, with barrel vaults and a dome at the crossing. Gargoyles caricaturing Gilbert, Woolworth, engineer Gunvald Aus, builder Louis Horowitz, and Lewis Peirson, president of one of the major tenants of the building, the Irving Bank, were placed at the crossing. The roof of the tower was originally gilded, and Woolworth was insistent upon a scheme of night lighting. Yet for all these aesthetic considerations, the building was still a commercial undertaking. In December 1911 Gilbert received a letter from Woolworth about his worries that the building might not be finished by its projected completion date of May 1913. He wrote: "In fact I cannot conceive or imagine what a terrible loss it would be to me personally if I were not able to get

FIGURE 3.19
F. W. Woolworth Company Building, New York City, roof and lantern of tower, September 28, 1911. T. R. Johnson, draftsman. Graphite, crayon on tracking paper, 20 in. × 13 in. on 21 in. × 15 in. mount.

(Cass Gilbert Collection, courtesy New-York Historical Society, neg. no. 72836)

FIGURE 3.20
F. W. Woolworth Company Building lobby, New York City, April 15, 1912. T. R. Johnson, draftsman. Watercolor, colored pencil, graphite on tracing paper, 15 in. × 10 in. on 18 in. × 14 in. mount.

(Cass Gilbert Collection, courtesy New-York Historical Society, neg. no. 70876)

tenants in that building on the first of May 1913, and it is, therefore, of the utmost importance that the work in your office should be expedited as fast as possible and every effort made to get out plans and specifications for the work as soon as it can be done."[73]

Woolworth was worried that the work on air cushions and lobby, both of which had been finalized fairly late in the process, might delay the building's completion. As construction progressed, an even greater concern was the delivery of the exterior terra-cotta cladding. By September 1912 the Atlantic Terra Cotta Company was slowly fabricating the terra-cotta and not delivering it fast enough to suit the contractors, architect, and owner. Finally, by the end of October all terra-cotta was on-site. A floor of model offices, in different color schemes and finishes, was installed during November 1912 to entice potential tenants.[74]

The exterior terra-cotta was complicated to fabricate due to its elaborate decoration and complex color scheme. Gilbert and the Atlantic Terra Cotta Company chose cream as the predominant color because it was warm in tone and more pleasing to the eye than a cold white. Gilbert also liked the slight variations in color, which he believed added light and life to the facade.[75] The color scheme also included a background of blue, green, and golden yellow, as well as faience colors, which were "used more to accentuate the natural shadows than to add their own color value."[76]

The project seems to have been largely free of the tensions and conflicts that plagued Gilbert's public commissions, yet Woolworth, who liked to inspect every aspect of the building, must have been a trying client. He complained that well-known lighting manufacturer Edward Caldwell's typical hallway fixtures were not up to standard and that Caldwell should be denied his final payment.[77] He objected to the designs for statues at the entrance by Donnelly and Ricci because they were "too monkish" and made the building still more of a cathedral.[78]

Gilbert synthesized a variety of sources for the Woolworth Building design. He credited the French Gothic style as the primary source of inspiration for the building. He wrote to the French ambassador to the United States, J. J. Jusserand: "My own study in France and my repeated visits to your beautiful country led me to adopt many of the architectural forms of the Fifteenth Century Gothic which are so pliable and expressive."[79] Yet Woolworth wanted the building to be based on London's nineteenth-century Gothic revival Houses of Parliament, and Gilbert may also have looked at medieval Guild Hall buildings in Belgium, as well as Venetian Gothic palazzi.

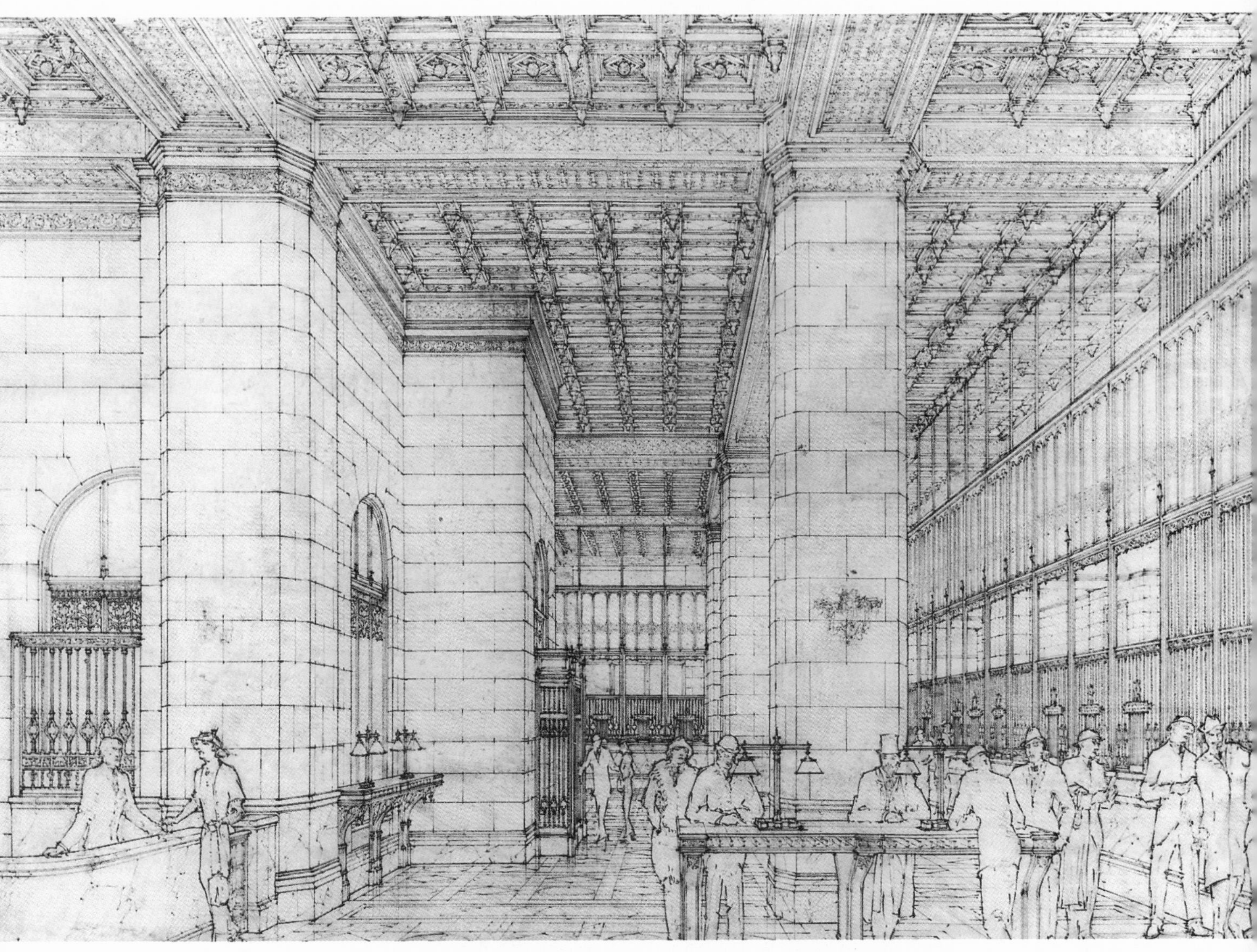

FIGURE 3.21

F. W. Woolworth Company Building, Banking Room, New York City, 1912. Hugh Ferriss, renderer. Graphite on trace, 21 in. × 30 in.

(Cass Gilbert Collection, courtesy New-York Historical Society, neg. no. 69601)

FIGURE 3.22.

F. W. Woolworth Company Building, New York City, 1912. Wurts Brothers, photographers. Photographs, 10 in. × 8 in.

(Cass Gilbert Collection, courtesy New-York Historical Society, neg. nos. 54744, 73195, 73194)

9-12

FIGURE 3.23
Interior view from the center of the lobby of the F. W. Woolworth Company Building, May 11, 1913. Gargoyles humorously caricaturing F. W. Woolworth *(left)* and Cass Gilbert *(right)* can be seen in the corners of the entrance to the south hallway. Unidentified photographer.

(Cass Gilbert Collection, courtesy New-York Historical Society, neg. no. 73094)

In 1915 several pieces of the terra-cotta failed, prompting arguments between Woolworth and Gilbert about whether the terra-cotta had been improperly set. Gilbert believed the failures were due to the expansion and contraction of joints, high winds, underground blasting, or tremors. He stated that "for any one of these causes the contractors could not be held liable, they were beyond our power of discerning when the building was built." While Woolworth complained about whistling windows and the terra-cotta, on the whole he was enormously pleased with the building. Recovering from a nervous collapse in Europe during the summer of 1914, Woolworth wrote Gilbert that he considered the building to be one of the great events in his life: "When it comes to the building and its wonderful beauty I always look to you as the great artist and architect and you alone deserve the praise that is constantly being [brought] up about its beauty and I sometimes wonder how you could have done it and in such a short space of time."[80]

The Woolworth Building dominated Gilbert's reputation, a fact he fought by insisting that any publication or exhibition of the Woolworth Building also include his other buildings. At times he found the Woolworth's fame difficult. In 1920 he wrote to the architect Ralph Adams Cram: "I sometimes wish I had never built the Woolworth Building because I fear it may be regarded as my only work and you and I both know that whatever it may be in dimension and in certain lines it is after all only a skyscraper."[81] Yet Gilbert was attuned to the energy and teamwork of American skyscrapers and could see it as the best of American culture. Of skyscrapers he wrote:

> The symbols of our national genius and unrestraint rise like the crags of a volcanic island still in process of upheaval. The scale is gigantic; the power, irresistible; the daring, licentious; and yet, to those that have eyes to see, there is the germ of the true art. And the Skyscraper is ours. It is conceived by business, half in economy of ground, half in extravagance of advertising; it is born of the mechanical ingenuity which evolved the steel frame and the express elevator; and it is sanctioned only by the least paternal of governments. Now because it is ours, because it expresses the most obvious side of our cosmos, because there are no alien conventions to follow, we are evolving, almost unconsciously, a new type of interest and even beauty.[82]

WOOLWORTH BUILDING

Turn-of-the-century American architects dreamed of reshaping whole sections of cities, and Cass Gilbert shared these visions. By the 1900s Cass Gilbert was actively engaged in planning issues that looked at large complexes of buildings or even entire cities. Oberlin College was one of Gilbert's early group plans; he remained involved with the college until his death in 1934, giving the office an opportunity to design and implement a plan over a span of three decades.[83]

The administration of Oberlin first approached Gilbert in early spring of 1904 with the proposal to design a new college chapel. The college had recently lost several buildings to fire; many others were severely out-of-date. In discussing the chapel, Lucien Warner, an Oberlin trustee, revealed that the college was also considering building an administration building and that it had retained the services of Frederick Law Olmsted to create a general design for the grounds. Asked if he was interested in designing the new chapel, Gilbert replied: "I told him that my father had been a student at Oberlin College and that I myself was a native of Ohio, so that from a sentimental point of view I should be interested in the work."[84] The themes of alma mater and sentiment would frequently recur in Gilbert's description of the Oberlin plan.

Gilbert received a copy of Olmsted's report. He marked several items pertaining to the general plan and long-range recommendations concerning various buildings envisioned by the administration. Of particular relevance was Olmsted's major recommendation to "clear the main campus of buildings and to keep it as a spacious and beautiful pleasure ground for the principal working buildings of the college to front upon."[85] Of equal significance was the firm's suggestion that the college's next step be the placement of buildings based on a general plan. While Gilbert's specific commission was to design and construct Finney Memorial Chapel (1904–8), this did not prevent him from making several sketches of a general plan.

When the college started to plan the Administration Building in 1909, Gilbert lobbied for a general plan. As discussions concerning the building continued into 1911, Gilbert pressed for the acquisition of more land; he discussed the grouping of buildings and gently pushed the administration toward developing an overall plan. On November 20, 1911, he announced his selection as general architect for the college.[86] Gilbert's plan kept the central part of the campus free of buildings, and he retained the Olmsted Brothers as landscape architects. Gilbert wanted to create an open, central

FIGURE 3.24

Oberlin College, perspective of quadrangle, Oberlin, Ohio. 1930. John T. Cronin, delineator. Watercolor, graphite on illustration board, 16 in. × 22 in.

(Cass Gilbert Collection, courtesy New-York Historical Society, neg. no. 72837)

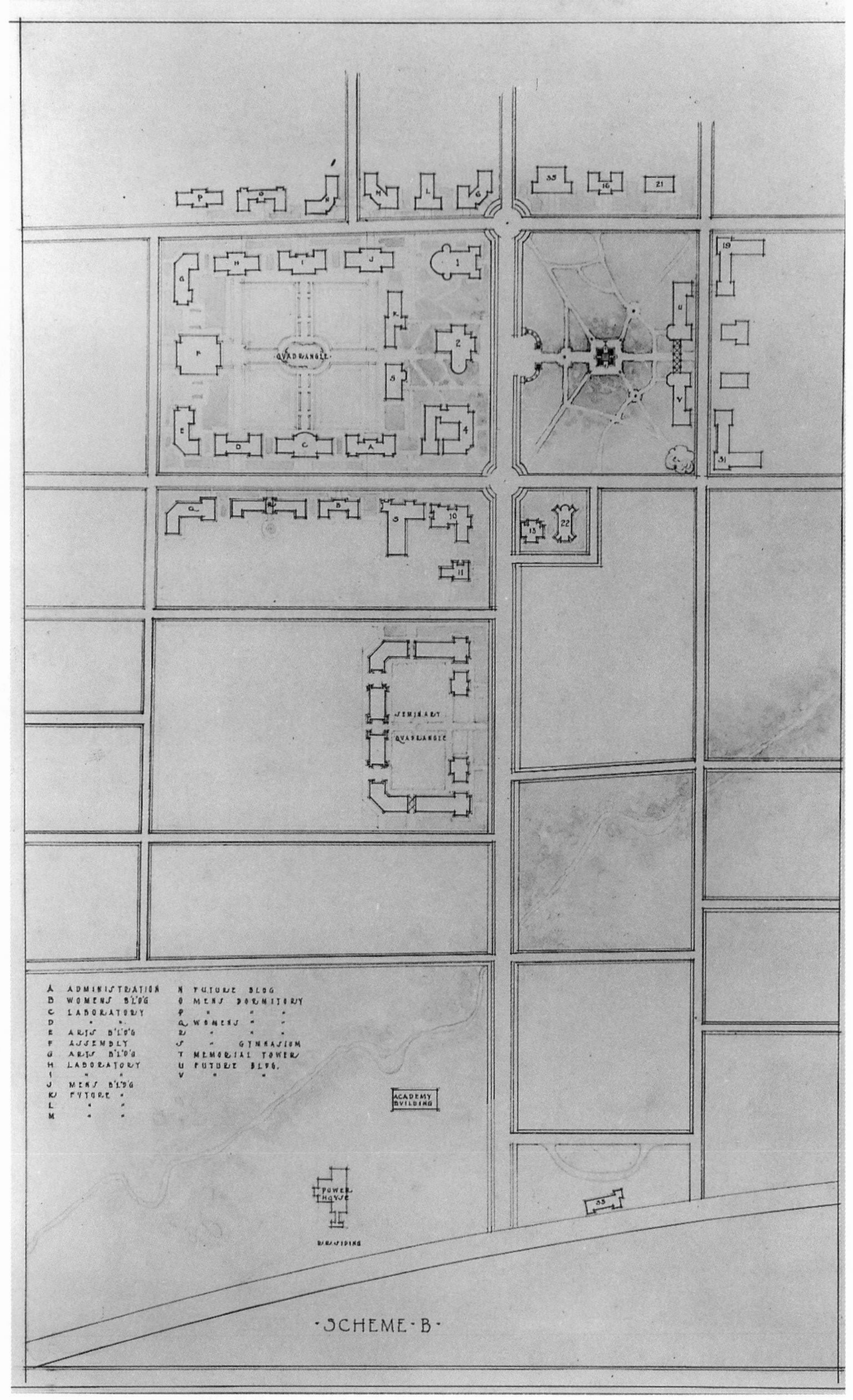
QUADRANGLE
SEMINARY
QUADRANGLE
A ADMINISTRATION
B WOMENS B'L'D'G
C LABORATORY
D " "
E ARTS B'L'D'G
F ASSEMBLY
G ARTS B'L'D'G
H LABORATORY
I " "
J MENS B'L'D'G
K FUTURE "
L " "
M " "
N FUTURE BLDG
O MENS DORMITORY
P " " "
Q WOMENS " "
R " " "
S " GYMNASIUM
T MEMORIAL TOWER
U FUTURE BLDG.
V " "
ACADEMY BUILDING
POWER HOUSE
R.R. SIDING
·SCHEME·B·

mall, yet shield the campus from the banal commercial buildings of the surrounding town.[87] While he applauded President King's idea of planning a civic center, he doubted that the college's funds were sufficient to accomplish such a scheme. Instead he advocated the occupation of the four corners of the campus to form a screen, shielding it from the surrounding city. This would leave the center free and make the central area look larger by closing down the perspective.[88]

FIGURE 3.25
Oberlin College, Scheme B, Oberlin, Ohio, no date. Unidentified artist. Ink wash, ink, and graphite on illustration board, 30 in. × 22 in.
(Cass Gilbert Collection, courtesy New-York Historical Society, neg. no. 72838)

While Gilbert was frequently pragmatic about budgets, he was capable of supporting added expenses for the sake of design. When the college eliminated paths from the campus, Gilbert argued: "Although the practical needs of circulation may be well served by fewer paths, plan composition in its relation to the ultimate unification of the various units demand such 'lines' and the accompanying vistas. This is especially true of this type of composition which accepts the planted campus as one of the principal features."[89] Gilbert sought to unify the campus by developing an overall approach to the visual forms of the various buildings.

> One of the most serious criticisms that can be made of college groups in this country is that with few exceptions no consistent scheme as to the style of buildings or as to the general plans has been carried out. The few exceptions to this rule have been so notably successful as to fully justify our intention of bringing Oberlin so far as possible into one harmonious style of architecture. When I first undertook work at Oberlin I found that the best of the buildings in existence there was the Warner Gymnasium which is a simple round arched so-called Romanesque style that could be adapted to the various needs of the college without too great an expense.

While the buildings Gilbert designed at Oberlin vary in style from Romanesque to Renaissance they share the same warmly colored materials and round-arched motif.

Gilbert's penultimate plan for Oberlin centered on a main axis starting with an auditorium complex, sweeping through Silsbee's Memorial Arch, and culminating in the administration complex with a tower. Gilbert was greatly attached to the tower design. He urged President King to make the tower a priority. "You would then have set a standard for the Oberlin of the future and have made a rallying point for its students and alumni. I think I can say that you would have a memorial tower that would be unrivalled in this country, for while it would not be elaborate in detail its majestic scale and fine proportions would give it such distinction that Oberlin would at once become a notable architectural center."[90] While the tower was "useless" in terms of housing the college's program, Gilbert felt it would serve a much-needed role at Oberlin.

> I hope the future of Oberlin with its great central tower, its arcade, cloisters and quadrangles, its richly ornamented doorways, its broad overhanging eaves and tile roofs, its loggias and terraces, its broad open grassy sunlit yards, its beautiful trees, will all combine to make a series of fascinating pictures which will have a permanent influence not only upon the student body while they are young and impressionable but always remain in the minds of the future alumni as the place which next to their own homes, they will love the best.[91]

Gilbert ultimately created five buildings or complexes at Oberlin: the Finney Chapel, Cox Administration Building (1915), Allen Memorial Art Museum (1917), Allen Memorial Hospital (1925), and the Graduate School of Theology (1931), an impressive legacy of his work. At his death in 1934 the office was designing one of the major components of the master plan, the auditorium complex. Unfortunately, Gilbert's death precluded that project's completion.

FIGURE 3.26
U.S. Army Supply Base, Brooklyn, pier end, June 20, 1918. Frederick G. Stickel, draftsman. Watercolor, conté crayon, gouache and graphite on paper, 12 in. × 17 in.
(Cass Gilbert Collection, courtesy New-York Historical Society, neg. no. 72839)

U.S. ARMY SUPPLY BASE

A self-described Republican and patriot, Cass Gilbert enthusiastically supported the United States' World War I efforts. When the United States entered the conflict in April 1917 Gilbert immediately offered his services. Not until January 1918, however, did Gilbert finally have the opportunity to serve his country. That month H. C. Turner, president of Turner Construction Company, approached Gilbert about collaborating on an extensive series of warehouses and docks for the War Department. Turner, one of many companies vying for the project, was proposing a site on the South Brooklyn waterfront.[92] The warehouse complex was part of a series of East Coast bases collecting goods and people for transportation to Europe. As the largest American port, New York City would also have the largest base. The economic benefits the base would bring to any neighborhood sparked intense competition between the various sectors of the New York harbor. Besides the South Brooklyn site, the War Department also considered locations in New Jersey, Jamaica Bay, Staten Island, and Manhattan.[93]

Why did Turner want to collaborate with the architect of the Woolworth Building and the U.S. Custom House on a warehouse complex? Gilbert's work at the Woolworth Building proved that the office could build a large-scale structure with complex structural and mechanical systems at a rapid pace. Gilbert also had experience as a warehouse designer,

FIGURE 3.27

U.S. Army Supply Base, Brooklyn, November 1919. Hugh Ferriss, renderer. Graphite on paper, 26 in. × 48 in.

(Cass Gilbert Collection, courtesy New-York Historical Society, neg. no. 72840)

constructing the Austin, Nichols and Company Warehouse in Brooklyn in 1913. Similar to the proposed U.S. Army Supply Base, the official name of the War Department complex, Austin, Nichols was a reinforced concrete structure with piers and rail lines.

By February, Gilbert, Turner, and Irving Bush, head of the New York war effort and owner of the adjacent Bush Terminals, met with General Goethals in Washington, D.C., and presented their plan. Gilbert commissioned Hugh Ferriss to render a series of dramatic perspectives for the proposal. These, together with a plot plan, formed the basis of the presentation. The scheme called for several piers—including three double-deck piers, a Gantry-loading pier, and a dock—two enormous warehouses, an administration building, power plant, and barracks. Gilbert, Turner, and Bush emphasized the purported advantages of the Brooklyn location as the connecting point with various forms of transportation, the accessibility of the site to workers from all parts of the city, and the proximity to other large industrial plants. The three men also stressed their proposal's advanced engineering. The buildings would be of reinforced concrete based on the latest advances in fireproof warehouse and factory construction. Additionally, they would employ a traveling crane system similar to that used in Henry Ford's Detroit automobile plant. In March 1918 the War Department selected the South Brooklyn site and Gilbert and Turner's designs.[94]

The commission set off intense rivalries within the War Department as to who would control and administer the project. Colonel R. C. Marshall was initially in charge of the project, but Gilbert disliked Marshall's views on Gilbert's design autonomy and fees. Instead, Gilbert managed to be hired as a consultant answering directly to General Goethals; he signed the contract in June 1918.[95]

Gilbert's final design for the complex called for two huge reinforced concrete warehouses connected by bridges. He specified a recently patented method of construction consisting of concrete slabs supported by specially reinforced columns. The warehouses lacked ornamentation but were enlivened by the arrangement of windows, projecting piers, and almost-decorative frieze of downspouts. Gilbert wrote: "The whole system of building is characterized by extreme simplicity—there is not one moulding or ornament of any kind. The structures are impressive and majestic because of their vast scale, severe design and fine proportions."[96] The larger warehouse, Building B, had a skylighted central court for unloading train cars. Traveling roof-level cranes, inspired by those in the Ford plant, loaded and unloaded cargo from the diagonally positioned balconies without in-

FIGURE 3.28

U.S. Army Supply Base, Brooklyn, interior of Building B, no date. Unidentified photographer. Photograph, 20 in. × 25 in.

(Cass Gilbert Collection, courtesy New-York Historical Society, neg. no. 72841)

FIGURE 3.29

U.S. Army Supply Base, Brooklyn, Building A, no date. Unidentified photographer. Photograph, 8 in. × 11 in.

(Cass Gilbert Collection, courtesy New-York Historical Society, neg. no. 72842)

terruption or long waits for elevators. The War Department made only one major alteration; it cut the size of Building B in half.

Of equal importance to the building's modern appearance was its modern method of functioning. Gilbert wrote: "The modern storage warehouse should no more be regarded as a *'tomb'* for merchandise than the modern high pressure boiler as a *tank* for water. If merchandise does not flow through it freely and easily, it is stagnant and unprofitable. It is worse than that, it is an 'aneurysm' on traffic; it is a cause of delay."[97]

Construction commenced during the summer of 1918. Only weeks into the project, Lt. Col. Herbert S. Crocker, the War Department official supervising the project, was accused of minimal and slack management. Gilbert believed this scandal was due to political in-fighting rather than any genuine negligence on Crocker's part.[98] While the accusations did not result in Crocker's removal, it did shift power from Crocker to an engineer named B. F. Cresson Jr., Goethals' consultant on docks. By August, Cresson and Gilbert were clashing on a number of issues, and Gilbert began complaining about Cresson's interference with the work.[99] Cresson questioned the feasibility of the overhead cranes. After detailed study, a subcommittee approved them. He forced Gilbert to redesign the pier ends because he found the original scheme to be too decorative.[100] Cresson then questioned the height of the parapets on the warehouses and the need for a connecting bridge.[101] Playing on the dual division of work that he had initially disliked, Gilbert went to his friend Irving Bush, who reported to Gilbert's one-time nemesis but now enthusiastic supporter R. C. Marshall. With Marshall's permission Bush sharply reprimanded Cresson, stating that the "Construction Division does not wish to take the attitude of overruling so competent an architect whose judgement and opinions are entitled to full respect and consideration."[102] After November, no more was heard of the troublesome Cresson.

Gilbert, who had had experience with railroads in Minnesota and New York, was concerned that the army's layout of rail lines within the complex was dangerous. He consulted with experts from the Long Island Railroad to redesign the yards. In his statements describing the base, Gilbert emphasized that architects designed buildings and planned complexes: "His planning of the storage yards, streets, ramps, railroads, lines of traffic, connecting bridges, tunnels, and in short all facilities of handling freight make it a practical achievement of notable character; and demonstrate that the work of the trained architect in the organization of a practical plan is of the highest values."[103]

By November 1918, with the war over, the War Department was considering its options, including selling the buildings to private owners as factories.[104] The base, however, remained under the army's control and was a major point of embarkation during World War II and the Korean and Vietnam Wars. Today it is owned by the New York City Economic Development Corporation and is used for a variety of purposes.

FIGURE 3.30

Detroit Public Library, front elevation, no date. T. R. Johnson, draftsman. Ink wash, ink, graphite on board, 15 in. × 30 in.

(Cass Gilbert Collection, courtesy New-York Historical Society, neg. no. 72843)

In designing and constructing the Detroit Public Library, Cass Gilbert drew upon artistic ideals and tactical skills that he had honed in more than twenty years of practice. The library embodied the ideals of the American Renaissance that Gilbert had first employed in the Minnesota state capitol, with its large, marble, classically styled building that set the tone for a surrounding civic center. It was embellished with sculpture, mosaics, murals, paintings, and other examples of the decorative arts as a symbol of civic pride and refined taste. Gilbert skillfully maneuvered through disappointed local contractors, wild swings in the economy, political reversals, and World War I.

Gilbert formulated his vision of the building and how it related to the site during the 1913 competition. He wrote that he "endeavored to make a design which should be as pure and as fine an example of the best period of the Renaissance." Additionally, he was very struck with the possibilities of the site and of making "a beautiful development of that particular section of the city."[105]

After receiving the contract, Gilbert spent the next year and a half developing the designs with chief librarian Adam Strohm. Gilbert faced several problems: the library commission was still acquiring land for the structure, and the program for the building was badly out-of-date, necessitating intensive restudy.[106] Public outcry about the dormant site created pressure to commence work. At Gilbert's suggestion, the library commission let contracts for the excavations, foundations, and structural steel in January and February 1915.[107] Gilbert recognized that prices for materials and labor were extremely low and urged the library commission to let the contracts for the general construction and stacks. His revised design, however, cost more than the funds available for the building. The commission had to submit the revised budget to public referendum, which failed in April 1915.[108] By November 1915 the foundations were complete; the structural steel was in place; and no further monies were available. Gilbert suspended work on the building until a bond could be passed.[109] He would wait a year until the citizens of Detroit finally voted in the affirmative, providing $750,000 in funds. The ongoing European war, however, had generated a vastly different economic situation, and Gilbert worried that the additional funds would not be sufficient for the building.[110] In April 1917 the voters approved a second bond of $250,000, thus guaranteeing, in Gilbert's words, "a thoroughly substantial building with handsome exterior and practical and

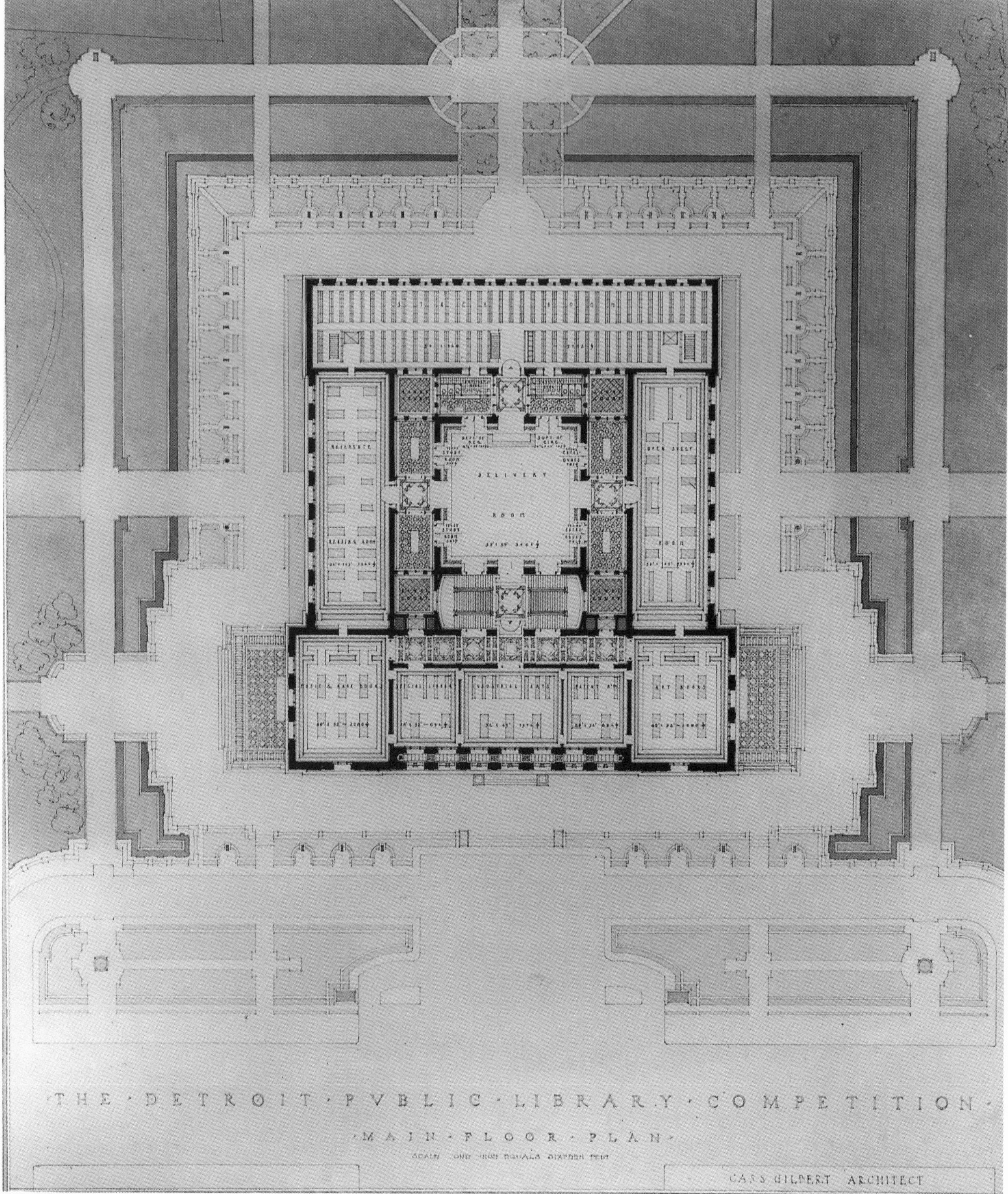
STACK ROOM
REFERENCE
READING ROOM
DELIVERY
ROOM
OPEN SHELF
ROOM
ART BOOKS
·THE·DETROIT·PVBLIC·LIBRARY·COMPETITION·
·MAIN·FLOOR·PLAN·
CASS GILBERT ARCHITECT

usable interior."[111] In other words, the library would have a marble exterior but a very plain interior, lacking the murals, sculptures, and other ornamental features.

After the approval of the bond, Gilbert and the commission turned to selecting a contractor. The commission wanted to hire the local contractor William Dall Company; Gilbert's own preference was the George Fuller Company, and the overall cost estimates favored his choice. Gilbert persuaded the commission to select Fuller. He, however, worked hard to appease Dall, since his previous experience with the Minnesota state capitol had taught him that disgruntled local contractors could ignite future political problems. As the contracts were awarded, the United States entered World War I, causing further shortages of material and labor. In August 1920 the building was slowly nearing completion, and Gilbert reminded Strohm of the extreme difficulties Fuller had faced: "At the time of the award of the contract to the Fuller Co., the world war was then in existence and at that time, the possibility of the completion of the building being delayed was admitted, as one of the conditions of the contract with the Fuller Co. Later, when the United States entered the war, the conditions became more acute and since the Armistice, conditions have not improved; on the contrary have developed even more serious."[112] Fuller finally completed the building in December 1920.

Although the budget did not include any funds for artwork or decorative embellishments, Gilbert hoped to incorporate these components into the building. As early as the summer of 1917, Gilbert explored obtaining private donations for art.[113] This, combined with the city's growing enthusiasm for the building, resulted in funding for almost all the envisioned decorative work. Pewabic Pottery and Frederick J. Wiley collaborated on mosaics for the entrance loggia; Samuel Yellin created a wrought-iron entrance gate to the Fine Arts Room; Edwin Blashfield painted murals for the main stair hall; Gari Melchers created decorative figure paintings in the Delivery Room; John Donnelly carved much of the exterior ornamental marble work including the signs of the zodiac under the main cornice.[114] John Polachek Bronze and Iron Company's work for the building included the main entrance doors illustrating the history of philosophy, science, and art. Gilbert believed this to be the most beautiful bronze work in the United States.[115] In addition to designing the loggia mosaics, Frederick J. Wiley created the decorative murals throughout the building, as well as designs for stained glass windows in the main stairway. By December 1920 the library commission perceived enough public goodwill and economic stability to

FIGURE 3.31
Detroit Public Library, Main Floor Plan, no date. Unidentified artist. Ink wash, ink on illustration board, 34 in. × 30 in.
(Cass Gilbert Collection, courtesy New-York Historical Society, neg. no. 72844)

AVENUE
AVENUE
MUSEUM BUILDING
THE DETROIT PVBLIC LIBRARY COMPETITION
BLOCK PLAN

FIGURE 3.32.

Detroit Public Library, Block Plan, no date. Unidentified artist. Ink wash, ink on illustration board, 34 in. × 30 in.

(Cass Gilbert Collection, courtesy New-York Historical Society, neg. no. 72845)

FIGURE 3.33

Detroit Public Library, perspective view of Delivery Hall, December 3, 1918. Frederick G. Stickel, draftsman. Graphite, ink wash on drawing paper, 30 in. × 49 in.

(Cass Gilbert Collection, courtesy New-York Historical Society, neg. no. 72846)

send Wiley to Rome, Florence, and Sienna to study Renaissance paintings as a basis for his decorations.[116]

Gilbert described the effect that a well-designed and beautiful library could have on an urban landscape: "It is one of the structures which will most be noted by citizens and strangers alike as the evidence of the civic spirit, the progressive character and the intelligence of the community."[117] Written in 1917 to persuade the citizens of Detroit to approve the bond for the building, Gilbert's statement accurately anticipated the pride Detroit would take in its public library and civic center during the 1920s. Today the library stands in a downtown that has been devastated by poverty and attempts at urban renewal, a mute reminder of another era's more optimistic belief in the power of architecture to generate beauty and civic responsibility.

Almost ten years in the making, the New York Life Insurance Company Building was Cass Gilbert's third and final version of the Gothic-styled skyscraper. In the interim between the Woolworth Building and the New York Life Insurance Company Building, profound changes had occurred in American building practices and in the economy. They resulted in a complex design and construction process that was deeply frustrating to Gilbert. The depression and political instability that followed World War I made the directors of the New York Life Insurance Company nervous about their financial investment in the building, which resulted in frequent changes. In addition, the introduction of zoning laws in 1916 and the increased importance of the general contractor in the construction process took many of the decisions and responsibilities away from the architect. Initially enthusiastic about the project, by 1927 Gilbert's office was simply approving or disapproving the contractor Starrett Brothers' decisions, largely without comment. Gilbert wrote to a professor at the University of North Carolina, "If the students realized the complicated detail and extent of these large buildings they would probably find it very discouraging."[118] The office's interest in the project only returned with the decoration of the major interior spaces.

The president of the New York Life Insurance Company, Darwin Kingsley, first approached Cass Gilbert about designing a new headquarters in 1919. The two met in December and discussed the zoning regulations and the requirements of a profitable and well-designed office building.[119] While Gilbert's office worked on designs for the building from 1920 through 1922, serious meetings about the structure did not begin until late 1923, probably due to the economic recession after World War I. By 1923 the company had decided on a site, the abandoned Madison Square Garden building on Madison Avenue at Twenty-sixth Street, and that they needed a large building of around 700,000 to 1 million square feet. The company equivocated about every other aspect of the design. At times Kingsley and other executives desired a large floor plan with space in the center for its extensive files. At other instances they preferred smaller, adequately lit spaces. They oscillated between desiring a plain business building and a more monumental structure. Three radically different massing solutions were also studied: a squat, massive ziggurat-like building, a high tower, and an interim solution of about twenty stories with a fairly large tower of 144 square feet.[120] Gilbert was in favor of the high tower solution and diplomatically but firmly kept emphasizing that scheme: "I told them that I had not yet given up the idea

FIGURE 3.34

New York Life Insurance Company Building, New York City, November 1923. F. G. Stickel, draftsman. Ink wash and graphite on illustration board, 28 in. × 9 in.

(Cass Gilbert Collection, courtesy New-York Historical Society, neg. no. 72847)

that this structure might be developed with a high tower, that their Company ought to have the most 'distinguished' thing that they could get in New York and without pressing the matter I still proposed to make at least one sketch showing how the structure would look carried to the height as suggested in previous sketches."[121] By November 1924 the New York Life Insurance Company finally reached a solution; while they admired the high tower scheme as a design, they were afraid of the large amount of rental space included in the building and opted for the interim solution. In light of the glut of office space in New York City during the Great Depression, the company's decision was probably economically wise.[122]

The company continued to revisit the design throughout 1924, with various officers asking Gilbert to create sketches of different schemes. Gilbert, however, focused on the interim solution and used that design as the basis of the working drawings and specifications.[123] One of the major issues was the amount of light needed for the interiors. While standard practice called for office space to be no farther away from a window than twenty-five to thirty feet, Gilbert felt that a deeper plan in this instance was practical with files, vaults, stairs, and elevators occupying the interior, and the office force placed around the perimeter of the building. He also pointed out that the company made extensive use of electric lights in their current building: "That in their own building, which was [an] exceptionally well lighted building for down town, I had been through their departments in the brightest sunny weather when every electric light over every desk and every ceiling light was going full blast."[124]

Gilbert tried desperately to save a portion of Madison Square Garden, designed by his mentor, Stanford White. Gilbert planned to save the tower of the Garden and reconstruct it on the Bronx campus of New York University, also a White design. Throughout the spring of 1925, Gilbert searched for a donor to pay for the hauling and reconstruction of the tower. By April 1925 it was apparent no donor was forthcoming and large portions of the building could not be preserved.[125]

In March 1926 the bids for construction came in significantly higher than either Gilbert or the New York Life Insurance Company expected. With working drawings and specifications completed, and steel being fabricated for the structure of the building, the company again revisited the design. A frustrated Gilbert wrote to Kingsley:

> If the exterior design were reduced to a perfectly plain brick building of the Army Supply Base type without cornices or ornamenta-

FIGURE 3.35

New York Life Insurance Company Building, New York City, October 1923. F. G. Stickel, draftsman. Watercolor and graphite on canvas mounted to board, 23 in. × 21 in.

(Cass Gilbert Collection, courtesy New-York Historical Society, neg. no. 72849)

FIGURE 3.36

New York Life Insurance Company Building, New York City, ca. 1930. Irving Browning, photographer. Photograph, 9 in. × 7⅝ in.

(Cass Gilbert Collection, courtesy New-York Historical Society, neg. no. 69089)

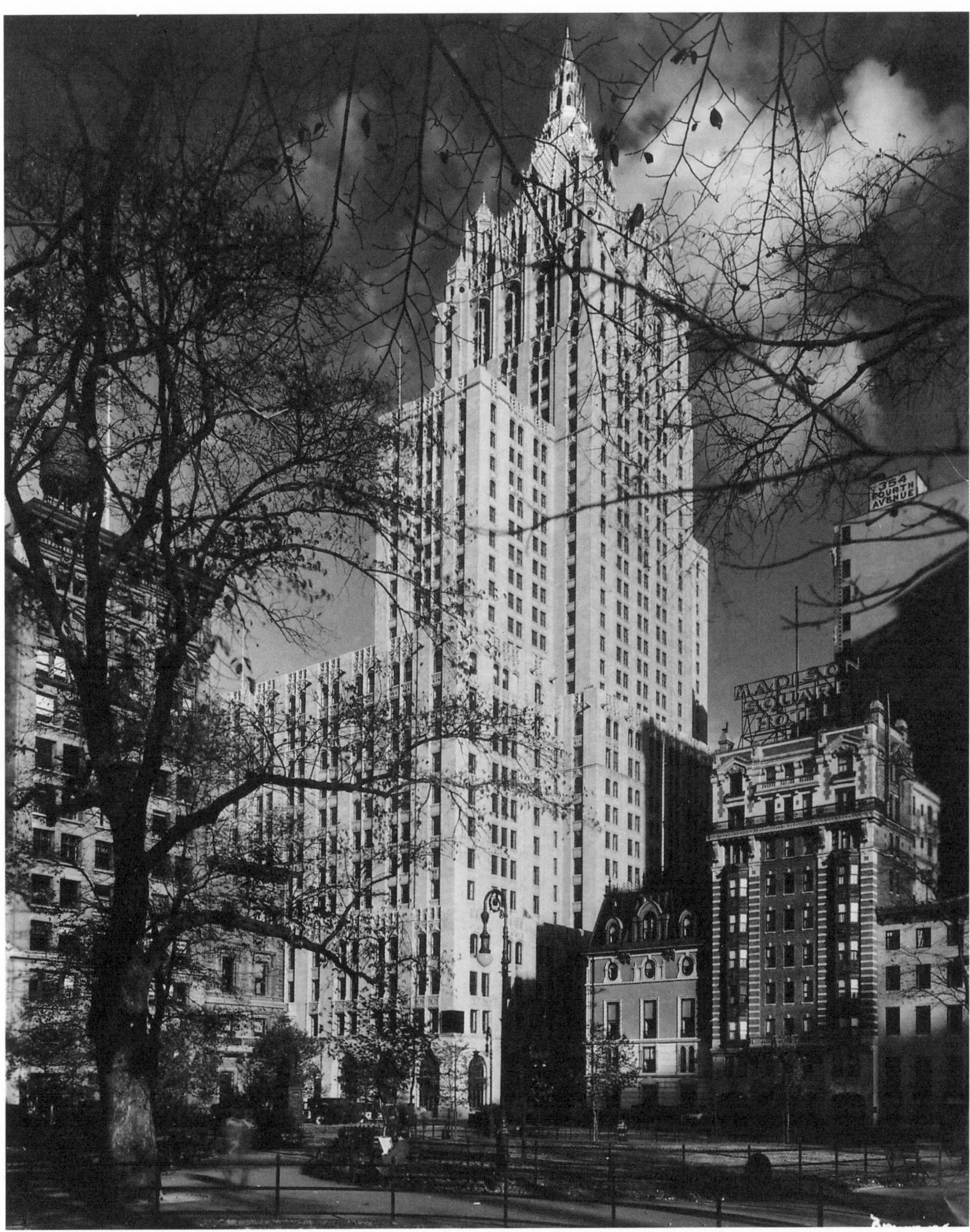
354
FOURTH
AVENUE
MADISON

> tion the cost could be still further reduced and estimates might be obtained thereon from your contractors as soon as sketches could be prepared. A building of this type, however, would not be in accord with your original instructions as to the character and types of structures desired by your company. It would, however, be more nearly in line with some of the buildings which have been quoted in the memorandum report to you.[126]

In April 1926 Kingsley suspended the fabrication of the structural steel, and Gilbert's office began to redesign the building in May and June.[127] Suggestions for variations on the design appeared from every firm involved with the project, including New York Life and Starrett Brothers, the general contractor. By June 1926 Gilbert and New York Life finally agreed on a design. Gilbert described the process to his colleague Aymar Embury: "Boiled down the story is very simply this. The company mentioned at first wanted a monumental building of a certain type and the drawings and specifications were prepared accordingly and received their approval and some contracts were let. Later they decided they would prefer to have a different type of building and we made a new design with which I understand they are very much pleased and it is under construction."[128]

While the overall design for the structure was agreed on, New York Life executives continued to change their mind about several aspects of the design, causing the completion date to be moved from May 1 to October 1, 1928, with people finally moving into the building in mid-November of that year. Pressed to complete the drawings, Gilbert wrote: "Starrett Brothers state that they must have in their hands all drawings by March 1st. Complete information as to any changes which may be contemplated should be in our hands prior to that time in order to give us ample time to revise and complete the drawings."[129] In the final design the company settled for a semimonumental building. Gilbert used limestone instead of marble for the exterior but created a distinctive gilded pyramidal roof. While the interiors lacked luxurious materials, they had elaborately painted decorations by Paris and Wiley in the lobby and ground floor corridors, murals by Edward Trumbull in various company dining rooms, and murals by Ezra Winter in the ground floor restaurant, Savarin.

While Gilbert did not construct the building he wanted, and the office was detached from a great deal of the construction process, he was apparently satisfied with the results. He described the New York Life Insurance Company Building:

The form of the building arises from the requirements of the set-back law which is so noticeably affecting the newer architecture of New York. The style of architecture has been called "American Perpendicular" but is distinctive in type from any other building. This style was inspired by studies of old European examples of towers, town halls and civic buildings of France and the Netherlands. Its special adaptation to American building has been largely developed by Cass Gilbert, Inc. Architect, in such structures as the Woolworth Building, the West Street Building, Army Supply Base in Brooklyn, and other buildings designed by that office.[130]

FIGURE 3.37

George Washington [Hudson River] Bridge, perspective of New York Tower and Plaza, July 1926. H. Radberg, draftsman. Graphite and conté crayon on drawing paper, 20 in. × 31 in.

(Cass Gilbert Collection, courtesy New-York Historical Society, neg. no. 70325)

In January 1926 the Port Authority announced that it had appointed Cass Gilbert as architect of the new Hudson River Bridge (now known as the George Washington Bridge). Discussions of a bridge crossing the Hudson River had been ongoing for several decades and numerous sites had been considered.[131] By the time of Gilbert's selection the definitive site had been selected; the bridge would extend from West 178th Street and Fort Washington Avenue over the Hudson to Fort Lee, New Jersey. As the architect, Gilbert's initial responsibilities were extensive: designing the cladding of the towers, anchorages, and the approaches; creating light standards, toll booths, plazas, and even sculpture for the cable ends. In addition to the large scope of the project, Gilbert struggled with the gigantic scale of the bridge. He wrote the bridge engineer, Othmar Ammann, that he was only getting used to the scale.[132] The scale and the complexity of the project caused Gilbert to modify his design process; on several occasions he used models to study design solutions for the bridge.[133] While the office had always used models, it tended to commission models sparingly because of the expense of fabrication.

While the George Washington Bridge was a large commission for Gilbert's office, it was clear that the major designer of the project was the structural engineer, Othmar Ammann. Gilbert wrote to bridge designer Gustav Lindenthal: "It is not my function to design the bridge but to take the engineer's design and develop the architectural forms in harmony with it. I am happy to say that far from making any criticism of the engineer's design I like it and I am working in hearty sympathy with it."[134]

Gilbert's penultimate design for the towers and anchorage called for simple Romanesque forms clad in granite. In creating the designs he relied upon both ancient and Renaissance architecture, melding the two to arrive at classical forms clad in rough-faced stone. He wrote that his studies in Europe during the summer of 1926 had convinced him that the simpler the structure was, the more impressive it would be.[135] In trying to design the surface of the stone cladding, Gilbert referred Ammann to photographs of the stonework of the fifteenth-century Pitti Palace in Florence.[136] Gilbert also wanted the bridge to be a monument, in the traditional sense of the term. He urged Ammann to include elevators, so the top of the towers could be used as observation decks and in one set of drawings included a restaurant with a boat drop-off in the New York tower.[137]

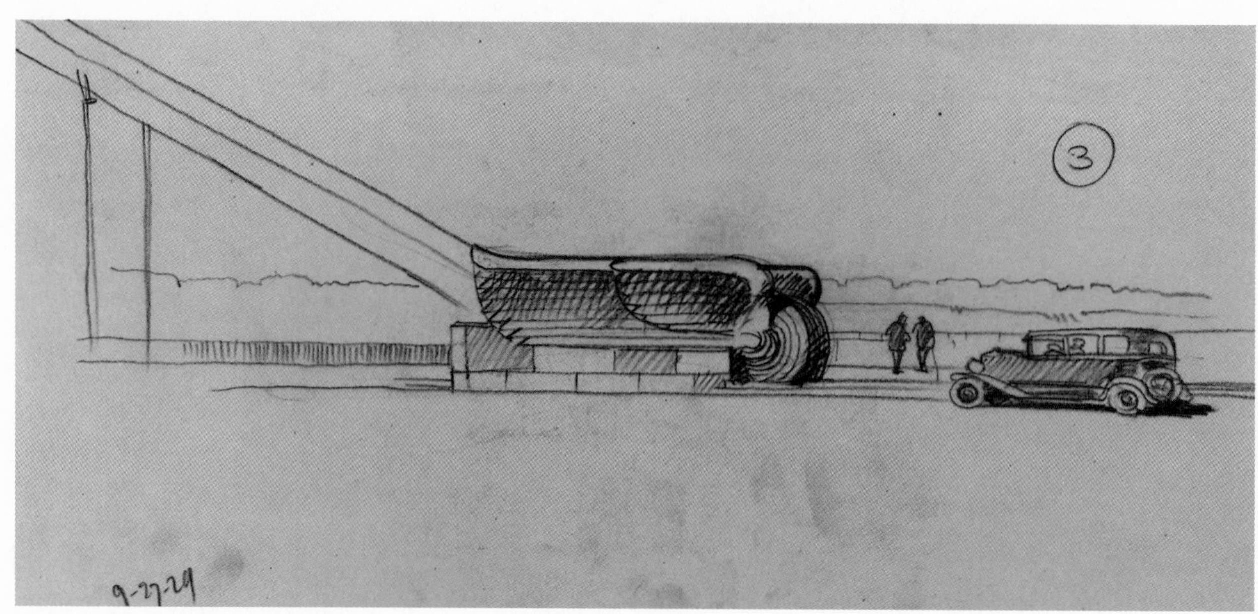

FIGURE 3.38

George Washington [Hudson River] Bridge, cable end, September 27, 1929. John T. Cronin, draftsman. Graphite on tracing paper, 17 in. × 49 in.

(Cass Gilbert Collection, courtesy New-York Historical Society, neg. no. 70320)

FIGURE 3.39

George Washington [Hudson River] Bridge, New Jersey Plaza, study for toll houses, 1931. B. Cronin and John T. Cronin, draftsmen. Graphite on tracing paper, 19 in. × 35 in.

(Cass Gilbert Collection, courtesy New-York Historical Society, neg. no. 70310)

The bridge was controversial because the anchorage and towers would take up space in Riverside Park, and the bridge would affect the scenery of the New Jersey palisades. Gilbert wrote to his colleagues George Kunz of the American Scenic and Historic Preservation Society and Frederick Law Olmsted seeking support for the project. He persuaded them to promote the scheme because he promised that the towers would harmonize with the Palisades and the project included adding additional land to Riverside Park.[138]

By May 1927 Gilbert decided to use Stony Creek granite for the towers, anchorages, and approaches. Gilbert preferred this stone for several reasons: there was a large supply, and its color and patterning blended well with the surrounding landscape. By January 1928, however, Ammann was looking for cheaper alternatives. Gilbert rejected using Palisades rock, because it was difficult to work and had an unpleasing slate gray color.[139] The use of Benedict stone, a compound of Portland cement and granite aggregate, was rejected on the grounds that it would not withstand the weather, and the bridge was being built to last not only for a few generations, but for centuries. Finally, Gilbert conceded that stones from different quarries could be used but the granite needed to be of "rich warm variable color and large crystallization." He reminded Ammann of the fierce opposition to the bridge's location due to concerns that it would destroy the beauty of the Palisades and Riverside Drive; only the promise of the bridge harmonizing with the landscape—in large part due to the use of an appropriate stone—persuaded the various civic societies to support the plan.[140] Undoubtedly the reality of the depression forced Gilbert to accept inferior materials, but he remained distinctly unhappy. In 1931 he wrote Ammann that he had inspected the stonework of the lower crossover bridge at Riverside Drive and was appalled by the Mount Waldo granite: "The color is so deadly even and the effect is so absolutely without the distinguished character which this work should have that I am moved to urge you strongly that this granite should not be used."[141]

Small portions of Gilbert's design were executed, such as the crossover bridges and retaining walls, but they were of inferior workmanship and materials. Gilbert's original schemes for the bridge treated it as a beaux arts monument with elaborate plazas decorated with fountains and sculptures, as well as sculptural embellishments of the cable ends. He had conferred with two sculptors, James Earle Fraser and Robert Aitken, about possible proposals for these pieces.[142] The majority of Gilbert's plans for the bridge were never implemented. In August 1931 Gilbert wrote to designer Charles R. Lamb that the ornamental aspects of the bridge had been deferred.[143]

FIGURE 3.40
George Washington [Hudson River] Bridge, New Jersey Plaza, study for toll houses, 1931. B. Cronin and John T. Cronin, draftsmen. Graphite on tracing paper, 19 in. × 35 in.
(Cass Gilbert Collection, courtesy New-York Historical Society, neg. no. 70310)

Ultimately the depression and changing tastes defeated Gilbert's design. The Port Authority decided it was cheaper to regularly paint the metal towers than to pay for granite, and critics and architects inspired by modernist aesthetics came to prefer the honesty of the structural steel towers over stone-clad schemes of vaguely historical origins.

Cass Gilbert's design for the New York County Lawyers' Association, located in downtown Manhattan at 14 Vesey Street, represents his increasing conservatism and preference for neoclassical forms during the last part of his career. The building was designed as a club (complete with library, lounge, and auditorium) for this legal association, which was founded in 1908. Notable members of the association included Benjamin Cardozo and Samuel Seabury. Gilbert had previously designed a building for the legal profession, the Essex County Courthouse, as well as a club, the Union Club, thus the firm had experience with the demands of both building types.

The association preferred a building in a classical revival style.[144] This meshed with Gilbert's interest in seventeenth- and eighteenth-century architecture, which had been stimulated by his 1907 purchase of a colonial house in Ridgefield, Connecticut, and involvement with planning New Haven, Connecticut, with its colonial-era green. For the law association, Gilbert believed that the colonial, or Georgian, style provided the building with a "simple, dignified and impressive" image.[145]

While Gilbert's reliance upon historical precedents remained a constant theme in his career, how he used history changed during the later half of his career. Rather than synthesizing numerous sources, their uses became more specific. The exterior of the Lawyers' Association was similar to the rowhouses of Lincoln's Inn Fields, London, whereas the second-floor auditorium was based on the interior of Independence Hall in Philadelphia. While these eighteenth-century references connected the building to its surroundings, particularly the adjacent Saint Paul's Chapel, both Gilbert and the association believed the historical references severed the building from the dominant context, the skyscrapers of lower Manhattan. A pamphlet on the building stated that "by its calm and serene character it is impressive in the locality which is characterized by structures of an entirely different type."[146]

The building differed from Gilbert's earlier work in other significant ways. Colors and materials continued to be rich, but details were flatter and more delicate. Rather than the robust sculptural forms of the U.S. Custom House or Woolworth Building, the New York County Lawyers' Association is austere on the exterior and subdued on the interior. Even the drawings produced by the office for the building differed from those created earlier. Presentation drawings of the building were made by Frederick G. Stickel,

COUNTY
LAWYERS
ASSOCIATION

FIGURE 3.41
New York County Lawyers' Association, no date. Wurts Brothers, photographers. Photograph, 13 in. × 10 in. on signed 20 in. × 16 in. mount.
(Cass Gilbert Collection, courtesy New-York Historical Society, neg. no. 72850)

FIGURE 3.42
New York County Lawyers' Association, Vesey Street, second floor stair hall, 1928. Unidentified draftsman. Black chalk, gouache, graphite on drawing paper, 18 in. × 24 in.
(Cass Gilbert Collection, courtesy New-York Historical Society, neg. no. 74124)

Cass Gilbert Jr., and John Cronin, and drawn in monochrome using ink wash, graphite, or conté crayon. These formed a striking contrast with earlier exuberant watercolors of Gilbert buildings created by Hughson Hawley, Thomas R. Johnson, and Birch Burdette Long. The tone of the office also changed. From the 1920s on, Cass Gilbert Jr. played an increasingly significant role in the office. On February 10, 1930, he accompanied the president of the association, William Cromwell, to select light fixtures at Black and Boyd. Cromwell did not like the metal fixtures picked by the firm, believing them to look like "bar-room fixtures." Cass Gilbert Jr. wrote: "I replied that I was glad that Mr. Cromwell did not like the fixture because that made me certain that the fixture was good. Mr. Cromwell looked odd and I added that I preferred Mr. Gilbert's taste [to] Mr. Cromwell's."[147] This rather impertinent response to a client would have been unimaginable in the earlier office.

The schedule for construction was tight, and the office had numerous problems with the Lawyers' Association. Cass Gilbert took great offense at a suggestion that he was in league with the contractors to milk the association for money.[148] Cass Gilbert Jr. had difficulties convincing the association that the office needed written authorization, a standard practice, to place orders for materials needed to begin work on the interiors.[149]

The conservative nature of both the association and Gilbert was evident in another aspect of the program. Initially both Gilbert and the association wanted to segregate any women using the space, whether they were members of the association or relatives of a member. The association wanted a balcony in the auditorium for wives.[150] Gilbert contemplated separate lounge and reception areas for the few female members.[151] In both cases, the added expense of providing these areas persuaded the association to allow women to mix with men.

The Lawyers' Association was pleased with the completed building. President Cromwell praised Gilbert for having the boldness "to cut loose from our modern architectural surroundings and to enter the sweetness, serenity, purity and charm of the Colonial period."[152] Ironically, one of the modern architectural surroundings was Gilbert's own Woolworth Building. In fact, most of Gilbert's later projects seem similarly estranged from their contemporary design context. The serene, austere classicism of the New York County Lawyers' Association is very distant from the jazz-age modernity of contemporary buildings such as the Empire State and Chrysler Buildings.

Yet if Gilbert during the final decade of his career no longer produced buildings that dealt with contemporary architectural concerns, he still suc-

FIGURE 3.43

New York County Lawyers' Association, Vesey Street Auditorium, January 26, 1928. Unidentified artist. Charcoal, conté crayon, gouache on paper, 18 in. × 25 in.

(Cass Gilbert Collection, courtesy New-York Historical Society, neg. no. 72851)

ceeded in meeting two of his primary goals: to make well-designed structures that employed the best workmanship and materials, and to make buildings that were enjoyed by their users. The New York County Lawyers' Association Building won prizes for its craftsmanship. William Cromwell wrote to Gilbert: "You have given to our Home of Law refinement, dignity and daintiness beyond compare, while furnishing every requirement of utility. Your amazing experience and practicality have become a part of the life of the law."[153] No better testimony to Gilbert's ability to understand and interpret the needs of a client exists than the fact that the building continues to be used and greatly appreciated by the organization that originally commissioned the structure.

Notes

1. The best summary of the history of the Minnesota state capitol is Neil B. Thompson, *Minnesota's State Capitol: The Art and Politics of a Public Building* (St. Paul: Minnesota Historical Society, 1974).
2. Cass Gilbert to Board of State Capitol Commissioners, May 2, 1898, Minnesota State Capitol Letter Book, 5/5/1897–1/15/1899, New-York Historical Society (hereinafter N-YHS).
3. Memorandum, n.d., Minnesota State Capitol Letter Book, 1/16/1899–11/19/1900, p. 103, N-YHS.
4. Memorandum, n.d., Minnesota State Capitol Letter Book, 6/1/1904–3/25/1905, p. 686, N-YHS.
5. J. Rachac [Rockart] to Cass Gilbert, September 10, 1901, Minnesota State Capitol Letter Book, 2/19/1901–2/1/1902, p. 378, N-YHS.
6. Cass Gilbert to Louis Comfort Tiffany, December 13, 1901, Minnesota State Capitol Letter Book, 2/19/1901–2/1/1902, p. 614, N-YHS.
7. Memorandum, n.d., Minnesota State Capitol Letter Book, 6/1/1904–3/25/1905, p. 606, N-YHS.
8. Cass Gilbert, memorandum, Minnesota State Capitol Letter Book, 1/16/1899–11/19/1900, p. 103, N-YHS.
9. Thompson, *Minnesota's State Capitol,* pp. 25–31.
10. Cass Gilbert to Editor, *Sentinel,* Lake City, Minnesota, August 2, 1899, Minnesota State Capitol Letter Book, 1/16/1899–11/19/1900, p. 247, N-YHS.
11. Thompson, *Minnesota's State Capitol,* pp. 37–49.

12. Cass Gilbert to Board, December 31, 1902, Minnesota State Capitol Letter Book, p. 462, N-YHS; Channing Seabury to Cass Gilbert, January 27, 1903, Minnesota State Capitol Correspondence, N-YHS.
13. Thompson, *Minnesota's State Capitol,* pp. 52–5.
14. Cass Gilbert to T. H. Anderson, March 4, 1903, Minnesota State Capitol Correspondence, N-YHS.
15. Thompson, *Minnesota's State Capitol,* pp. 65–72.
16. Cass Gilbert to Kenyon Cox, August 1, 1904, Minnesota State Capitol Letter Book, 6/1/1904–3/25/1905, p. 208, N-YHS.
17. Cass Gilbert to Edward Simmons, December 6, 1904, Minnesota State Capitol Letter Book, 6/1/1904–3/25/1904, p. 495, N-YHS.
18. Cass Gilbert to Channing Seabury, November 14, 1904, Minnesota State Capitol Letter Book, 6/1/1904–3/25/1905, p. 414, N-YHS.
19. Cass Gilbert to Channing Seabury, December 27, 1904, Minnesota State Capitol Letter Book, 6/1/1904–3/25/1905, p. 559, N-YHS.
20. Cass Gilbert to Joseph Wheelock, Editor, *St. Paul Daily Pioneer-Press,* August 8, 1901, Minnesota State Capitol Letter Book, 2/19/1901–2/1/1902, p. 257, N-YHS; Thompson, *Minnesota's State Capitol,* p. 75.
21. Sharon Irish, "Cass Gilbert's Career in New York, 1899–1905," Ph.D. diss., Northwestern University, 1985, pp. 146–208.
22. Cass Gilbert to William Martin Aiken, March 18, 1899, Miscellaneous Letter Book, 3/1899–9/1899, p. 41, N-YHS.
23. Cass Gilbert to Steve Haskell, April 15, 1899, Broadway Chambers Letter Book, 3/1899–1/1900, p. 120, N-YHS.
24. Cass Gilbert to George Fuller Company, March 4, 1899, Broadway Chambers Letter Book, 8/1898–3/1899, p. 448, N-YHS.
25. Cass Gilbert to Steve Haskell, April 14, 1899, Broadway Chambers Letter Book, 3/1899–1/1900, p.106, N-YHS.
26. Cass Gilbert to T. B. Townsend Brick and Contracting Co., May 25, 1899, Broadway Chambers Letter Book, 3/1899–1/1900, p.177, N-YHS.
27. Steve Haskell to Cass Gilbert, June 3, 1899, Broadway Chambers Letter Book, 5/1899–3/1900, p. 47, N-YHS.
28. Steve Haskell to George Fuller Company, June 14, 1899, Broadway Chambers Letter Book, 5/1899–3/1900, p. 91, N-YHS; Edward Andrews to Cass Gilbert, November 24, 1899, Broadway Chambers Correspondence, N-YHS.
29. Cass Gilbert to George Fuller Company, April 12 1899, Broadway Chambers Letter Book, 3/1899–1/1900, p. 104, N-YHS.
30. Susan Tunick, *Terra-Cotta Skyline* (New York: Princeton Architectural Press, 1997), p. 55.
31. Cass Gilbert to Perth Amboy Terra Cotta Company, February 21, 1900, Broadway Chambers Letter Book, 5/1899–3/1900, p. 609, N-YHS.

32. Steve Haskell to Cass Gilbert, February 5, 1900, Broadway Chambers Letter Book, 5/1899–3/1900, p. 580, N-YHS.
33. Edward Andrews to Gilbert, July 25, 1899, Broadway Chambers Correspondence; Cass Gilbert to Edward Andrews, December 2, 1899, Broadway Chambers Letter Book, 5/1899–3/1900, p. 361; Edward Andrews to Cass Gilbert, January 18, 1900, Broadway Chambers Correspondence; Cass Gilbert to Edward Andrews, memorandum, April 29, 1901, Broadway Chambers Correspondence, N-YHS.
34. Steve Haskell to Edward Andrews, June 6, 1900, Broadway Chambers Letter Book, 3/15/1900–1/14/1901, p. 312, N-YHS.
35. Edward Andrews to Cass Gilbert, May 10, 1900, Broadway Chambers Correspondence, N-YHS.
36. Memorandum by Edward Andrews, April 29, 1901, Broadway Chambers Correspondence, N-YHS.
37. Irish, "Cass Gilbert's Career in New York," pp. 184–5.
38. Cass Gilbert to William T. Andrews, February 17, 1925, Broadway Chambers Correspondence, N-YHS.
39. Cass Gilbert, Essex County Courthouse Competition Memorandum, April 17, 1901, Essex County Courthouse Correspondence, 2, N-YHS.
40. Steve Haskell, Essex County Courthouse Memorandum, July 8, 1902, Essex County Courthouse Correspondence, 2, N-YHS.
41. Steve Haskell, Essex County Courthouse Report, December 12, 1902, Essex County Courthouse Correspondence, 1, 2, N-YHS.
42. George Brown and Co. to Cass Gilbert, November 9, 1903, Essex County Courthouse Correspondence, N-YHS.
43. V. J. Hedden and Son Company to Cass Gilbert, October 3, 1904, Essex County Courthouse Correspondence, N-YHS; Cass Gilbert to George Brown, January 12, 1904, Essex County Courthouse Letter Book, 12/4/1903–4/17/1905; F. H. Keese, "Report Essex County Court House," January 28 and 29, 1904, Essex County Correspondence, N-YHS.
44. Cass Gilbert to Leslie D. Ward, November 14, 1906, Essex County Courthouse Letter Book, 8/1906–11/1907, p. 450, N-YHS; Cass Gilbert to T. D. Wadelton, June 9, 1906, Essex County Courthouse Letter Book, 1/23/1906–8/28/1906, p. 425, N-YHS.
45. Cass Gilbert to T. D. Wadelton, July 30, 1906, Essex County Courthouse Letter Book, 1/23/1906–8/28/1906, pp. 591–2, N-YHS.
46. Cass Gilbert to Andrew O'Connor, June 6, 1906, Essex County Courthouse Letter Book, 1/23/1906–8/28/1906, p. 426, N-YHS.
47. Leslie D. Waid to Cass Gilbert, November 27, 1906, Essex County Courthouse Correspondence, N-YHS.
48. Cass Gilbert to Mr. J. T. William, November 30, 1910, Miscellaneous Letter Book, 4/1910–1/1911, p. 552, N-YHS.

49. The best account of the Custom House commission is Irish, "Cass Gilbert's Career in New York," pp. 256–322.
50. Cass Gilbert to James Knox Taylor, April 22, 1899, Miscellaneous Letter Book, 3/1899–9/1899, p. 115, N-YHS.
51. Cass Gilbert to Stevens Haskell, July 18, 1899, Broadway Chambers Letter Book, 3/1899–1/1900, p. 321–2, N-YHS; Cass Gilbert to Stevens Haskell, July 24, 1899, Broadway Chambers Letter Book, 3/1899–1/1900, p. 351, N-YHS.
52. Cass Gilbert to Thomas Holyoke, September 18, 1899, Miscellaneous Letter Book, 4/1899–11/1899, N-YHS.
53. Geoffrey Blodgett, "Cass Gilbert and the Politics of Public Architecture," paper delivered at "Cass Gilbert, Life and Work: From Regional to National Architect" symposium, November 14, 1998, Alexander Hamilton U.S. Custom House at Bowling Green, New York City. Dr. Blodgett gave an excellent summary of Gilbert's ethical problems in the competition.
54. Entry November 28, 1899, [Cass Gilbert Office] Journal 1899–1909, p. 76, N-YHS.
55. Cass Gilbert to Stevens Haskell, January 3, 1900, U.S. Custom House Letter Book, 11/9/1899–6/19/1908, p. 41, N-YHS.
56. Cass Gilbert to the Secretary of the Treasury, May 2, 1910, U.S. Custom House Correspondence, N-YHS; "Painters and Sculptors New York Custom House," undated memorandum, U.S. Custom House Correspondence, N-YHS, lists Ross Turner, C. Y. Turner, F. Hopkinson Smith, E. H. Blashfield, Florian Peixotto, and Douglas Volk. Elmer Garnsey, "United States Custom House, New York City, Description of Decorative Painting," memorandum of May 5, 1911, U.S. Custom House Correspondence, N-YHS.
57. Cass Gilbert to Henry Bell, February 10, 1921, CGP Letter Book, 12/1920–2/1922, p.142, N-YHS. Gilbert complained that both the Custom House and the Minnesota state capitol were overembellished.
58. Irish, "Cass Gilbert's Career in New York," pp. 209–55, and Irish, "A 'Machine That Makes the Land Pay': The West Street Building in New York," *Technology and Culture* 30 (April 1989): 376–97, are the best studies on the West Street Building.
59. Cass Gilbert to General Howard Carroll, September 29, 1905, West Street Letter Book, 4/29/1905–12/26/1906, p. 35, N-YHS.
60. Cass Gilbert to General Howard Carroll, April 11, 1906, West Street Letter Book, 4/29/1905–12/26/1906, p. 150, N-YHS.
61. Cass Gilbert to John Peirce, May 9, 1906, West Street Letter Book, 4/29/1905–12/26/1906, p. 201, N-YHS.
62. Cass Gilbert to John Peirce, September 7, 1906, and Cass Gilbert to Frederick J. Wiley, November 17, 1906 West Street Letter Book, 4/29/1905–12/26/1906, p. 438, N-YHS.

63. Cass Gilbert to John Peirce, October 4, 1905, West Street Letter Book, 4/29/1905–12/26/1906, p. 43, N-YHS; Cass Gilbert to John Peirce, May 3, 1906, West Street Letter Book, 4/29/1905–12/26/1906, p. 175, N-YHS.
64. Cass Gilbert to John Peirce, April 26, June 8, 1906, West Street Letter Book, 4/29/1905–12/26/1906, pp. 165, 244, N-YHS.
65. Cass Gilbert to John Peirce, June 1, 1906, West Street Letter Book, 4/29/1905–12/26/1906, p. 231 N-YHS.
66. Cass Gilbert to Boyd Equipment Company, February 16, 1906, West Street Letter Book, 12/26/1906–6/26/1907, p. 208, N-YHS.
67. Cass Gilbert to John Peirce, January 21, 1907, West Street Letter Book, 12/26/1906–6/26/1907, p.105, N-YHS.
68. Irish, "Cass Gilbert's Career in New York," p. 218.
69. Cass Gilbert to John Peirce, January 5, 1907, West Street Letter Book, 12/26/1906–6/26/1907, p. 36, N-YHS.
70. Cass Gilbert to E. C. Simmons, March 12, 1907, West Street Letter Book, 12/26/1906–6/26/1907, p. 324, N-YHS.
71. Gail Fenske, "The 'Skyscraper Problem' and the City Beautiful: The Woolworth Building," Ph.D. diss., MIT, 1988, is the most complete account of the Woolworth Building.
72. Cass Gilbert to John Beverly Robinson, September 6, 1918, CGP Letter Book, 8/1917–8/1918, p. 702, N-YHS.
73. Frank Woolworth to Cass Gilbert, December 27, 1911, Woolworth Correspondence, N-YHS.
74. Memorandum, October 31, 1912, Woolworth Correspondence N-YHS; memorandum, November 21, 1912, Woolworth Correspondence, N-YHS.
75. Atlantic Terra Cotta Co. to Cass Gilbert, August 22, 1912, Woolworth Correspondence, N-YHS.
76. Atlantic Terra Cotta Co., undated statement on letterhead, Woolworth Correspondence, N-YHS.
77. John Rockart, memorandum, October 7, 1913, Woolworth Correspondence, N-YHS.
78. Memorandum, April 25, 1914, Woolworth Correspondence, N-YHS.
79. Cass Gilbert to J. J. Jusserand, January 14, 1915, Woolworth Correspondence, N-YHS.
80. "Woolworth Building Terra Cotta," memorandum, July 27, 1915, Woolworth Correspondence, N-YHS; Frank Woolworth to Cass Gilbert, July 27, 1914, Woolworth Correspondence, N-YHS.
81. Cass Gilbert to Ralph Adams Cram, December 23, 1920, CGP Letter Book, 12/1920–2/1922, p. 45, N-YHS.
82. Cass Gilbert, "Indigenous Architect" undated typescript, in Woolworth Correspondence, N-YHS.

83. Barbara Christen, "Cass Gilbert and the Ideal of the City Beautiful: City and Campus Plans, 1900–1915," Ph.D. diss., Graduate Center, City University of New York, 1997, discusses Oberlin and other group plans in depth.
84. Cass Gilbert, Report, March 16, 1904, Oberlin College Correspondence, 1, 2, N-YHS.
85. Olmsted Brothers to Dr. H. C. King, June 20, 1903, Oberlin College Correspondence, 2, N-YHS.
86. Cass Gilbert to Joseph Lyman Silsbee, November 20, 1911, Oberlin College Letter Book, 9/29/1905–2/15/1912, p. 695, N-YHS. Much to Gilbert's dismay, he discovered that the college had a previous commitment with architect Jacob Lyman Silsbee to design the Administration Building. While Gilbert offered to step aside in favor of Silsbee, as long as the latter conformed to his overall scheme, when the college finally offered the Administration Building commission to Gilbert, he accepted with alacrity.
87. Geoffrey Blodgett, *Oberlin Architecture, College and Town: A Guide to Its Social History* (Oberlin, Ohio: Oberlin College and Kent State University Press, 1985).
88. Cass Gilbert to H. C. King, January 16, 1914, Oberlin College Letter Book, 3/1/1912–11/10/1915, p. 241, N-YHS.
89. Cass Gilbert to H. C. King, March 20, 1914, Oberlin College Letter Book, 3/1/1912–11/10/1915, p. 320, N-YHS.
90. Cass Gilbert to H. C. King, June 9, 1916, Oberlin College Letter Book, 11/1916–5/1924, p. 76, N-YHS.
91. Cass Gilbert to A. H. Shaw, February 18, 1921, Oberlin College Letter Book, 1/1916–5/1924, p. 447, N-YHS.
92. Memorandum, January 22, 1918, U.S. Army Supply Base Correspondence, N-YHS.
93. Clippings in U. S. Army Supply Base Correspondence, including "Committee Picks South Brooklyn for War Base," *New York Evening Mail,* 16 March 1918, N-YHS.
94. "Preliminary Plans for War Department Supply Base South Brooklyn, N.Y.," February 16, 1918, U.S. Army Supply Base Correspondence, N-YHS.
95. Memorandums, April 3, April 8, 1918, on problems with Marshall; memorandum, June 10, 1918, records that Gilbert signed the contract on June 8, U.S. Army Supply Base Correspondence, N-YHS.
96. "The Brooklyn Army Supply Base," December 30, 1919, U.S. Army Supply Base Correspondence, N-YHS.
97. "U.S. Army Supply Base," undated memorandum (ca. 1919), U. S. Army Supply Base Correspondence, N-YHS.

98. Cass Gilbert, memorandum, June 29, 1918, U.S. Army Supply Base Correspondence, N-YHS.
99. Daily report, Cass Gilbert, August 20, 1918, U.S. Army Supply Base Correspondence, N-YHS.
100. Memorandums, June 3, August 13, 1918, U.S. Army Supply Base Correspondence, N-YHS.
101. Memorandum, Bush to Cresson, September 24, 1918; Minutes of Conference, November 15, 1918, U.S. Army Supply Base Correspondence, N-YHS.
102. Memorandum, Bush to Cresson, September 24, 1918, U.S. Army Supply Base Correspondence, N-YHS.
103. Memorandum, November 21, 1918, U.S. Army Supply Base Correspondence, N-YHS; U.S. Army Supply Base pamphlet, U.S. Army Supply Base Correspondence, N-YHS.
104. Memorandum, November 29, 1918, U.S. Army Supply Base Correspondence, N-YHS.
105. Cass Gilbert to Fred Farnsworth, May 18, 1913, Detroit Public Library Letter Book, 6/16/1913–10/8/1915, p. 8, N-YHS.
106. Cass Gilbert to Detroit Library Commission, February 18, 1915, Detroit Public Library Letter Book, 6/16/1913–10/8/1915, p. 346; Cass Gilbert to Adam Strohm, March 8, 1917, Detroit Public Library Letter Book, 10/1915–6/1917, pp. 514–5, N-YHS.
107. Cass Gilbert to Adam Strohm, December 8, 1914, Detroit Public Library Letter Book, 6/16/1913–10/8/1915, p. 165; Cass Gilbert to Adam Strohm, March 28, 1917, Detroit Public Library Letter Book, 10/1915–6/1917, p. 515–6, N-YHS.
108. Gilbert to Detroit Library Commission, February 18, 1915, Detroit Public Library Letter Book, 6/16/1913–10/8/1915, p. 346; Gilbert to Strohm, March 28, 1917, Detroit Public Library Letter Book, 10/1915–6/1917, p. 515, N-YHS.
109. Gilbert to American Bridge Co., November 5, 1915, Detroit Public Library Letter Book, 10/1915–6/1917, p. 65, N-YHS.
110. Cass Gilbert to Adam Strohm, March 28, 1917, Detroit Public Library Letter Book, 10/1915–6/1917, pp. 516–7, N-YHS.
111. Ibid. p. 513.
112. Cass Gilbert to William Dall Co., April 11, April 16, 1917, Detroit Public Library Letter Book, 10/1915–6/1917, pp. 519, 524–5, N-YHS. Gilbert believed that disgruntled local builders were behind the Minnesota state legislature's 1903 investigation of Gilbert's management of the state capitol construction.

    Cass Gilbert to Adam Strohm, August 18, 1920, Detroit Public Library Letter Book, 7/1920–1/1921, p. 104, N-YHS.

113. Cass Gilbert to Charles Moore, July 31, 1917, Detroit Public Library Letter Book, 6/1917–3/1918, p. 68, N-YHS.
114. Cass Gilbert, "Detroit Public Library," October 1920, Detroit Public Library Letter Book, 7/1920–1/1921, pp. 299–305, N-YHS.
115. Cass Gilbert to John Polachek Bronze and Iron Co., November 17, 1920, Detroit Public Library Letter Book, 7/1920–1/1921, p. 342, N-YHS.
116. Cass Gilbert to Gorham Stevens, December 22, 1920, Detroit Public Library Letter Book, 6/1920–1/1921, p. 446, N-YHS.
117. Gilbert to Strohm, March 28, 1917, Detroit Public Library Letter Book, 10/1915–6/1917, p. 517, N-YHS.
118. Cass Gilbert to Erich Zimmerman, February 24, 1927, New York Life Insurance Building Letter Book, 3/31/1926–2/24/1927, p. 495, N-YHS.
119. Cass Gilbert to Darwin Kingsley, December 16, 1919, New York Life Insurance Building Correspondence, and Gilbert to Kingsley, June 28, 1928, New York Life Insurance Building Letter Book, 5/3/1928–8/11/1928, p. 417, N-YHS.
120. Cass Gilbert, "New York Life Building—Madison Square Site," memorandums, December 24, 1923, January 23, April 17, April 24, June 11, 1924, New York Life Insurance Building Correspondence, N-YHS.
121. Cass Gilbert, "New York Life Building—Madison Square Site," memorandum, January 23, 1924, New York Life Insurance Correspondence, p.7, N-YHS.
122. John Rockart, "New York Life Insurance Building," memorandum, November 6, 1924, New York Life Insurance Building Correspondence, N-YHS.
123. Cass Gilbert, "New York Life Insurance Building," memorandums, June 1, April 24, 1924, New York Life Insurance Company Correspondence, N-YHS.
124. Cass Gilbert, "New York Life Insurance Building," memorandum, April 24, 1924, New York Life Insurance Company Correspondence, p. 3, N-YHS.
125. Cass Gilbert to A. L. Aiken, April 10, 1925, New York Life Insurance Letter Book, 3/8/1924–3/30/1926, p. 198, N-YHS.
126. Cass Gilbert to Darwin Kingsley, April 8, 1926, New York Life Insurance Building Letter Book, 3/31/1926–2/24/1927, p.32, N-YHS.
127. Cass Gilbert to Darwin Kingsley, April 12, 1926; Cass Gilbert to A. L. Aiken, May 5, 1926; June 6, 1926, New York Life Insurance Building Letter Book, 3/31/1926–2/24/1927, pp. 34, 99, 100, N-YHS.
128. Cass Gilbert to Aymar Embury, May 21, 1927, New York Life Insurance Building Letter Book, 2/24/1927–8/16/1927, p. 200, N-YHS.
129. Cass Gilbert to A. L. Aiken, January 25, 1928, New York Life Insurance Building Letter Book, 12/9/1927–2/24/1928, p. 264, N-YHS.

130. Cass Gilbert to Albert Ashforth, October 2, 1928, New York Life Insurance Building Letter Book, 8/1928–11/1928, p. 442, N-YHS.

131. James W. Doig, "Joining New York City to the Greater Metropolis: The Port Authority As Visionary, Target of Opportunity, and Opportunist," in David Ward and Olivier Zunz, eds., *Landscape of Modernity: Essays on New York City, 1900–1940* (New York: Russell Sage Foundation, 1992), pp. 76–105.

132. Cass Gilbert to O. H. Ammann, February 25, 1926, Hudson River Bridge Letter Book, 1/1926–6/1929, p. 11, N-YHS.

133. Cass Gilbert to O. H. Ammann, April 29, 1926; Cass Gilbert to O. H. Ammann, June 11, 1926; Cass Gilbert to O. H. Ammann, January 26, 1927, Hudson River Bridge Letter Book, 1/1926–6/1929, pp. 30, 39, 122, N-YHS.

134. Cass Gilbert to Gustav Lindenthal, October 5, 1927, Hudson River Bridge Letter Book, 1/1926–6/1929, p. 225, N-YHS. Lindenthal was the engineer for the Hell Gate, Manhattan, and Queensboro Bridges.

135. Cass Gilbert to Charles E. Fowler, October 19, 1926, Hudson River Bridge Letter Book, 1/1926–6/1929, p. 94, N-YHS.

136. Cass Gilbert to O. H. Ammann, April 26, 1929, p. 581, Hudson River Bridge Letter Book, 1/1926–6/1929, p. 581, N-YHS.

137. Cass Gilbert to O. H. Ammann, March 1, 1926, Hudson River Bridge Letter Book, 1/1926–6/1929, p. 13, N-YHS; George Washington Bridge drawings call for a restaurant in the New York tower with elevators connecting boats and cars to the restaurant at the top.

138. Cass Gilbert to Frederick Law Olmsted, April 22, 1927, Hudson River Bridge Letter Book, 1/1926–6/1929, p. 173; Cass Gilbert to George Kunz, April 23, 1927, Hudson River Bridge Letter Book, 1/1926–6/1929, p. 172, N-YHS.

139. Cass Gilbert to O. H. Ammann, April 29, 1927, January 25, 1928, Hudson River Bridge Letter Book, 1/1926–6/1929, pp. 182, 406, N-YHS. The office also used Stony Creek granite on the Broadway Chambers building.

140. Cass Gilbert to O. H. Ammann, August 2, 1929, October 15, 1930, Hudson River Bridge Letter Book, 6/1929–1/1934, pp. 14, 147, N-YHS.

141. Cass Gilbert to O. H. Ammann, February 6, 1931, Hudson River Letter Book, 6/1929–1/1934, p. 198, N-YHS.

142. Cass Gilbert to O. H. Ammann, May 26, 1930, Hudson River Bridge Letter Book, 6/1929–1/1934, p. 91, N-YHS.

143. Cass Gilbert to Charles R. Lamb, August 21, 1931, Hudson River Bridge Letter Book, 6/1929–1/1934, p. 298, N-YHS.

144. "Dedicatory Ceremonies of the Home of Law of the New York County Lawyers' Association, Vesey Street Facing St. Paul's Churchyard" (New York: New York County Lawyers' Association, ca. 1930).

145. *Year Book of New York County Lawyers' Association* (New York: New York County Lawyers' Association, 1930), p. 424.
146. "Dedicatory Ceremonies of the Home of Law."
147. Cass Gilbert Jr., "Memorandum New York County Lawyers' Ass'n. Building," February 13, 1930, New York County Lawyers' Association Correspondence, 1, N-YHS.
148. Cass Gilbert, memorandum, September 24, 1929, New York County Lawyers' Association Correspondence, N-YHS.
149. Cass Gilbert Jr., "Memorandum New York County Lawyers' Ass'n.," February 28, 1930, New York County Lawyers' Association, N-YHS.
150. Cass Gilbert Jr., memorandum, June 28, 1929, New York County Lawyers' Association Correspondence, N-YHS.
151. Ibid.
152. William Cromwell to Cass Gilbert, June 3, 1930, New York County Lawyers' Association Correspondence, N-YHS.
153. Craftsmanship Award, New York County Lawyers' Association Building, April 19, 1930, Committee on Recognition of Craftsmanship of the New York Building Congress; William Cromwell to Cass Gilbert, June 3, 1930, New York County Lawyers' Association Correspondence, N-YHS.

CASS GILBERT COLOR PLATES

PLATE I.

U.S. Custom House, perspective drawing, ca. 1902. T. R. Johnson, delineator. Gouache, graphite on paper, 40 in. × 17 in.

(Cass Gilbert Collection, courtesy New-York Historical Society, neg. no. 72903T)

PLATE 2.

Edwin Howland Blashfield sketch for "Mercy" figure, Essex County Courthouse mural, 1905. Charcoal, graphite, and conté crayon on paper, 33 in. × 45 in.

(Cass Gilbert Collection, courtesy New-York Historical Society, neg. no. 72909T)

PLATE 3.

Minnesota state capitol, 1901. T. R. Johnson, delineator. Watercolor, gouache, graphite on drawing paper, 26 in. × 46 in.

(Cass Gilbert Collection, courtesy New-York Historical Society, neg. no. 72898T)

PLATE 4.

"Perspective View of Entrance Hall, Detroit Public Library," October 21, 1918. F. G. Stickel, delineator. Graphite, ink wash on illustration board. 21¾ in. × 19⅔ in.

(Cass Gilbert Collection, courtesy New-York Historical Society, neg. no. 72899T)

PLATE 5.

U.S. Custom House, 1902. Hughson Hawley, delineator. Watercolor on paper, 38 in. × 63 in.

(Cass Gilbert Collection, courtesy New-York Historical Society, neg. no. 72078T)

PLATE 6.
Broadway Chambers Building, New York City, November 3, 1897. Thomas Holyoke, draftsman. Watercolor, ink, graphite on drawing paper, 18 in. × 27 in.
(Cass Gilbert Collection, courtesy New-York Historical Society, neg. no. 69616T)

PLATE 7.

West Street Building, New York City, no date. Birch Burdette Long, draftsman. Color wash and conté crayon on paper, 54 in. × 22 in.

(Cass Gilbert Collection, courtesy New-York Historical Society, neg. no. 71465T)

PLATE 8.

Oberlin College, study for Finney Chapel, Oberlin, Ohio, ca. 1905. Unidentified draftsman. Watercolor, graphite on drawing paper, 14 in.× 21 in.

(Cass Gilbert Collection, courtesy New-York Historical Society, neg. no. 71478T)

PLATE 9.

New York Life Insurance Company Building, corridor, no date. E.W. (?), draftsman. Graphite and crayon on tracing paper, 4 in. × 26 in.

(Cass Gilbert Collection, courtesy New-York Historical Society, neg. no. 72897T)

PLATE 10.

Oberlin College Administrative Group, with Tower, ca. 1915. Cass Gilbert, delineator. Pastel and wash on drawing paper mounted on board, 20 in. × 38 in.

(Cass Gilbert Collection, courtesy New-York Historical Society, neg. no. 72900T)

PLATE 11.

Proposal for New Haven Railroad Station: Renaissance revival version, ca. 1907. Cass Gilbert, delineator. Ink and wash on drawing paper mounted on board, 21 in. × 35 in.

(Cass Gilbert Collection, courtesy New-York Historical Society, neg. no. 72901T)

PLATE 12.

Perspective of F. W. Woolworth Company Building, New York City, April 25, 1910. T. R. Johnson, delineator. Graphite and conté crayon on board, 17 in. × 8 in.

(Cass Gilbert Collection, courtesy New-York Historical Society, neg. no. 45871T)

PLATE 13.

General Electric Building, Augusta, Georgia, 1920. Unidentified artist. Pastel and charcoal on tracing paper, 34 in. × 24 in.

(Cass Gilbert Collection, courtesy New-York Historical Society, neg. no. 72027T)

CHAPTER FOUR

Barbara S. Christen

THE ARCHITECT AS PLANNER: CASS GILBERT'S RESPONSES TO HISTORIC OPEN SPACE

Cass Gilbert was a planner as much as he was an architect. During his career he received a wide range of invitations and requests for advice on municipal art matters, town and park planning, and architectural materials for municipal building groups. Representatives of cities as diverse as Baltimore, Atlanta, Cleveland, and Seattle, as well as smaller towns such as Grand Rapids, Michigan; Winona, Minnesota; Halesite, New York; and settlements in Montana sought his opinion as a planner.[1] Organizations such as the New York City Planning Commission, the Municipal Art Society, the National Housing Association, and the American Association of Highway Improvement asked him to join their groups. Publishers and statistics experts requested information and articles from him.[2]

Gilbert himself thought his talents and contributions as a planner equaled those of his as an architect. When a colleague requested names of architects who had extensive experience in the planning of building groups, Gilbert not only supplied the expected names of California architect John Galen Howard; Eames and Young of St. Louis; McKim, Mead, and White, George B. Post, and others from New York but also included his own name.[3] Some years later, when asked to name "the best city planners in the country," Gilbert again could not resist including himself on the list of illustrious designers and planners. In his company, Gilbert included Frederick Law Olmsted, Edward H. Bennett, Arnold Brunner (who, like

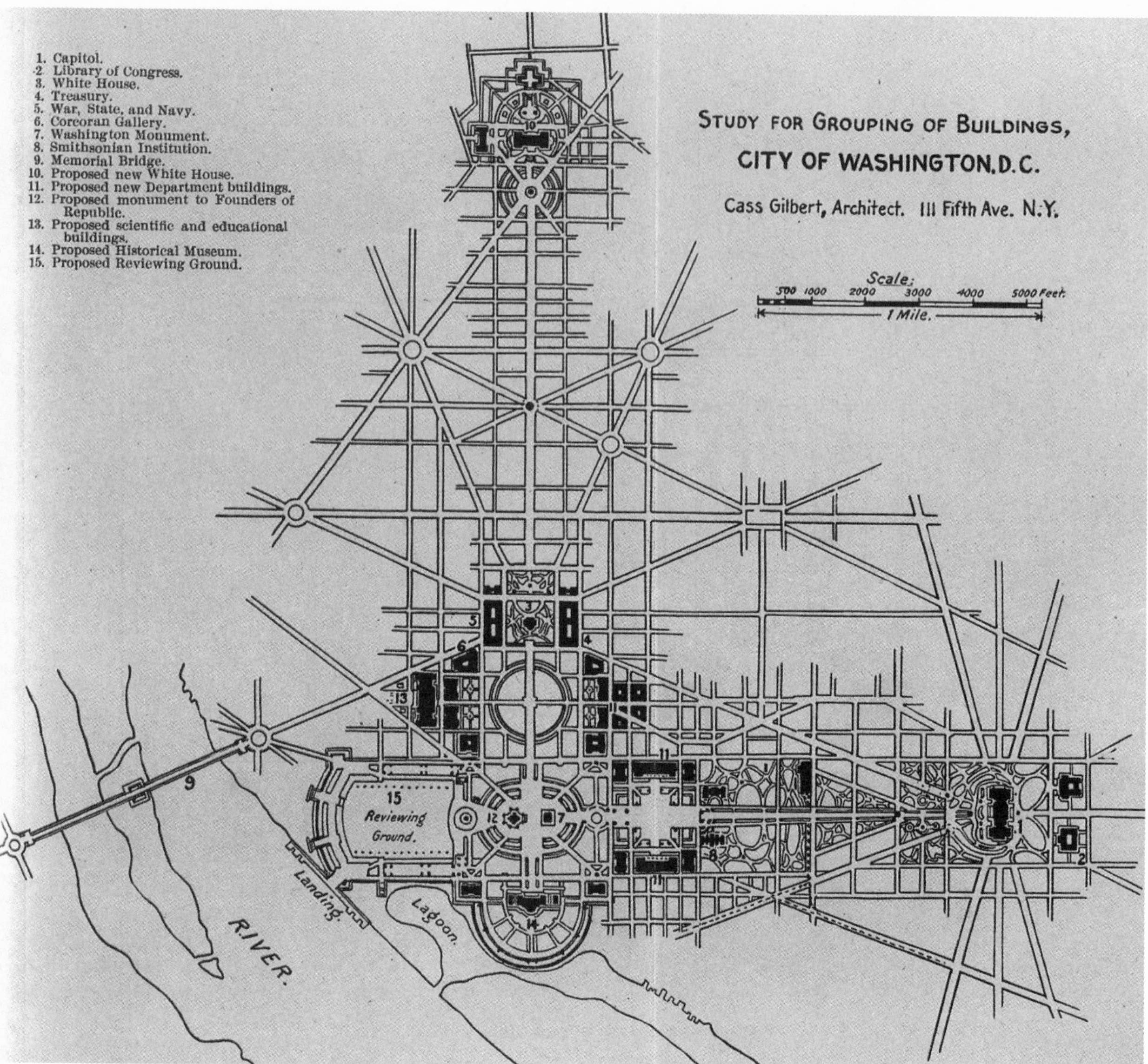

FIGURE 4.1

Study for Grouping of Buildings, City of Washington, D.C., 1900.

Cass Gilbert, delineator.

FIGURE 4.2

University of Minnesota, Minneapolis, Minnesota, plan and section, October 1909. W. P. Foulds, delineator.

(Courtesy University of Minnesota, University Archives)

UNIVERSITY OF MINNESOTA
MINNEAPOLIS MINNESOTA
CASS GILBERT ARCHITECT

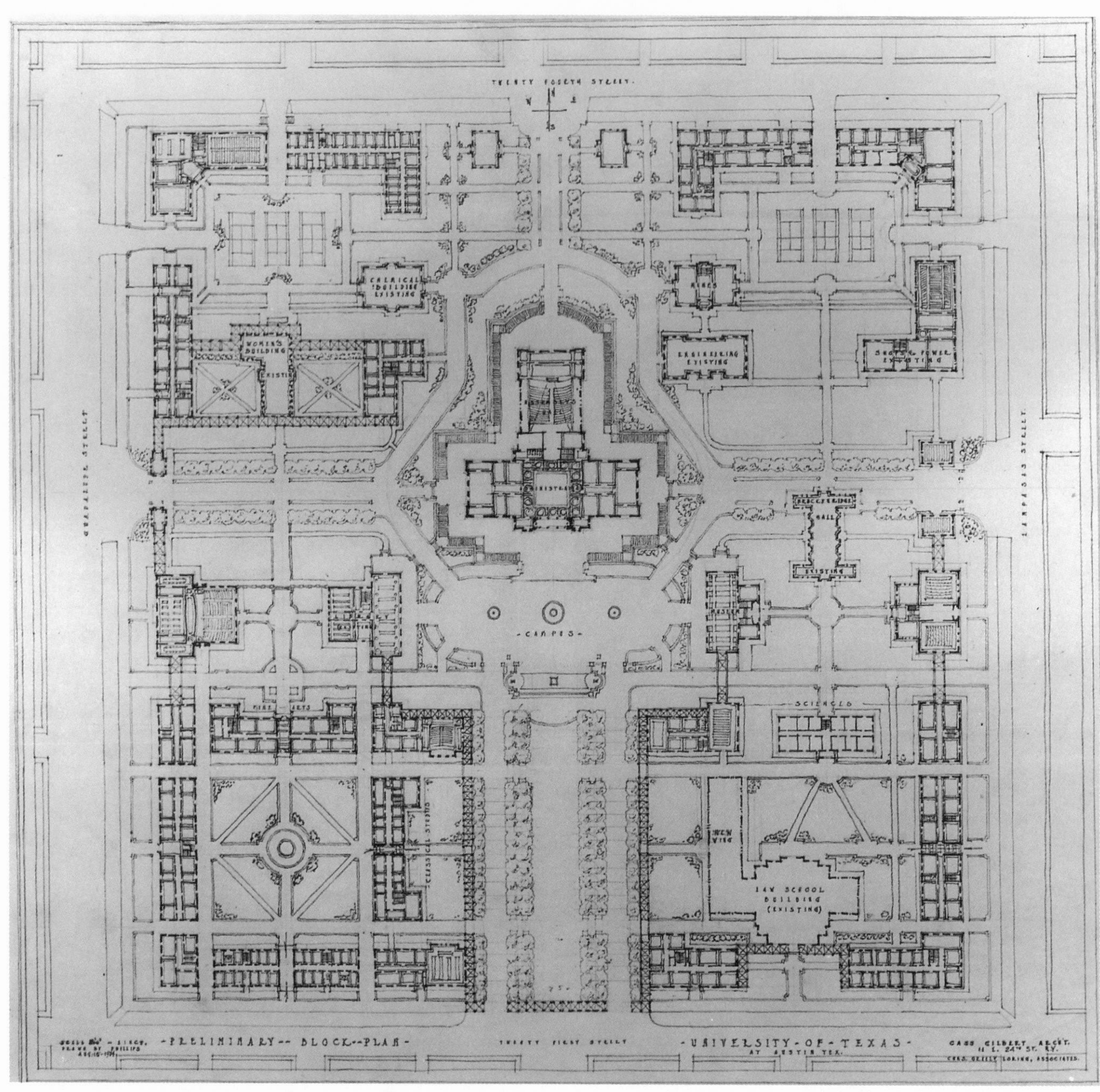

TWENTY FOURTH STREET
CHEMICAL BUILDING EXISTING
WOMAN'S BUILDING
ENGINEERING EXISTING
CAMPUS
FINE ARTS
SCIENCES
CLASSICAL STUDIES
LAW SCHOOL BUILDING (EXISTING)
GUADALUPE STREET
LAVACA STREET
TWENTY FIRST STREET
-PRELIMINARY--BLOCK--PLAN-
-UNIVERSITY-OF-TEXAS-
AT AUSTIN TEX.
CASS GILBERT ARCHT.

Gilbert, had "been connected with several city plan enterprises"), and the author of the Canberra, Australia, plan, Walter Burley Griffin.[4]

Gilbert was no stranger to grand schemes. At the behest of Glenn Brown, secretary of the American Institute of Architects, he had published an essay and plan for the reshaping of Washington, D.C. in 1901 (fig. 4.1), predating the McMillan Commission plan. In the first decade of the twentieth century, Gilbert also experimented with master plans in his proposals for the University of Minnesota (1907–9; fig. 4.2) and the University of Texas at Austin (1909–16; fig. 4.3). Both these plans presented complex building groups that addressed the changing needs of the early twentieth-century university, and both were only partially realized.[5]

Although Gilbert was reluctant to become directly involved with many planning groups as his career was on the rise, his work on two large-scale projects, a campus plan for Oberlin College in Ohio and a city plan for New Haven, Connecticut, suggests his commitment to the historic preservation of open space. In the case of Oberlin, Gilbert's campus development, particularly between 1903 and 1915, responded to the public space called Tappan Square, which was shared by the college and town. This thirteen-acre parcel was named for the New York merchant and abolitionist Arthur Tappan, who had aided the college during a financial crisis.[6] A village green that dated back to the town's settlement in 1833, Tappan Square had become a center for community life (fig. 4.4). Likewise, at New Haven, between 1906 and 1910, Gilbert based his ideas on his respect for the open space of the historic green at the center of the New England city (fig. 4.5). The New Haven Green, which dated to the earliest origins of the colonial town in 1639, was the central of nine squares in the city and, at approximately seventeen acres, was comparable in size to Oberlin's square. In 1912 the green still held the distinction of being the largest public square in the United States.[7]

Gilbert's work with these two spaces is illuminated through examination of three factors: patronage by an informed institutional representative who was influential in decision-making in each project; Gilbert's development of building groups, both in accord with beaux arts principles and with an awareness of the City Beautiful movement; and his reliance on the concept of vista to establish how these building groups were to be perceived. Although his work at Oberlin and at New Haven had preexisting conditions, special stipulations, site requirements, and budget constraints that affected the outcome of the proposals, in each case Gilbert developed

FIGURE 4.3
Preliminary Block Plan, University of Texas at Austin, Texas, August 15, 1914. Phillips, delineator. Ink and graphite on drawing paper, 25 in. × 26 in.
(Cass Gilbert Collection, courtesy New-York Historical Society, neg. no. 59142)

FIGURE 4.4
View looking northeast, across Tappan Square and Oberlin College campus, Oberlin, Ohio, 1860. Unidentified photographer.
(Courtesy Oberlin College Archives)

a plan that sought to utilize the historic core of the community for maximum effect while also respecting the traditions of past projects and ideas.

For the Oberlin and New Haven projects, Gilbert was fortunate to have found patrons who fully supported his ideas and with whom he developed a strong rapport. In the case of Oberlin, his work, which developed over the course of several years, was championed by Henry Churchill King, president of Oberlin College from 1902 to 1927. King first contacted Gilbert in late 1903 and came to regard him as "the best thing Oberlin [had] seen in architectural lines."[8] Under King's leadership, plans for the campus flourished.[9] From early in his tenure, King envisioned the college, and by extension the town, as a cultural center. His commitment to campus development was vital to a design process that produced several buildings, including Finney Memorial Chapel (1907–8), Cox Administration Building (1911–2), and the Allen Memorial Art Museum (1914–7). These buildings, in turn, contributed to Gilbert's comprehensive vision for the Oberlin campus.[10]

At Oberlin, Gilbert's initial experience, which put him on a firm footing with President King, occurred in 1907 when he was engaged by the college to design a chapel. An older chapel building, located at the southwest corner of Tappan Square, had served since 1854 as a central feature of the college and of the community. When it burned down on January 25, 1903, the need for a new meeting place for religious and secular activities became acute. Frederick Norton Finney, president of the Missouri, Kansas, and Texas Railway Company, donated substantial funds for the construction of a new chapel that would honor his father, the evangelist and former Oberlin College president Charles Grandison Finney. The Finney homestead, located just opposite the northwest corner of Tappan Square, was chosen as the new site. This location fundamentally changed the course of how the campus would be developed in future years.[11]

When King rejected proposals made by architects from Indianapolis and Boston, he turned to Finney for advice. The railroad financier gave King the names of two architects who might be interested in building the chapel: "Kim," which referred to Charles Follen McKim, one of the founding partners of the New York architectural firm of McKim, Mead, and White, and Cass Gilbert, who was noted as "a very artistic fellow."[12] In the meantime, King assured the community that no plan would be adopted until "the very best advice to be had in America" was sought.[13]

Over the course of their many years of work together, Gilbert and King greatly respected one another's cordiality, sense of fairness, and talents in de-

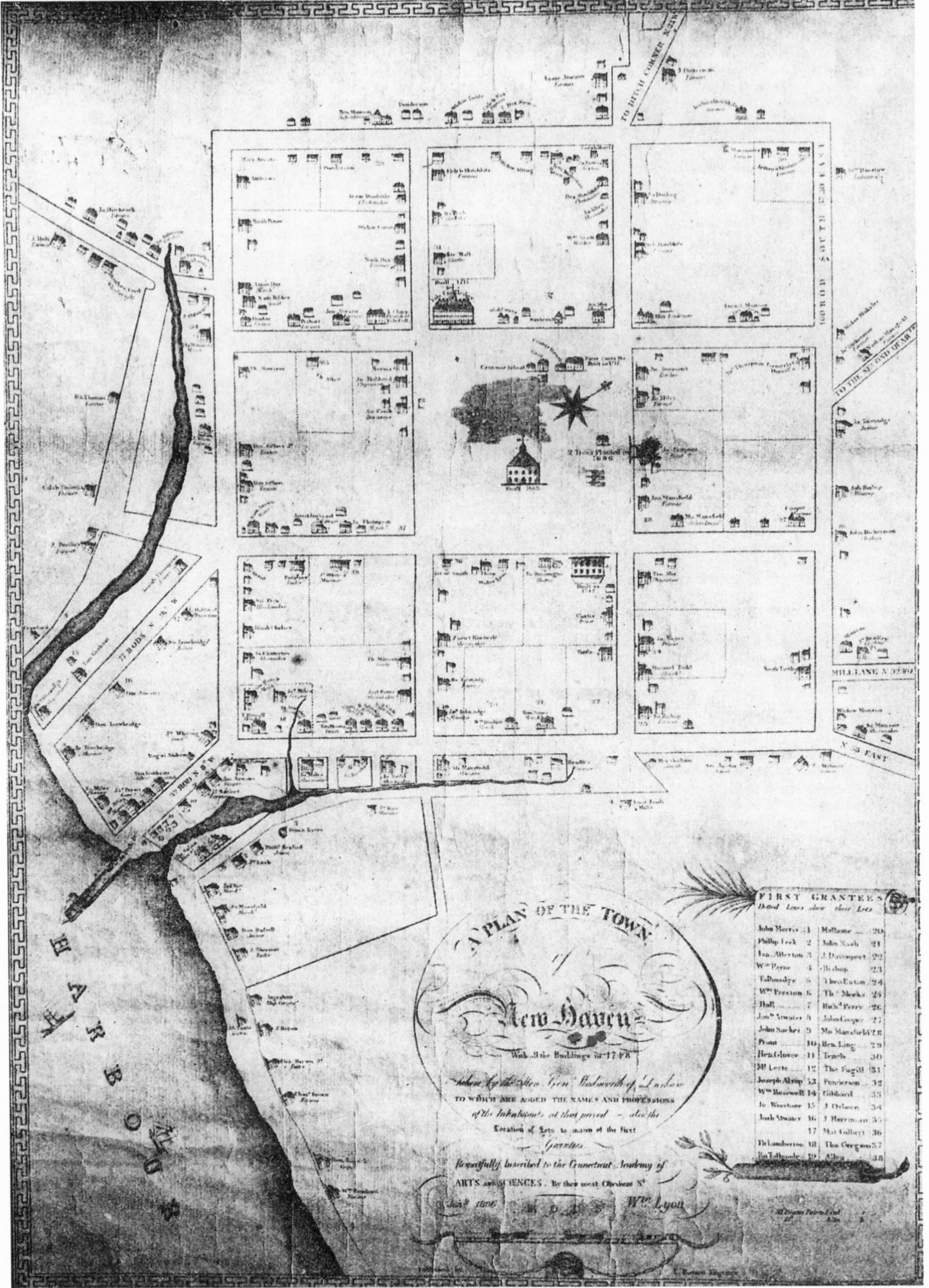

A PLAN OF THE TOWN
of
New Haven
With all the Buildings in 1748
TO WHICH ARE ADDED THE NAMES AND PROFESSIONS
of the Inhabitants at that period — also the
Location of Lots to many of the first
Grantees
Respectfully Inscribed to the Connecticut Academy of
ARTS and SCIENCES. By their most Obedient St
Wm. Lyon
FIRST GRANTEES
Dotted Lines shew their Lots
John Morris 1
Phillip Leek 2
Isa. Allerton 3
Wm. Payne 4
Tallmadge 5
Wm. Preston 6
Hall 7
Jonth. Atwater 8
John Sacket 9
Prout 10
Hen. Glover 11
Mr. Leete 12
Joseph Alsop 13
Wm. Bosewell 14
Jo. Winstone 15
Josh Atwater 16
17
Th. Lamberton 18
Mallbone 20
John Nash 21
J. Davenport 22
Bishop 23
Theo. Eaton 24
Ths. Meeks 25
Richd. Perry 26
John Cooper 27
Mo. Mansfield 28
Ben. Ling 29
Tench 30
Tho Fugill 31
Pencierson 32
Gibbard 33
J. Osborn 34
J. Harriman 35
Mat Gilbert 36
Tho Gregson 37
Allen 38
TO DITCH CORNER
60 RODS TO THE
TO THE SECOND QUARTER
MILL LANE
HARBOUR

veloping future plans for the college. When Gilbert, for example, acknowledged receipt of a pamphlet addressing the future campus needs at Oberlin, he noted that he found King's optimism and faith as expressed in the publication "just what [he] needed."[14] That Gilbert, with King's strong support, intended to use Finney Memorial Chapel and the southern Romanesque masonry building Warner Gymnasium (Norman Patton, architect; 1901–12) as the core of the campus soon became evident. This choice was due in large part to the architect's admiration of Warner Gymnasium, which was being constructed west of Tappan Square at the time Gilbert was engaged to design the chapel.[15] Warner Gymnasium was held up by Gilbert as a model, first for the chapel and later for other buildings.[16] He praised this structure as "the only building of architectural merit" on the campus. The other buildings seemed to him to be "fussy or stupid, and not of a style that would be well to continue."[17] Gilbert selected the gymnasium because he believed it was at once "serious, quiet, and not extravagant."[18]

Gilbert was also open to King's ideas. For example, the architect praised King's foresight in urging him to place the Art Building at the southeast corner of North Main and East Lorain Streets. Although initially skeptical of King's recommendation, Gilbert applauded the college president for looking at the plan "in a bigger way" than he had. Gilbert also urged King to "take the next step, [and] clear the ground for a really fine effect" by developing plans for the auditorium.[19]

Finney, however, proved to be a difficult client, often petulant and critical of Gilbert's design and budget.[20] Finney persisted in trying to obtain a spatially complex building without supplying the necessary funds for it. Although Finney did not understand the problems faced by the architect or by the college, Gilbert strove to placate the fault-finding donor by trying to incorporate some of Finney's suggestions, such as the inclusion of a widened central hall and narrower side aisles.[21] Gilbert, however, successfully defended to the railway executive his overall position and choice of design due largely to the force of his own and King's vision for what the campus might become.[22]

As at Oberlin, Gilbert's proposal for New Haven developed over the course of several years, after commencing with a project for a single building. At New Haven the new railroad station for the New York, New Haven, and Hartford Railroad most likely provided Gilbert's introduction in 1906 to George Dudley Seymour, a Yale-trained patent attorney, author of regional history, and civic leader in New Haven. (Seymour, an avid art collector, may also have met Gilbert at a lecture Gilbert delivered in 1907 for

FIGURE 4.5
"A Plan of the Town of New Haven, 1748." Used as frontispiece to Cass Gilbert and Frederick Law Olmsted, *Report of the New Haven Civic Improvement Commission.*
(New Haven: Tuttle, Morehouse, and Taylor, 1910).

the Trowbridge Lecture Series at the Yale School of Art.[23]) Seymour did not directly oversee the railroad project but the New Haven leader no doubt was familiar with the project that would greatly influence later discussions about the core of the New England city.

For the New York, New Haven, and Hartford Railroad, Gilbert had designed a handful of smaller suburban passenger stations, few of which were built.[24] With the advent of the company's absorption of various independent rail entities, the line had gained control of the sole route into the Northeast for both passenger and freight service. Charles S. Mellen, president of the New Haven line, who had been an executive at the Northern Pacific Railroad in the upper Midwest, likely had been impressed by Gilbert's work for McKim, Mead, and White in the early 1880s.[25] Mellen initially gave Gilbert carte blanche to design a monumental station that would serve as a gateway to the city.[26]

Gilbert and Seymour had experienced remarkably similar lives with complementary interests. Both had been born in 1859 (indeed, within six weeks of each other); both were avid art and furniture collectors with an abiding interest in colonial architecture and history; and both had traveled the world over. They shared similar political views as staunch Republicans and, professionally, they had earned respect within their individual disciplines. Gilbert's reputation was on the way to becoming established. Seymour's, outside his profession, was founded on his interest in Nathan Hale and other topics in regional colonial history. He was active in community welfare, civic progress, and historical research, and in 1906 led a successful campaign to keep the green clear of new buildings. From 1913 to 1924 he served as secretary to the New Haven Civic Improvement Commission, a position that allowed him to work closely with Gilbert.[27]

Just as Gilbert had praised King's foresight on issues relating to campus planning, he expressed admiration for his colleague's work and foresight in the reshaping of downtown New Haven. Gilbert noted Seymour's "courageous confidence in the intelligence of the community" in working toward civic improvement in the city. Gilbert later wrote, "You have started a great movement in New Haven. . . . It is the ideal of citizenship and public duty that a man may influence the community in which he lives that the generations that follow shall be better for his having lived. This is what you have done and are doing now."[28] Gilbert admired Seymour for his commitment and his resolve to leave a distinctive, historically sensitive mark on the physical landscape.

Seymour's vision was to develop a plan for constructing new public buildings on the northeast and southeast sides of the green, and on this topic he consulted with Gilbert. In response to Seymour's plan, which was addressed to the city's mayor and aldermen (and later published in local papers), Gilbert advised Seymour that the strongest part of his argument was in setting forth objections to haphazard development. Gilbert further noted:

> When attention is called to the objections, the intelligent American people are apt to seek a remedy. The first step in effecting the remedy is, as you urge, the employment of an expert or a commission of experts to carefully study the whole subject and to devise a plan whereby the conditions could be bettered. . . .
>
> I would suggest that . . . you add to your argument the fact that in the early days of the Republic the importance of a definite plan was fully understood. That President Washington and the Congress of the United States saw to it that a definite plan was adopted for the city of Washington and obtained the services of Major L'Enfant . . . to plan the Capital City. Detroit was also planned in [a] like manner. You have only to recur to the original idea of the New England towns and particularly to New Haven itself to illustrate that in the early days of this country the merit of a civic center was fully appreciated.[29]

Of particular interest to Gilbert was the "good effect" of grouping public buildings around such a space as the green, a lesson he had learned from recent expositions that had demonstrated "the value of grouping buildings."[30] Their exchange in 1907 sealed Gilbert and Seymour's professional relationship, and for more than nine years they corresponded and conferred regularly about the New Haven project.

At Gilbert's urging Seymour pushed for the implementation of plans to develop the New Haven Civic Improvement Commission. Initially, Seymour had hoped to engage Charles Follen McKim, Frederick Law Olmsted Jr. (son of the Boston-based landscape architect and designer of Central Park), and Gilbert as the "experts" to work with the commission. But he was unable to secure McKim's participation.[31] Gilbert suggested William Rutherford Mead, one of McKim's partners. Of these colleagues, Gilbert wrote, "there are no two men that I know of with whom it would be more agreeable to be associated than Mr. Mead & Mr. McKim."[32] Seymour, however, was well aware of the cachet that McKim's name would lend to the project, replying to Gilbert that Mead, since he had "always kept in the background . . . would not speak with anything like Mr. McKim's authority."[33]

Seymour worked mainly with Gilbert on the general concept of the city plan, while Olmsted (whom Seymour had succeeded in engaging on the project) appears to have focused on gathering economic, social, health, and topographical statistics for the report solicited by the commission.[34] Gilbert and Olmsted were each paid $1,250, with $500 additional expenses for the preparation of their drawings.[35] Their *Report to the New Haven Civic Improvement Commission* was published in 1910. This report became Seymour's rallying cry for planning reform in the city core. Gilbert's drawings for this project and his consultations with Olmsted (with Seymour's resounding support) make clear their treatment of the city as a growing organism with interconnected systems for traffic, sanitation, and recreation. It also addressed how the city's environs would be affected by changes that were expected to occur because of increasing industrialization and population growth.[36]

That Gilbert was hired to work on such a project is not surprising; in 1906 he had published a similar report for the Minnesota State Capitol Commission.[37] Considering the thrust of Seymour's advocacy for municipal reform through civic and planning changes, as outlined in his publications, Gilbert clearly found in him a citizen of a like mind.[38] They shared a passionate dedication to development of a civic center in the growing Connecticut city. Seymour expressed this interest when he wrote, in 1912, that the historic purpose of the green should be taken into account since the founders of the city "did not design the Green for use as a park, but as a market place or civic center."[39] The idea of the green as a civic center embodied the features proposed in Gilbert and Olmsted's plan.

At both Oberlin and New Haven Gilbert's building groups illuminate his interest in beaux arts education and ideals, concepts that had already been manifested in several of the City Beautiful projects in America. The Ecole des Beaux-Arts had been founded in Paris in the early seventeenth century, originally as a group of diverse royal art academies.[40] The atelier system, which allowed students to apprentice under established architects, was developed at the Ecole. It informed architectural education and practice in both Europe and America in the late nineteenth and early twentieth centuries. Although Gilbert did not study at the Ecole, he paid for some of his office staff to attend the school and hired special renderers who had studied there when he competed for the U.S. Custom House commission.[41] Gilbert revered the principles of Ecole training: the reliance on architectural elements of a classical past, balance and symmetry in architectural massing, a hierarchical arrangement of buildings in a grander scheme, clear circulation patterns within and between buildings in a group, and lavish visual representations of these ideas.[42]

These formal beaux arts elements and planning ideals were often embraced by projects that were part of the City Beautiful movement, a phenomenon at the turn of the century in America that yoked the beaux arts movement to a complex cultural, political, and environmental agenda. Initially, the movement was expressed in small-scale projects that reflected its origins in municipal art, civic improvement, and outdoor art.[43] As its aims became clearer, the projects grew more ambitious, so much so that the advocates of the movement strove to improve the visual, moral, and social quality of life in small towns and large cities alike. Formal beaux arts features are clear in Gilbert's most significant Oberlin plan, that of 1912–5 (fig. 4.6).[44] Developed after years of wrangling over site location for the Administration Building and the auditorium and negotiations about design and project costs, this proposal hinged upon an earlier precedent set by the landscape architects the Olmsted Brothers (stepbrothers Frederick Jr. and John Charles Olmsted), whose firm carried on the legacy of their father, Frederick Law Olmsted Sr. Like the Olmsted brothers' plan (fig. 4.7), which was produced in 1903 as accompaniment to an insightful report, Gilbert's proposal cleared Tappan Square of three buildings that formed the center of the campus. Specifically, he (like his Boston-based predecessors) called for the moving or demolition of Society Hall (no. 8), French Hall (no. 9), and Spear Library (no. 10), identified on a plan of 1902 (fig. 4.8). Above all, the landscape architects had recommended that Tappan Square be kept "as a spacious and beautiful pleasure ground" that, while owned and controlled by the college, would serve as a public park.[45] In this recommendation, Gilbert heartily concurred.[46]

Gilbert emphasized the east-west axis of the open space, as had the Olmsted brothers. This axiality was also influenced by the recent completion of the Memorial Arch (Joseph Lyman Silsbee, architect; 1903), a monument formed as an exedra, a semicircular outdoor seat, that commemorated Oberlin missionaries who had died in the Chinese Boxer Rebellion. The Olmsteds' plan, however, had not provided a clear axial link to the west, where a massive, Richardsonian building, Peters Hall (Weary and Kramer, architects; 1887; no. 2 on the Olmsteds' plan) was located directly west of Tappan Square on Professor Street. This building was to become a

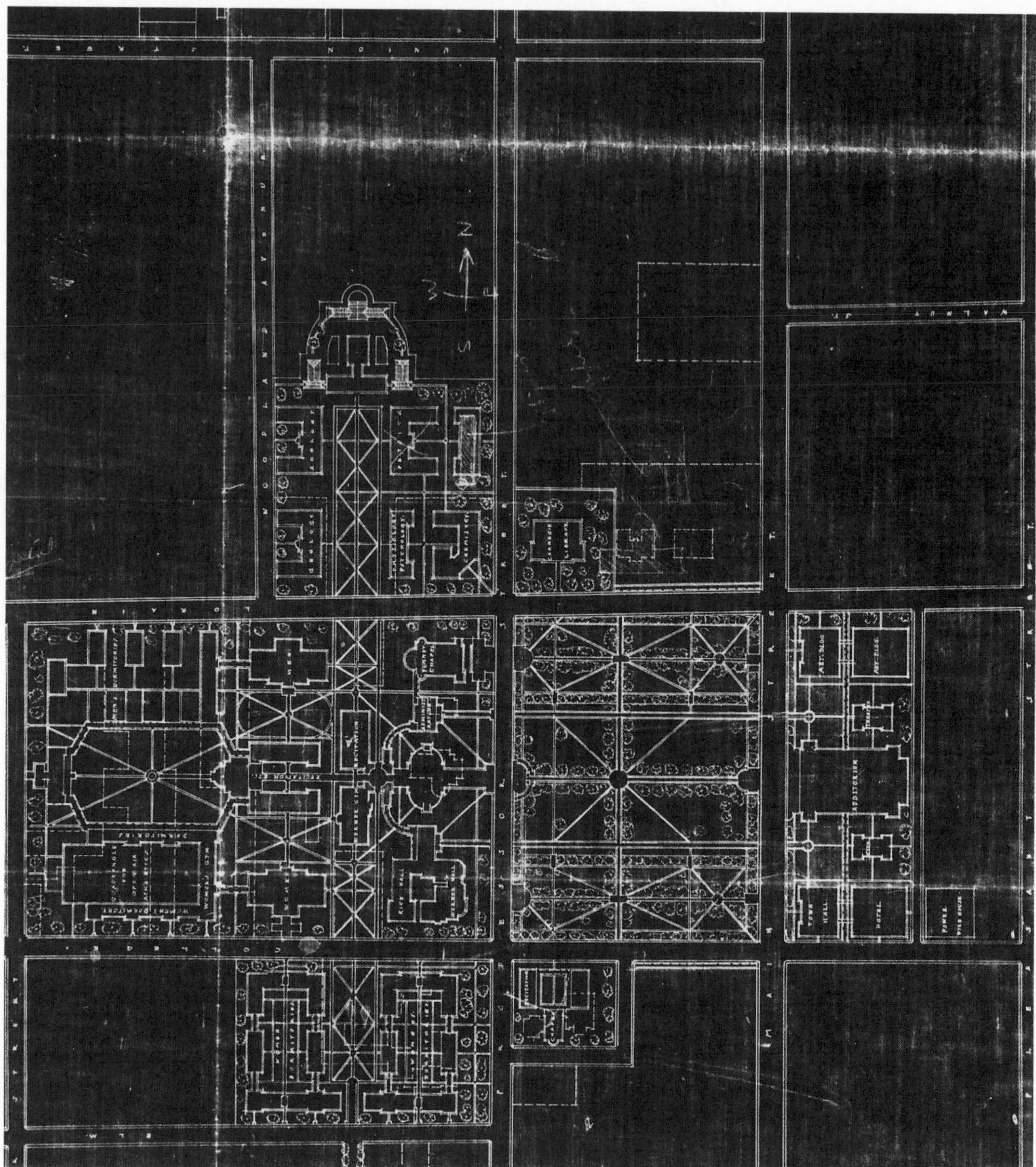

point of contention for Gilbert; from early on he had hoped to remove it entirely from the campus. Indeed, in various versions of his comprehensive plan, Gilbert either removed it completely from view or denoted the building as a dotted outline, since he hoped it would soon be gone.[47]

In the 1914–5 plan Finney Memorial Chapel (located at the southwest corner of West Lorain and Professor Streets) served as a touchstone for the overall development, just as Gilbert and King had intended.[48] The Prudential Committee (the college governing group) had supported Gilbert's chapel proposal and pledged to find the necessary funds for the tower and other features they and Gilbert felt were necessary to the design.[49] Although Finney wanted Gilbert to place the tower on the north end of the chapel, Gilbert was successful in his demands that this asymmetrical feature be placed at the south corner.

This decision reflects Gilbert's consideration of a broader general plan that Finney did not fully comprehend. Gilbert hoped the chapel would become the most important building of the campus group; he envisioned later buildings taking their cue from the characteristic features of the chapel exterior so that the group of buildings would "compose harmoniously *toward* the center instead of *away* from the center of the group."[50] In other words, he hoped the chapel tower would form a compositional anchor at the north end of a building group (yet to be realized) that would be dominated by an even larger tower located to the south of the chapel. Although willing either "to leave off the tower [and] make the [chapel] building as plain as a warehouse" made of brick or to reduce the overall size of the project, Gilbert did not, in that case, wish to be held responsible for the end result.[51] The Prudential Committee agreed and believed the structure should be the college's most monumental building, rather than a "mutilation" of another design. The 1912–5 plan, when compared to a perspective drawing of approximately the same date (plate 10), conveys the focus of the east-west axis at the monumental tower, which compositionally proclaimed the dominance of the building group in relation to Tappan Square.

Notably, in an earlier comprehensive plan for Oberlin, King had to mediate between the trustees, the faculty, and splinter groups within them, where each group lobbied for its own interests.[52] One dissenting voice was heard from a trustee who objected to any closed quadrangle building groups and who expressed the feeling that Gilbert's plan "was too much like a city plan, and not sufficiently adjusted to the country situation."[53] Certainly the complex building group Gilbert proposed for the small lib-

FIGURE 4.6
Oberlin College, February 8, 1915. Blueprint.
(Cass Gilbert Collection, courtesy New-York Historical Society, neg. no. 72871)

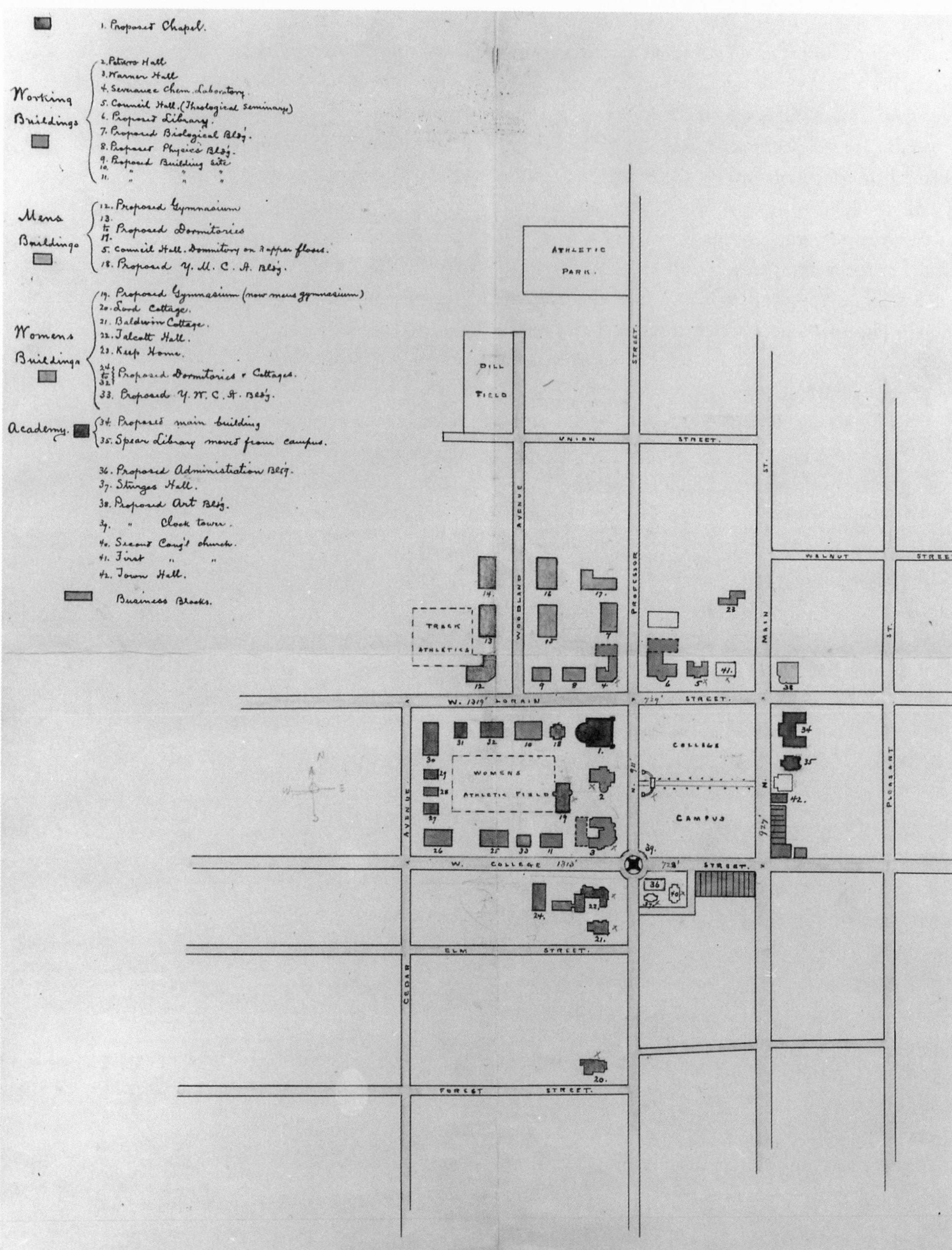
1. Proposed Chapel.
Working Buildings
2. Peters Hall
3. Warner Hall
4. Severance Chem. Laboratory.
5. Council Hall. (Theological Seminary)
6. Proposed Library.
7. Proposed Biological Bldg.
8. Proposed Physics Bldg.
9. Proposed Building site
10. " " "
11. " " "
Mens Buildings
12. Proposed Gymnasium
13. to 17. Proposed Dormitories
5. Council Hall. Dormitory on 3 upper floors.
18. Proposed Y. M. C. A. Bldg.
Womens Buildings
19. Proposed Gymnasium (now mens gymnasium)
20. Lord Cottage.
21. Baldwin Cottage.
22. Talcott Hall.
23. Keep Home.
24 to 32 Proposed Dormitories & Cottages.
33. Proposed Y. W. C. A. Bldg.
Academy.
34. Proposed main building
35. Spear Library moved from campus.
36. Proposed Administration Bldg.
37. Sturges Hall.
38. Proposed Art Bldg.
39. " Clock tower.
40. Second Cong'l church.
41. First " "
42. Town Hall.
Business Blocks.
ATHLETIC PARK.
DILL FIELD
UNION STREET.
WALNUT STREET
TRACK ATHLETICS
WOODLAND AVENUE
PROFESSOR STREET.
MAIN ST.
PLEASANT ST.
W. LORAIN STREET.
COLLEGE CAMPUS
WOMENS ATHLETIC FIELD
AVENUE
W. COLLEGE STREET.
ELM STREET.
CEDAR
FOREST STREET.

eral arts college was overwhelming to the uninitiated viewer: it proposed a dramatic reshaping of public and institutional space in the name of a grand plan.

FIGURE 4.7
Oberlin College campus, detail of plan, ca. 1903. Olmsted Brothers, delineators. Ink and wash on drawing paper, 22 in. × 17 in.
(Cass Gilbert Collection, courtesy New-York Historical Society, neg. no. 72872)

Gilbert first articulated his ideas about campus development in his plans for the University of Minnesota in Minneapolis. As practitioners of the City Beautiful movement believed, a city's or university's building groups, if imbued with visual order and a hierarchy and symmetry of form, as well as compositional and functional clarity, would create an environment that would instruct and guide the citizenry. In the case of the University of Minnesota, Gilbert spoke eloquently about his hope:

> I can say with confidence that upon that site could be planned one of the most effective and noble groups of educational buildings to be found anywhere. The last few years have brought me very much in contact with matters of this kind. . . . It is not necessary that University buildings should be ponderous and monumental, but [it] is essential that they should be well-ordered, well-grouped, well-arranged, and well-proportioned and that they should leave a definite and ennobling impression upon those who might visit or use them.[54]

Gilbert almost certainly had similar goals for his Oberlin College building group: to create a beneficial moral and social effect on those who came into contact with the physical environment that he envisioned.

This beaux arts-informed City Beautiful orientation is apparent in Gilbert's encounter with similar difficulties in New Haven for the city's proposed railroad station. The railroad station was not realized in specific accord with many of Gilbert's designs, such as a proposed Renaissance-revival version (plate 11), because of project delays, funding problems, and changes in the railroad administration.[55] But in each version of Gilbert and Olmsted's proposals, the station was to serve as a gateway, a feature embodying the ideals of City Beautiful authors such as Charles Mulford Robinson, who had written about the importance of the railroad station as a significant threshold to a community. It was probably Seymour who placed an editorial in a local New Haven newspaper stating that with designs such as Gilbert's "New Haveners will be able to point to [the railroad station] with pride. Indeed the day is shortly coming when we will no longer feel as though we had to hurry our arriving guests away from the depot just as quickly as possible for fear they may get a wholly unaesthetic

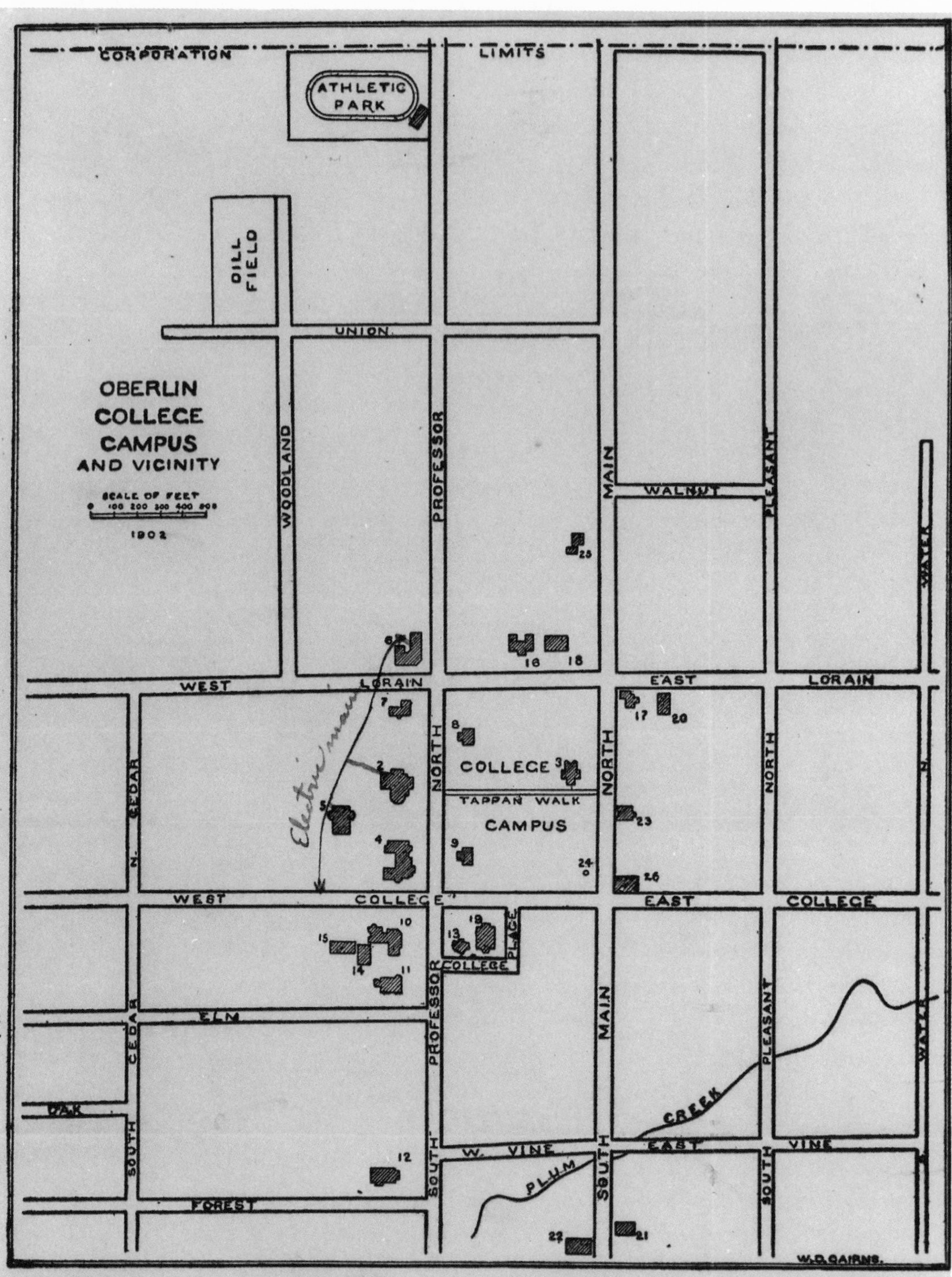

2 Peters Hall.
3 Spear Library.
4 Warner Hall.
5 Warner Gymnasium.
6 Severance Chemical Laboratory.
7 Finney House.
8 Society Hall.
9 French Hall.
10 Talcott Hall.
11 Baldwin Cottage.
12 Lord Cottage.
13 Soldiers' Monument.
14 Women's Gymnasium.
15 Rockefeller Skating Floor.
16 Council Hall.
17 Stewart Hall.
18 First Congregational Church.
19 Second Congregational Church.
20 Baptist Church.
21 First M. E. Church.
22 Episcopal Church.
23 Oberlin Town Hall.
24 Historic Elm.
25 Keep Home.
26 Park Hotel.

FIGURE 4.8
Oberlin College Campus and Vicinity, 1902. Whiteprint, 10 in. × 17 in.
(Cass Gilbert Collection, courtesy New-York Historical Society, neg. no. 72873)

FIGURE 4.9
New Haven, perspective view, looking south toward railroad station, ca. 1910. Cass Gilbert, delineator. Conté crayon on brown paper, 18 in. × 41 in.
(Cass Gilbert Collection, courtesy New-York Historical Society, neg. no. 72874)

impression of the city."[56] The railway station became a monumental terminus, both aesthetic and functional, at the end of a wide thoroughfare, which connected northward to the green (fig. 4.9).

Gilbert and Olmsted's published proposal makes the railroad boulevard integral to the heart of the historic city. Although Gilbert's overall arrangement of buildings and of new development was not symmetrical and balanced in massing (both beaux arts features), he was most concerned in this project with circulation within the city. Gilbert and Olmsted were particularly interested in reducing congestion at the corner of Church and Chapel Streets.[57] They proposed the development of a high-rise hotel and, later, of a post office (neither of which was built on the site) to mark the pivotal circulation point connecting the grand boulevard from the railroad station to Temple Street, leading to the New Haven Green. As a corollary to this reworking of existing city thoroughfares (fig. 4.10), they proposed a grand scheme of public buildings to be arranged around the perimeter of the open space. This matter, which Gilbert and Seymour discussed at length, was published in Olmsted and Gilbert's more fully developed comprehensive plan (fig. 4.11).

Gilbert also had a role in the new public library. Seymour had successfully blocked the original campaign to place the library on the green, and Gilbert fully agreed with his position. In early 1907 Gilbert stated that what he liked most about New Haven was the magnificent green at the center of the city. When he learned of the proposition "to spoil the Green by the erection of a public library on it and by cutting it up with [a] trolley line," he urged citizens "not [to] let the city do it" since the green "was too beautiful to be desecrated in any way."[58] Later that year, Gilbert was engaged to design a public library building, funded by a generous gift of $300,000 from New Haven widow Mary E. Ives.[59]

The library, as Seymour and Gilbert saw it, was the first building to be constructed as part of the new civic building group on the northeast edge of the green. Gilbert's credibility for this project was enhanced by his recently having received the commission for the St. Louis Public Library, a $1.25 million project that had received a fair amount of publicity.[60] Initially, Seymour envisioned the New Haven civic center along the northeast edge of the green as having a library, courthouse, hall of records, and possibly a new post office and bank. But Gilbert advised Seymour that "a sufficient space should be reserved" around the library for later changes.[61]

Cass Gilbert considered it necessary for his buildings to be surrounded by ample space in order to achieve the maximum visual effect. For both

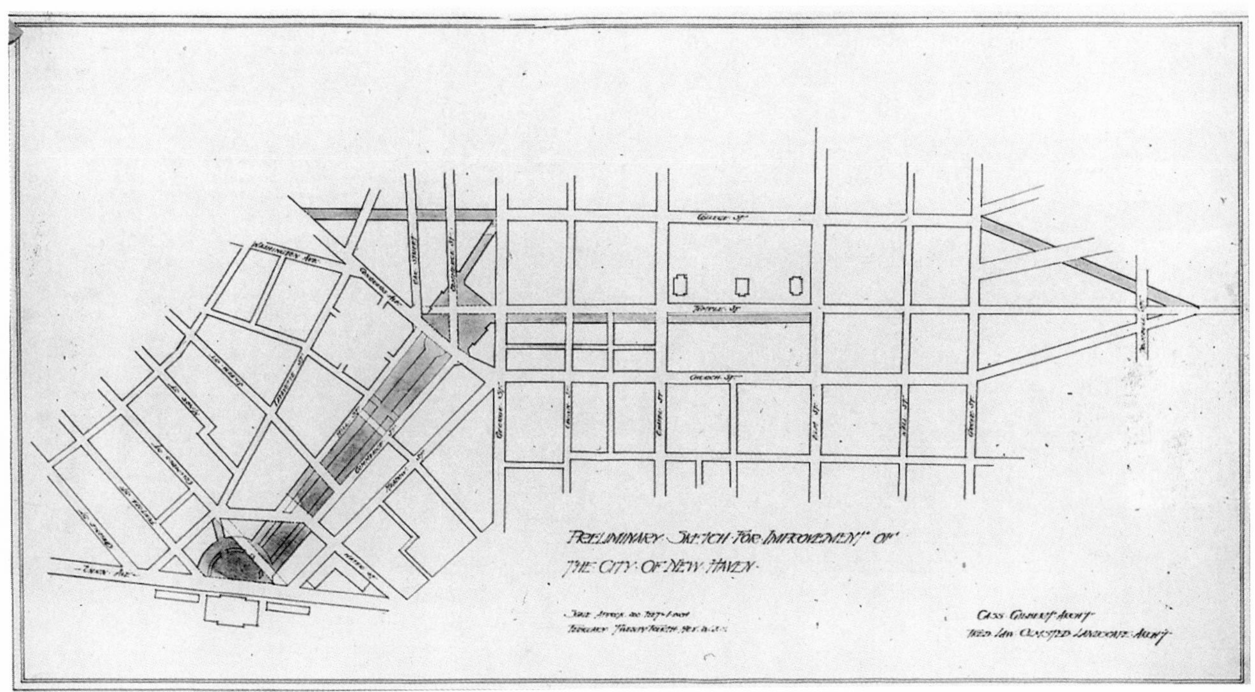

FIGURE 4.10

Preliminary sketch for the improvement of New Haven, February 24, 1908. W. J. S., delineator. Ink, wash, and graphite on drawing paper mounted on board, 24 in. × 39 in.

(Cass Gilbert Collection, courtesy New-York Historical Society, neg. no. 72875)

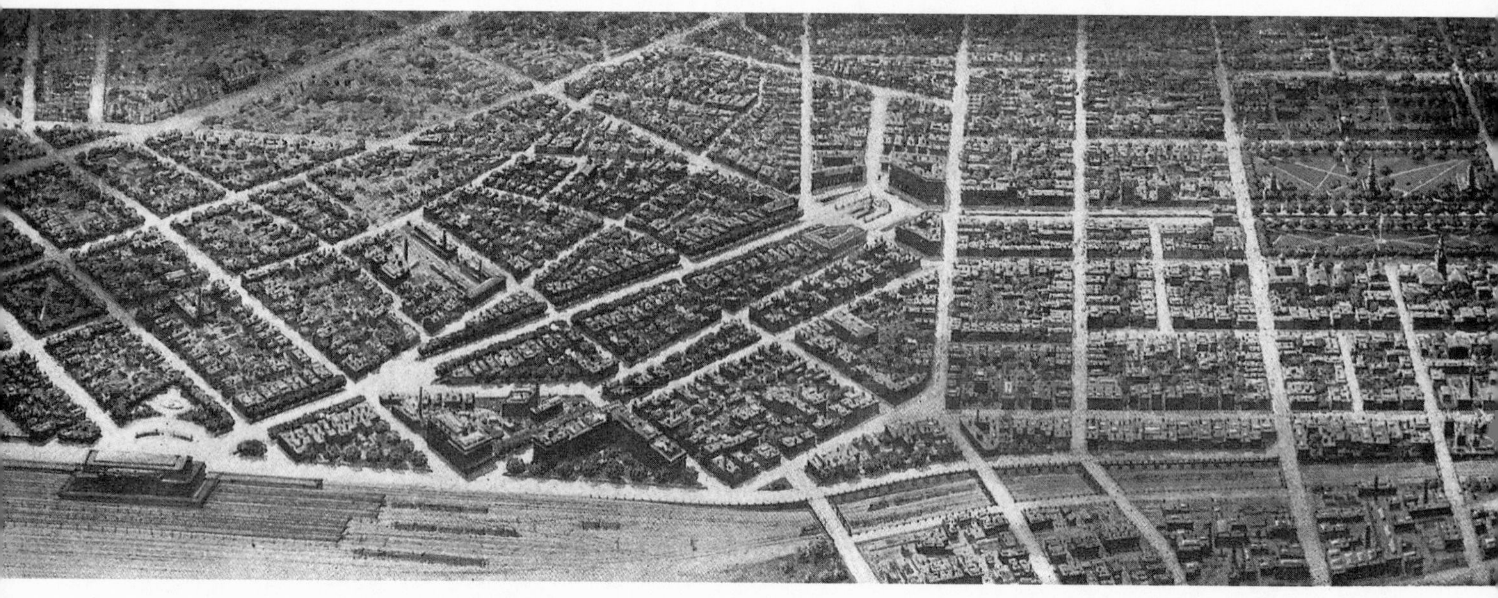

FIGURE 4.11
New Haven, bird's-eye view of proposed avenue from the Station to the Green through the proposed Square, ca. 1910.

Oberlin and New Haven, the building groups at the edge of their respective squares simultaneously demonstrate Gilbert's regard for open space, his respect for the existing architecture around it, and his utilization of the entire framework as a setting for his own buildings. The viewer's perception of a unified, stylistically consistent building group was of the utmost importance to Gilbert. Although King and college alumnus Lucien Warner had advocated the use of a Gothic exterior for the chapel (a style favored by some faculty), Gilbert convinced them that the hybrid of southern Romanesque and Renaissance classicism was more appropriate. Despite delays with constructing individual buildings, Gilbert remained hopeful that a new building group, east of Tappan Square, still might be realized. He expressed this hope to President King: "Every time I think of one of these buildings for Oberlin I am more and more impressed with the desirability of having a general plan where the buildings could be located so that they can be co-related to one another. I should keep them all in the style of the Finney Memorial [Chapel] though, of course, they would vary in design and I think we could make a most interesting group if we did so."[62]

Even before the Administration Building plans had been fixed, Gilbert was thinking about the long-term potential of relating several buildings to his first project for the college. Gilbert agreed with King's inclination not to use the Gothic style for the new auditorium (as advocated by its donor, Charles Martin Hall), explaining that while he appreciated that medieval theme for some buildings, it was more important for him "to consider the College as a unit rather than as a series of individual units. For that reason I have been endeavoring to keep the buildings all of one general architectural style. One of the most serious criticisms that can be made of College groups in this country is that, with few exceptions, no consistent scheme as to the style of buildings or as to general plans has been carried out." Gilbert felt that campus planning, as it had been manifested thus far in the early twentieth century, justified his decision. In his mind, to adopt a single Gothic building would have been a "mistake."[63]

This new building group, east of Tappan Square along Main Street, was subject to various phases of development. The new Art Building was the most pressing project, as it had been discussed for several years. But a new hotel, town hall, and high school were also part of this eastern campus proposal. The town-oriented function of these buildings made the more-finished 1915 plan a sort of micro–town plan, or at the very least an augmentation of the existing town. Existing buildings in this area east of Tappan Square included the college's Stewart Hall, the town's Methodist Church, the town hall, and a small hotel. By blurring the boundaries between campus and town, this master plan by Gilbert addressed the needs of the growing college, as well as those of the town, both of which required the facilities for several different functions.[64]

Compositionally, the east side development of the Art Building and the auditorium carried out the east-west orientation depicted in the 1914–5 plan, which visually terminated to the west with Memorial Tower. To counter the effect of the administrative group, an impressive screen of buildings was proposed to the east, which included the Art Building, the auditorium, and an unidentified "Future Building," located on Main Street (fig. 4.12, *left to right*).[65] In between and in back of the arcades that connected the flanking buildings were secondary unidentified structures. Gilbert reasoned that these subsidiary buildings "would help the composition besides giving greater justification for the destruction of existing structures."[66]

Although funds were so limited that the college could not afford to remove poorly constructed existing buildings, let alone construct new ones, Gilbert unrealistically lobbied for the development of a row of several buildings. He explained: "Of course, as you know, I have always advocated the occupation of the Campus forming, as you once expressed it, a screen to enclose the Campus and to some extent mask the common and uninteresting structures that surround it, particularly on the east and the south. It would leave the whole center of the Campus free and would make it look larger by closing down the perspective to some extent."[67]

The focal point for the building group and plan that he hoped to realize was a massive central tower, on the west side of Tappan Square and placed on the main axis (see fig. 4.9). Gilbert utilized the tower form not only in plans for Oberlin but also in other university projects, such as those at Minnesota and Texas. In these tower proposals, he capitalized on the multistory form he had successfully used in projects such as New York's West Street Building (1905) and the Woolworth Building (1911–3), and he translated it into a powerful campus symbol.[68] In one series of proposals, Gilbert offered an imposing array of tower designs for Oberlin's long-term development.[69] Gilbert wanted the three-hundred-foot Memorial Tower to "dominate the entire landscape and be visible for miles around. It should be simple, vigorous, and impressive." He considered Magdalen Tower at Oxford University in England a noteworthy model of smaller dimensions.[70] Since Gilbert continued to produce tower studies well into the 1920s, not only for the Memorial Tower project but also for Oberlin's

FIGURE 4.12

Elevation view of proposed east sector of the Oberlin College Campus, ca. 1914. Cass Gilbert, delineator. 32 in. × 64 in.

(Photograph courtesy Allen Memorial Art Museum, Oberlin, Ohio)

FIGURE 4.13

Administration Building, Oberlin College, July 22, 1912. W. P. Foulds, delineator. Ink and wash on drawing paper, mounted on board, 25 in. × 39 in.

(Cass Gilbert Collection, courtesy New-York Historical Society, neg. no. 72876)

Theological Seminary, clearly this building typology remained important to him.[71]

Gilbert's interest in enhancing a viewer's perception of the "whole" of a design is suggested by his use of framing devices. At Oberlin, development of this framing feature probably arose from his similar treatment of the group plan in his proposals for the University of Texas in 1909–10, which adapted a series of connecting arcades between buildings to be constructed on a hilly site just north of the capitol in Austin. Noteworthy in this regard at Oberlin is a rendering by William P. Foulds that portrays arcades extending directly north and south of the Administration Building (fig. 4.13). This and other arcade proposals for the Ohio college may represent Gilbert's specific architectural response to Silsbee's exedra in Tappan Square. The arcades and the attempt to create a cloisterlike setting may also have reflected Gilbert's favorable impression of Theodate Pope's design for the Westover School in Middlebury, Connecticut. After visiting this school in August 1912, Gilbert recommended Pope's work to a colleague as "beautifully designed and beautifully planned" and characterized by "very refined and scholarly" details and admirable proportions. Gilbert also felt that her design was "a rather extensive one forming four sides of a large quadrangle or cloister," which he found refreshing in its charm and simplicity.[72] The Administration Building, however, was realized without these connective elements. Today, the rear of this building serves as a modest reminder of Gilbert's grander proposals.

Gilbert also used lamp standards to enrich the viewer's perception of his buildings from afar. His proposals for these elements are detailed in sketches he sent to New York marble merchant Rafaello Batelli. These fanciful columns, with bases depicting lions, were ultimately realized in more sedate form. When the standards were complete, they enhanced the slightly terraced effect near the front entrance of the chapel. With these columns Gilbert had hoped to create a rich, coloristic effect similar to that which he had wanted to create in the facade stonework. Although this effect was not achieved (the white Carrera marble of the capitals and bases of the lamp standards were not, as Gilbert had directed, "stained to an antique color" and combined with red Verona marble shafts), the columns nevertheless set off the chapel from the rest of the campus. Dismantled sometime after 1946, these columns and others such as those at Cox Administration Building (fig. 4.14) had provided a link between the Gilbert's built environment and the natural surroundings of Tappan Square, providing a transitional zone between architectural mass and open space.[73]

FIGURE 4.14

Cox Administration Building, detail of lamp standards, Oberlin College, Oberlin, Ohio. Unidentified photographer. Photograph.

(Courtesy Oberlin College Archives)

FIGURE 4.15

Preliminary sketch for New Court at New Haven, January 25, 1909. W. J. S., delineator. Ink and wash drawing, 18 in. × 33 in.

(Cass Gilbert Collection, courtesy New-York Historical Society, neg. no. 72877)

In New Haven, these same issues regarding the contextual aspects of style, framing devices, and importance of the vista came into play in Gilbert's plans. The unobstructed view of public buildings across the green, Gilbert believed, was a condition to be preserved and highly prized.[74] Gilbert thought New Haven was one of the most beautiful cities in the world, and he was especially gratified to design a building that faced the green, where he could be sure of how it would be perceived across the open space.[75]

When working on the library and the later courthouse designs (fig. 4.15), Gilbert and Seymour agreed that the structures should be Georgian in style and designed to be in harmony with the United (North) Church (David Hoadley, architect; 1814–5), as well as other buildings in the historic core of the city.[76] Gilbert advocated the use of local brick trimmed with granite to be "proportioned to the churches on the Green," a step that would be most important in "the presentation of the beauty of New Haven."[77] He wanted to make "the building distinctive and monumental and at the same time to preserve the proportions and spirit" of the colonial architecture of New Haven. He also admitted that had the United Church and the Center Church not existed, his own library designs would have been distinctly different.[78] He even went so far as to complete a set of measured drawings of the exterior of the United Church so that the proportions of the library "would be brought into harmony" with those of the church. He regarded this church as one of the best examples of colonial architecture in America, one that offered a rare opportunity for historic preservation.[79] Gilbert and Seymour also advocated restoring the Center Church (Ithiel Towne, architect; ca. 1815) on the Green and the United Church, which had been "submerged . . . in a bath of colored paint" in the mid-nineteenth century, to their original red brick appearance. Seymour wistfully referred to the day when the two buildings might be preserved, so that "we should then begin to recover for New Haven something of its old-time air [and] . . . nothing would help so much to preserve for New Haven its old-time distinction nor to impress visitors with the fact that this community is alive to its obligations to preserve for posterity the monuments of the past."[80]

Although Gilbert did not utilize such features as arcades or classically inspired columns in his designs for New Haven, he very directly addressed how City Beautiful ideas might be useful there. At the Yale School of Fine Arts, as part of the 1907–8 Trowbridge Lecture Series about civic improvement, he delivered a lecture entitled "The Grouping of Public Buildings,"

FIGURE 4.16
Plan of Civic Center at New Haven, no date. Cass Gilbert, delineator. Graphite, conté crayon, or both on tracing paper, 9 in. × 19 in.
(Cass Gilbert Collection, courtesy New-York Historical Society, neg. no. 72878)

a talk in which the rhetoric of the City Beautiful was apparent. As in his early sketches for the New Haven plan (fig. 4.16), Gilbert's articulation of what was at stake was characterized by a comprehensive, overall approach. His method was to examine building groups, both from smaller cities and from larger ones like Washington, D.C., and Paris, that he thought applicable to civic improvement in New Haven.[81]

Gilbert hoped to create an effect at New Haven similar to the east sector treatment at Oberlin. By 1907–8 Gilbert and Seymour advocated the development of a series of buildings that would have included a hall of records, the New Haven County Courthouse, a bank, and a hotel, as depicted in a phalanx of buildings in elevation and seen from afar (fig. 4.17). Gilbert obliged what appears to have been Seymour's particular interest in trying out various building arrangements and treatments of a central courthouse tower, probably for the northeast edge of the green, including one proposal in which he instructed his office staff to make the dome look more like the silhouette of Christopher Wren's Royal Naval Hospital at Greenwich, England (1707). On this latter sketch, with reference to the central tower, Gilbert scrawled, "The high mass emphasized the dissymmetry *[sic]* of the group. Make no more studies of this motif. See Greenwich Hospital. Pediment even unnecessary." Gilbert produced dozens of sketches working on this compositional problem, perhaps in an attempt to address how Henry Austin and David Russell Brown's city hall (1861; fig. 4.18), in grand Victorian Style, might be counterbalanced in both symbolic municipal function and massing. Like Wren, Gilbert was captivated by the concept of the vista, controlling how his buildings would be perceived from afar.

At New Haven, Gilbert and Seymour thought the New Haven Green at the core of the city should be preserved as open space around the three churches that had been constructed in the early nineteenth century. The space itself was what the architect wanted to preserve, as a period postcard in his collection suggests (see fig. 4.18). He did not want the green to be filled with functionally diverse structures. In fact, Gilbert discussed the need to keep such space open and unfettered:

> The present generation of New Haven has inherited a beautiful city with at least one feature of surpassing merit, namely—The Green. The original beauty of New Haven has been encroached upon in recent years by so-called "modern improvement" and buildings have

FIGURE 4.17

Elevation of New Haven Building Group, ca. 1907; *left to right:* records, courthouse, bank, hotel. Cass Gilbert, delineator. Graphite on tracing paper, 13 in. × 28 in.

(Cass Gilbert Collection, courtesy New-York Historical Society, neg. no. 72879)

FIGURE 4.18

The Green from Temple and Chapel Streets, ca. 1905. (Henry Austin City Hall, tall building just right of center on postcard.) Postcard, 3 in. × 11 in.

(Cass Gilbert Collection, courtesy the New-York Historical Society, neg. no. 72880)

> been erected regardless of the environment and without harmony of style. . . .
>
> Public buildings should be located with a view to the convenience of the public and not at the caprice or interests of individuals. They should be grouped so that they do not interfere with the traffic of the city nor make it necessary for a citizen to pass across busy streets or thoroughfares, or through long distances to transact business with public officials. A public building on a street of retail stores has been known to ruin the business of the street. . . .
>
> Such matters [as preparing a general plan] ought not to be left to chance or whim. The details of such a general plan would doubtless be modified in execution, but it would form a consistent basis for future development. . . . If it is true that new public buildings must within the near future be erected in New Haven, it seems equally true that they should be located in a systematic and orderly manner.[82]

His respect for past architecture, particularly the colonial revival, was palpable when his New Haven library was constructed. The site, located at Temple and Church Streets, in an area that had been known as "Quality Row" (referring to large, elegant private homes), held a mansion that had been owned by the Bristol family. By the time of Gilbert's work in New Haven, these homes had fallen into disrepair.[83] When it became apparent to Gilbert that the wrecker's ball would demolish this fine home (1803), which had been designed by New Haven architect David Hoadley, Gilbert obtained the entrance porch and much of the interior woodwork. He later installed the woodwork in his summer home at Ridgefield, Connecticut.[84]

With these projects in Oberlin, Ohio, and New Haven, Connecticut, Cass Gilbert leaves a rich legacy that makes clear his knowledge and fluency in addressing questions of history and context. Through these experiences at the midpoint of his career, he examined and considered the interaction between the built and the natural environment. His responses reflect his wide-ranging interest in and respect for the recent past. They also suggest that his growth and development as a designer were enhanced by the happy circumstance of working with two institutional representatives, Henry Churchill King and George Dudley Seymour, who revered and championed his proposals. Although the grand schemes at Oberlin and at New Haven were not fully realized, they provide evidence of Cass Gilbert's commitment to planning concerns in America at the turn of the century.

Notes

ABBREVIATIONS

AIA	American Institute of Architects
AIA/OFSO	AIA, office of the secretary, outgoing
AMAM	Allen Memorial Art Museum
CGC	Cass Gilbert Collection
CGP	Cass Gilbert personal correspondence
CGPprs	Cass Gilbert papers
Chron.	Chronological correspondence
F	Folder
FF	Flat file
GDS	George Dudley Seymour papers
LB	Letter book
LCMSS	Library of Congress, Manuscript Collection
LCPP	Library of Congress, Prints and Photographs Division
Misc.	Miscellaneous correspondence
N-YHS	New-York Historical Society
OCA	Oberlin College Archives
PC	Project correspondence
P-KC	President—Henry Churchill King correspondence
SB	Scrapbook
VF	Vertical file

FREQUENTLY CITED CORRESPONDENTS

CG	Cass Gilbert
FLO	Frederick Law Olmsted Jr.
FNF	Frederick Norton Finney
GDS	George Dudley Seymour
HCK	Henry Churchill King
OB	Olmsted brothers

The author thanks Geoffrey Blodgett, Sharon Irish, Gail Fenske, and Mary Beth Betts for their insightful comments and suggestions regarding the manuscript. She also thanks Margaret Heilbrun for her editorial suggestions.

1. Regarding Atlanta, see Thomas H. Morgan to CG, January 13, 1913, CGC, Chron., Box: 1913/no. 2, F: no. 103 M–P; Baltimore, see CG to William W. Emmart, October 31, 1904, CGC, PC, Box: MSC/no. 6, F: 7; Cleveland, Charles S. Howe to CG, September 24, 1906, CGC, Misc., Box: 1906, F: H–M; Seattle, CG to W. R. B. Willcox, April 20, 1910, AIA/OFSO, RG 801 SR4, Box: 1, F: 6 (AIA) and W. R. B. Willcox to CG, March 28, April 27, and May 4, 1910, CGC, Chron., Box: 1910/no. 2, F: no. 103-W; W. R. B. Willcox to CG, January 25, 1911, CGC, Chron., Box: 1912/no. 1, F: Misc., and W. R. B. Willcox to CG, October 28, 1911, CGC, Misc., Box: 1911, F: U–Y.

   For inquiries made from small towns, regarding Halesite (for town and park plan), C. D. McDonough to CG, August 31, 1914, CGC, Misc., Box: 2, 1914, F: no. 103 M–P; Grand Rapids (for a comprehensive plan), John Ihlder to CG, ca. March 14, 1908, CGC, Misc., Box: 1907–8/no. 7, F: New Business/no. 6; Winona (for park system), Warren P. Laird to CG, September 6 and 18, October 6, 1906, CGC, Misc., Box: 1906, F: H–M; Montana towns, CG to George Hollis Carsley, December 1, 1916; CG to Frederick Law Olmsted Jr. and CG to Working, March 14, 1917, CGC, CGP-LB 10/16–7/17. All correspondence listed above is from N-YHS, unless otherwise noted.

2. Although these were invitations he often did not accept, Gilbert was clearly thought of as a source of advice on planning issues. In 1910 Frederick Law Olmsted Jr. introduced Gilbert to Flavel Shurtleff, who was then secretary of the National Planning Conference. Shurtleff was gathering data about the legal and administrative problems of city planning in the United States, and Olmsted hoped Gilbert could aid the planning administrator in this project, especially by placing him in contact with the appropriate people in St. Paul, Minneapolis, and other cities where Gilbert had completed work. FLO to CG, September 28, 1910, CGC, Chron., Box: 1910/no. 1, F: no. 103; also see Flavel Shurtleff to CG, September 30, 1910, Chron., Box: 1910/no. 2, F: no. 103 (both N-YHS).

   Gilbert was elected to the General Committee for the National Committee on City Planning but was not able to accept the honor. When Shurtleff tried to corral Gilbert into delivering a talk at the Detroit Planning Conference of 1915, Gilbert declined to give a formally prepared speech. Shurtleff continued to try to secure Gilbert's participation in later years, for example, with the 1925 National Conference on City Planning, but Gilbert declined the invitation. CG to Flavel Shurtleff, July 26, 1913, CGC, CGP-LB 7/12–10/13 (N-YHS); Flavel Shurtleff to CG, May 26, July 21, and December 13, 1915, CGC, Chron., Box: 1915/no. 2, F: no. 103 R-T (N-YHS); CG to G. B. Ford, June 23, 1915, CGC, CGP-LB 12/14–12/15 (N-YHS); Report on conference, June 8, 1915, CGPprs, Box: 16 (LCMSS); CG to Edward H. Bennett, April 27, 1915, CGC, CGP-LB 12/14–12/15 (N-YHS); and CG to Flavel Shurtleff, December 22, 1921, CGC, CGP-LB 12/20–2/22 (N-YHS).

Gilbert became familiar with the work of landscape architect and planner John Nolen after making inquiries to his colleagues. Robert Craik McLean to CG, October 20, 1910, CGC, Chron., Box: 1910/no. 2, F: no. 103 (N-YHS); and Frederick Law Olmsted Jr. to CG, October 26, 1910, CGC, Chron., Box: 1910/no. 1, F: no. 103 (N-YHS). See also Gilbert's inclusion in his scrapbook of John Nolen, "The City Planning Movement," *Charlotte (North Carolina) News,* June 25, 1917, in CGC, oversize-SB, p. 229 (N-YHS). Landscape architect George Kessler admired Gilbert's work, including certain details of the architect's design for the St. Louis Public Library; William Hodgkinson to CG, January 23, 1914, CGC, Misc., Box: 1914, F: no. 103 A-C (N-YHS). Gilbert was apparently instrumental in adding Kessler's name to the membership list of the National Arts Commission, although President Taft deleted his name before forming the Fine Arts Commission. Gilbert's familiarity with their work and that of other landscape architects prompted him to serve as a clearinghouse for information on landscape issues, a service taken advantage of by Warren P. Laird, who was on the architectural faculty of the University of Pennsylvania; see, for example, Warren P. Laird to CG, June 29, 1916, CGC, Misc., Box: 1911–8, F: no. 103 I-L (N-YHS).

As with many other solicitations, Gilbert (who was addressed as "city planner") declined to join the National Housing Association (National Housing Association to CG, July 14, 1915, CGC, Chron., Box: 1915/no. 2, F: M-P [N-YHS]); the American Association for Highway Improvement (Thomas N. Page to CG, March 9, 1912, CGC, Chron., Box: 1912/no. 2, F:no. 103 I-L [N-YHS] and F. A. Vanderlip to CG, October 26, 1915, CGC, Chron., Box: 1915/no. 3, F: no. 103 A-D [N-YHS]); and the New York City Planning Commission (Robert Grier Cooke to CG, April 29 and June 12, 1912, CGC, Chron., Box: 1912/no. 2, F: no. 103 [N-YHS] and CG to Cooke, May 9, 1912, CGP-LB 6/11–6/12 [N-YHS]). The Municipal Art Society turned to him to take advantage of his experience and discriminating artistic judgment with respect to the subject of limiting building height in New York (Laurel Harris, July 1, 1913, CGC, Chron., Box: 1913/no. 2, F: no. 103 M-P [N-YHS]).

For more background with respect to a Philadelphia statistician's request for city planning information, see George W. B. Hicks to CG, February 12 and 20, 1912, CGC, Misc., Box: 1907–12, F: no. 164; and CG to George W.B. Hicks, February 15, 1912, CGC, CGP-LB 2/11–6/12 both (N-YHS).

3. CG to Warren P. Laird, February 23, 1910, CGC, CGP-LB 2/09–5/10 (N-YHS).

4. CG's notes on Warren P. Laird to CG, April 15, 1918, CGC, Misc., Box: 1917–8, F: no. 103 I-L (N-YHS).

5. See Cass Gilbert, "Grouping Buildings and Development of Washington," in Glenn Brown, comp., *Papers Relating to the Improvement of the City of Washington, District of Columbia* (Washington, D.C.: U.S. Government Printing Office, 1901), pp. 78–82, and plan.

For a general discussion of the changing needs of universities, see Paul Venable Turner, *Campus: An American Planning Tradition* (New York: Architectural History Foundation and Cambridge, Mass.: MIT Press, 1990). For specific studies of Gilbert's early experiments in campus planning and of the Minnesota and Texas plans, see Barbara S. Christen, "Cass Gilbert and the Ideal of the City Beautiful: Campus and City Plans, 1900–1916," Ph.D. diss., Graduate Center, City University of New York, 1997, pp. 212–43, 247–358, and 359–435, respectively.

6. For further background on the history of Tappan Square, see Geoffrey Blodgett, *Oberlin Architecture, College and Town: A Guide to Its Social History* (Oberlin, Ohio: Oberlin College and Kent State University Press, 1990), pp. 1–2.

7. Anthony N. B. Garvan, *Architecture and Town Planning in Colonial Connecticut* (New Haven: Yale University Press, 1951), p. 45; Floyd Shumway and Richard Hegel, eds., *New Haven: An Illustrated History* (Woodland Hills, Calif.: Windsor Publications and New Haven Colony Historical Society, 1981), pp. 8–20; George Dudley Seymour, *Our City and Its Big Needs: A Series of Four Articles,* reprinted from the *New Haven Journal-Courier,* December 16–9, 1912, p. 7. Each of the nine squares measured 52 by 52 rods, the equivalent of 16.9 acres.

8. HCK to CG, December 15, 1903, CGC, PC, Box: OC 1903–19/no. 1, F: 1903–4/King (N-YHS). Gilbert was very interested in the project because he claimed that his father, Samuel A. Gilbert, had been a student at Oberlin College. According to Geoffrey Blodgett, no evidence supporting this claim has been found; CG Report, March 16, 1904; and also CG to HCK, December 19, 1903, CGC, PC, Box: OC 1903–19/no. 1, F: 1903–4/King (N-YHS).

9. HCK to CG, August 6, 1904, CGC, PC, Box: OC 1903–19/no. 1, F: 1903–4 (N-YHS). King's contributions to the campus development process have been illuminated by Geoffrey Blodgett in several articles and talks. For a general survey of Gilbert's architectural work as a function of his politics, see Geoffrey Blodgett, "The Grand March of Oberlin Campus Plans," March 1995, lecture, typescript from the author; Blodgett, "Cass Gilbert, Architect: Conservative at Bay," *Journal of American History* 72 (December 1985): 615–36; and with respect to Gilbert and King, Blodgett, "President King and Cass Gilbert: The Grand Collaboration," *Oberlin College Observer,* February 4, 1982, pp. 3–4, February 18, 1982, pp. 4–5. A different version of this essay may also be found in *Oberlin College Alumni Magazine* (winter 1983): 15–9; and Blodgett, "Oberlin College Architecture: A Short History" (Oberlin: Oberlin College Office of Communications, 1992).

10. Later buildings, such as the Theological Seminary, Allen Memorial Hospital, and several unbuilt proposals are not examined because Gilbert's son, Cass Jr., was put in charge of these projects in the 1920s. The seminary, now known as Bosworth Hall, was begun in 1919 and completed in 1931; Allen Memorial Hospital was begun in 1920 and completed in 1925. Certainly by the 1920s Oberlin had become less of a priority to the senior Gilbert than it had been during the midpoint of his career.

    Unbuilt projects include proposals for athletic fields and grandstands, a boiler house, an auditorium, an alumni building, the College Inn, a recitation building, the First Methodist Episcopal Church, the Memorial Tower, and the Women's Department and Gymnasium. See the CGC presentation drawings (catalog no. 123.01–123.62) and VF photographs (N-YHS) for representations of many of these projects.

11. "College Chapel Burned," *Oberlin News,* January 27, 1903, p. 1, and "Oberlin's Need of a Large Auditorium," *Oberlin News,* May 12, 1903, p. 4. The sense of urgency to replace the structure was expressed in period accounts. As one editorial noted, "the destruction of the building [made] imperative the construction of a new chapel at once." An article entitled "A Chapel Memorial," *Oberlin News,* March 3, 1903, p. 4, also suggested the preservation and restoration of the chapel entrance, an idea that was not implemented.

    "In Memory of Finney," *Oberlin News,* June 22, 1908, pp. 2 and 4, provides a report of the dedication of the new building.

12. Blodgett, "President King and Cass Gilbert," pp. 15–9.

13. "With Reference to the Placement of College Buildings," *Oberlin News,* May 1, 1903, p. 4.

14. CG to HCK, March 10, 1914, CGC, CGP-LB 12/13–12/14 (N-YHS).

15. The southern portion of the building was completed in 1904; the northern section was finished in 1912.

16. CG report, April 21, 1904, CGC, PC, Box: OC 1903–19/no. 1, F: 1903–4 (N-YHS).
17. CG to Patton and Miller, March 22, 1905, CGC, PC, Box: OC 1903–19/no. 1, F: 1905 (N-YHS).
18. CG to FNF, January 18, 1905, P-KC, Box: 30, F: 1905 (OCA). These qualities, particularly the lack of extravagance, provided a worthy solution to the budgetary constraints of Finney's memorial gift. Gilbert explained that the style of the Warner building, inspired by the architecture of southern France and northern Italy, was extremely suited to construction from local Ohio stone and would not require high costs; CG to FNF, April 8, 1905, CGC, PC, Box: OC 1903–19/no. 1, F: 1905 (N-YHS).

    The only major difference between the gymnasium's style and Gilbert's proposed treatment for the chapel was in Gilbert's wanting to create a richer, more coloristic effect in his chapel stonework than Patton had done in his building. For the chapel columns at the main entrance, Gilbert had hoped to use several colors of local sandstone combined with bands of Indiana sandstone and another densely colored stone, such as marble or granite; CG report, May 8, 1905, CGC, PC, Box: OC 1903–19/no. 1, F: 1905 (N-YHS). He likely envisioned later buildings that would be treated in a similar fashion.
19. CG to HCK, July 21, 1915, CGC, OC-LB 3/12–11/15 (N-YHS). King also had the foresight to include a ramp so that people in "wheeled chairs" could have access to the programs held in the auditorium; HCK to CG, September 21, 1915, CGC, PC, Box: I. OC 1915–8/no. 2, F: Art Building 1915 (N-YHS) and copy in P-KC (OCA).
20. See Christen, "Cass Gilbert and the Ideal of the City Beautiful," pp. 448–52.
21. Gilbert had abandoned the separate apse he had initially envisioned for the organ, and instead of creating a separate transept (as he had done on plans from fall 1904), he redesigned the interior to create an auditorium that was one large room. Finney's somewhat unreasonable demands also included the designing of an auditorium that would garner such praise as "the best on the continent."

    In contrast to these early critiques of Gilbert's work, by September 1905, Finney changed course to insist upon Gilbert's production of a fine acoustical space, no matter "how it looks outside, if it is only in good taste"; FNF to CG, September 12, 1905, CGC, PC, Box: OC 1903–19/no. 1, F: 1905 (N-YHS). This change of heart probably was due to the protracted financial negotiations about the design. Finney was not without suggestions for the interior, however, as he tried to convince Gilbert to use brick, not plaster, for the interior walls. Finney quickly capitulated to

Gilbert's choice of materials, based on the argument that brick might be detrimental to the acoustics; FNF to CG, September 16, 1905, CGC, PC, Box: OC 1903–19/no. 1, F: 1905 (N-YHS).

Privately, Gilbert expressed his frustration to the college president about the client's persistent inquiries. The architect explained to King that "questions of proportion, ornament, and detail must be left to me, or my services will be of no value"; CG to HCK, April 1, 1905, CGC, Chron, Box: 1905/no. 3, F: Misc. (N-YHS).

Despite his many criticisms of Gilbert's chapel design, Finney thought well enough of Gilbert's work to invite the architect to submit a proposal for a railroad depot in Denison, Texas. Gilbert accepted the invitation, not surprisingly, given his experience working for the Northern Pacific Railroad in the 1890s and probably felt confident he could get the job. Citizens in Denison prevented the job from being realized, for reasons that remain unclear; FNF to CG, May 26, 1905, CGC, Chron., Box: 1905/no. 3, F: 14 (N-YHS); FNF to CG, March 17, 1906, CGC, Misc., Box: 1906, F: New work (N-YHS).

22. FNF to CG, March 25, 1905 and CG to FNF, April 8, 1905, CGC, PC, Box: OC 1903–19/no. 1, F: 1905 (N-YHS).

23. John F. Weir to CG, January 4, 23, and 27, 1907, CGC, Box: 7, F: 1907 (LCMSS). The other participants that year were artists Kenyon Cox and Loredo Taft and architects Grosvenor Atterbury and Ralph Adams Cram. Gilbert's lecture was entitled "Some Phases of the Renaissance in Architecture."

24. See "Along the 'Harlem River Branch,' " *Architectural Record* 24 (December 1908): 417–29; proposed designs for the Pelham Manor, Port Morris, Westchester Avenue stations (LCPP); and the drawing record for several stations, CGC, (N-YHS).

25. That Mellen was impressed by Gilbert's work for McKim, Mead, and White is suggested by a clipping from the *New Haven Register,* November 24, 1907, in CGC, SB (1907–10), n.p. (N-YHS).

26. By 1907 Gilbert and Mellen were in contact through railroad vice president E. H. McHenry; CG-EHMcH, May 21, 1907, CGC, CgP-LB 11/06–6/07 (N-YHS).

27. "George Dudley Seymour," in Hamilton Traub, ed. *The American Literary Yearbook* (1919; reprint, Detroit: Gale Research, 1968), p. 185; and Everett Hill, ed., *A Modern History on New Haven and Eastern New Haven County* (New York and Chicago: S. J. Clarke, 1918), pp. 185–6.

28. CG to GDS, June 4, 1907, CGC, CGP-LB 2/07–12/07 (N-YHS); CG to GDS, November 19, 1907, CGP-LB 2/07–12/07 (N-YHS).

29. CG to GDS, May 22, 1907, CGC, CGP-LB 11/06–6/07 (N-YHS). Re-

garding publication plans, see GDS to CG, May 29 and June 3, 1907, CGC, Misc. Box: 1907–12, F: no. 164 (N-YHS). Gilbert claimed he was a descendent of someone who had been connected to New Haven. In the case of New Haven, it was Matthew Gilbert, "one of the 'seven pillars' " on which one of the churches on the Green was founded in 1648.

30. CG to GDS, May 22, 1907, CGC, CGP-LB 11/06–6/07 (N-YHS).
31. GDS to CG, June 12, 1907, CGC, Box: Misc., F: 1907–12 (N-YHS).
32. CG to GDS, June 13, 1907, CGC, CGP-LB 2/07–12/07 (N-YHS). Granville T. Snelling and Walter Cook were other names bandied about for the third "expert." See George B. Post to CG, July 20, 1907, CGC, Misc., Box: 1907–12, F: 6 (N-YHS) and CG to FLO, August 5, 1907, CGC, CGP-LB 2/07–12/07 (N-YHS).
33. GDS to CG, June 28, 1907, CGC, Misc., Box: 1907–12, F: 6 (N-YHS).
34. FLO to GDS, August 26 and November 2, 1907, CGC, Misc., Box: 1907–12, F: 6 (N-YHS).
35. GDS to CG, October 9, 1907, CGC, Misc., Box: 1907–12, F: 6 (N-YHS).
36. In some respects, Gilbert and Olmsted's report is related in content to Daniel H. Burnham and Edward H. Bennett's *Plan of Chicago* (1909), particularly in relation to the role of transportation and park systems in the broader urban framework. The main difference was that the depth and breadth of the Chicago plan overshadowed the very focused project for New Haven. Burnham and Bennett's *Plan of Chicago,* in fact, was a volume well-known to Gilbert; he owned a copy and on occasion loaned it to colleagues, such as Alfred Morton Githens; CG to Alfred Morton Githens, September 23, 1909, CG, CGP-LB 2/09–5/10 (N-YHS).
37. *Report of the Capitol Approaches Commission to the Common Council of the City of St. Paul* (St. Paul, Minn.: Pioneer Press, 1906).
38. George Dudley Seymour, *New Haven* (New Haven: Tuttle, Morehouse, and Taylor, 1942).
39. Seymour, "Our City and Its Big Needs," p. 7.
40. Richard Chaffee, "The Teaching of Architecture at the Ecole des Beaux-Arts," in Arthur Drexler, ed., *The Architecture of the Ecole des Beaux-Arts* (1977; reprint, New York: Museum of Modern Art and Cambridge, Mass.: MIT Press, 1983), pp. 60–109. See also Donald Drew Egbert, *The Beaux-Arts Tradition in French Architecture* (Princeton, N.J.: Princeton University Press, 1980), pp. 11–57. By 1819 the Ecole taught architecture, which remained a part of the curriculum until 1968.
41. Sharon Irish, "Cass Gilbert's Career in New York, 1899–1905," Ph.D. diss., Northwestern University, 1985, pp. 301–7.
42. For an in-depth discussion of aspects of composition in Ecole training, see

David Van Zanten, "Architectural Composition at the Ecole des Beaux-Arts from Charles Percier to Charles Garnier," in Drexler, ed., *The Architecture of the Ecole Beaux-Arts,* pp. 110–323.

43. Jon Peterson, "The City Beautiful Movement: Forgotten Origins and Lost Meanings," *Journal of Urban History* 2 (August 1976): 415–35. For other studies of this movement, see Jon A. Peterson, "The Origins of the Comprehensive Planning Ideal in the United States, 1840–1911," Ph.D. diss., Harvard University, 1967; William H. Wilson, *The City Beautiful Movement* (Baltimore: Johns Hopkins University Press, 1989), pp. 1–95; William H. Wilson, "The Ideology, Aesthetics, and Politics of the City Beautiful Movement," in Anthony Sutcliffe, ed., *The Rise of Modern Urban Planning, 1800–1914* (New York: St. Martin's Press, 1980), pp. 165–98; Mario Manieri-Elia, "Toward an 'Imperial City': Daniel H. Burnham and the City Beautiful Movement," in Giorgio Ciucci et al., *The American City: From the Civil War to the New Deal,* trans. B. L. La Penta (Cambridge, Mass.: MIT Press, 1979), pp. 1–142. Period articles include Mary Caroline Robbins, "The Art of Public Improvement," *Atlantic Monthly* 78 (December 1898): 742–51; Sylvester Baxter, "The Beautifying of Village and Town," *Century* 63 (April 1902): 844–51; Andrew Jackson Downing, "On the Improvement of Country Villages," in Downing, *Rural Essays,* ed. George William Curtis, (New York: George P. Putnam, 1853); Charles Zueblin, *American Municipal Progress* (1902; reprint, New York: Macmillan, 1916); Charles Mulford Robinson, *Modern Civic Art; or, the City Made Beautiful* (1918; reprint, New York: Arno Press, 1970).

For local examinations of the movement, see, for example, Harvey A. Kantor, "The City Beautiful in New York," *New-York Historical Society Quarterly* 57 (April 1973): 149–71; Margaret French Cresson, *The Laurel Hill Association, 1853–1953* (Pittsfield, Mass.: Eagle Printing and Binding, 1953); Daniel Bluestone, *Constructing Chicago* (New Haven: Yale University Press, 1991); Gail G. Fenske, "The 'Skyscraper Problem' and the City Beautiful: The Woolworth Building," Ph.D. diss., MIT, 1988; and Barbara Christen, *City Beautiful in a Small Town: The Early History of the Village Improvement Society in Oberlin* (Elyria, Ohio: Lorain County Historical Society, 1994).

44. The earliest general form of this plan dates to ca. November 1912, as suggested by the following correspondence: William P. Foulds to HCK, November 22, 1912, P-KC, Box: 30, F: 1912 (OCA) and HCK to CG, December 10, 1912, CGC, PC, Box: OC 1912–29/no. 1, F: 1912 (N-YHS). This date is also suggested since Gilbert sent this plan in early 1913 to *Hi-O-Hi,* the campus yearbook; CG to HCK and CG to John W. Love, March 20, 1913, CGC, OC-LB 3/12–11/15 (N-YHS). Subsequent changes were made by 1914–5.

45. The Olmsted brothers had been engaged to work on a campus plan for the project only a few months before King contacted Gilbert. Gilbert made notations about existing campus buildings on his copy of the Olmsted plan. See OB to HCK, June 20, 1903, BT, Box: 10 and blueprint of map (1903) (OCA); original drawing with Gilbert's notations (AS no. 88. 6. 23) filed in CGC, Schools/Presentation Drawings (N-YHS); "With Reference to the Placement of College Buildings," *Oberlin News* May 1, 1903, p. 4; and "Encouraging Outlook for Oberlin College," *Oberlin News,* November 20, 1903, p. 1.

The Olmsteds' other recommendations concentrated on the spatial organization and the upkeep of the campus. They wanted buildings to face Tappan Square, with dormitories placed on the periphery; they also addressed questions of general site and maintenance of the landscape, such as the thinning of trees, soil grading, and the formation of a system of walkways.

46. On specific planning points, Gilbert and his office staff debated some questions as to the arrangement of buildings. In late 1904 Gilbert had produced a general plan that he felt was so important he placed it in "the hands of one of his best draughtsman," Lawrence F. Peck. Gilbert gave some of the work to Thornton M. Carson, who worked in his office and had produced drawings for details of the Essex County Courthouse in Newark, New Jersey, and to H. K. Culver and Maxime Boyer. Peck offered several options for the placement of dormitories in the general plan. He was critical of the Olmsted brothers' practical recommendations to relegate the student quarters to the periphery. Concerned that these buildings would be too dispersed from the center of campus, Peck reminded Gilbert of the social disadvantages of such placement away from the main area of activity. "Cases in point at Harvard," he explained to Gilbert, "have become standing college jokes"; CG to HCK, October 17, 1904, CGC, PC, Box: OC 1903–19/no. 1, F: 1903–4 (N-YHS); Thornton M. Carson to CG, October 22, 1904, CGC, PC, Box: OC 1903–19/no. 1, F: 1904 (N-YHS); Time record, November 7, 1904, CGC, Chron., Box: LPR 1904 *[sic],* F: St. Paul *[sic]* (N-YHS); and Lawrence F. Peck to CG, October 19, 1904, CGC, PC, Box: OC 1903–19/no. 1, F: 1904 (N-YHS).

In one sketch, Peck placed dormitories on either side of the campus, even though he still believed the buildings were located too far away from the heart of the campus. Other options, such as placing a row of dormitories "with the expanse of 900 feet of campus in front," were considered to be too cheerless and too cold an arrangement for a small college. Peck laid out in other proposals the plans for separate "enclosures" as he called them—features that were modeled after the standard English quadrangle.

47. Ironically, Peters Hall has since become an important symbol of the college.

48. CG to FNF, January 18, 1905, CGC, PC Box: OC 1903–19/no. 1, F: 1904 *[sic];* also see early sketches from November 24, 1904, in CGC, FF: Dwr. 3 (N-YHS). Gilbert spent two years working out changes to this design. Beginning in October 1904 he produced several studies (including blueprint sketches of a section, elevations, and a plan); CGC, PC, Box: OC 1903–19/no. 1, F: 1905 *[sic]* (N-YHS); and CG to HCK, October 17, 1904, CGC, PC, Box: OC 1903–19/no. 1, F: 1903–4 (N-YHS). The general plan of 1904 has not been located.

    Among the other drawings were *Studies for Finney Chapel,* including elevations, plans, and an interior view now held at the N-YHS. The date of these drawings is suggested from their marked similarity to the blueprint sketches of October 8, 1904; CGC, PC, Box: OC 1903–19/no. 1, F: 1905 *[sic]* (N-YHS). Notably, this general proposal did not include a tower positioned to the south of the building, the feature that later became part of the final design. Instead, Gilbert chose to articulate the southern corner as a mirror image of its northern counterpart so that the ends of the building would give the viewer an indication of the double-height nave, flanked by single-story side aisles, that lay within. This early proposal also made more overt references to southern Romanesque architecture with its variegated masonry, as suggested by stripes of shading in the facade.

    During the following month, Gilbert prepared a new set of studies, including a perspective rendering of November 24, 1904, depicting the new chapel, which is related to a later March 1905 study published in *American Architect and Building News*. See *American Architect and Building News* 92 (October 5, 1907); and *Oberlin News,* June 20, 1908, p. 1. (The original was given by Gilbert to the National Academy of Design upon his election as a member).

    Other designs were not fixed until late spring, since in May 1905 Gilbert was producing alternative studies that portrayed the front elevation of the chapel with and without a tower. These studies illustrate Gilbert's continued interest in a more severe, simplified Romanesque style. For more information about these OC sketches, see drawings filed with presentation drawings/FF (N-YHS).

49. HCK to CG, April 25, May 12 and 22, 1906, CGC, PC, Box: OC 1903–19/no. 1, F: 1905–6 (N-YHS). As cost estimates rose 50 to 150 percent above the available $100,000 budget, the committee's promise to find additional funds became increasingly difficult to fulfill. Various features such as exterior details (including the architectural frieze and figural sculpture on the facade), expensive building materials, and the hall's high seating capacity eventually were omitted from the contract. Thus although King and

the Prudential Committee fully backed Gilbert's plan, certain compromises had to be made when the building was constructed. See GHW to FNF, August 15, 1905, P-KC, Box: 30, F: 1905 (OCA); FNF to CG, August 18, 1905 and HCK to CG, October 6, 1905, CGC, PC, Box: 1903–19, F: 1905–6 (N-YHS); Miranda to CG, August 8, 1905, CGC, Misc., Box: 1904–5, F: Sc. 1905 (N-YHS); Modifications list, February 6, 1906, CGC, PC, Box: OC 1903–19/no. 2, F: 1907 (N-YHS).

Construction was delayed until 1907, in part to avoid the high building costs of the previous year. Some proposals suggested the omission of the side galleries and the reduction of the height of the side walls but these were rejected; HCK to CG, May 5, 1906; FNF to HCK, April 30, 1906, CGC, PC, Box: OC 1903–19/no. 1, F: 1905–6 (N-YHS); CG to HCK, May 7, 1906, P-KC, Box: 30, F: 1906 (OCA); and CG to HCK, June 2 and 9, 1906, P-KC, Box: 30, F: 1906 (OCA); WFB to G, June 13, 1906, and HCK to CG, June 19, 1906 CGC, PC, Box: OC 1903–19/no. 1, F: 1905–6 (N-YHS).

50. CG to FNF, April 8, 1905, and FNF to CG, March 25, 1905, CGC, PC, Box: OC 1903–19/no. 1, F: 1905 (N-YHS).

Finney also criticized the tiny window designs on the first floor and the rose window above, which he compared to a windlass on a ship. Gilbert believed the former features were practical elements that would filter light into the vestibule and narthex. With respect to the latter criticism, Gilbert and Finney wrangled for several years about the design and shape of the window; FNF, HCK, KC, and CG letters in PC, OC correspondence (N-YHS); and Geoffrey Blodgett, "The Changing Functions and Appearance of Oberlin's Finney Chapel," talk delivered at Society of Architectural Historians Conference, Philadelphia, 1994, for the session, "Political Uses of Built Space." For further reference to Finney's suggestions about how to change this design, see CG and HCK correspondence from March through May 1906, CGC, PC, Box: OC 1903–19/no. 1, F: 1905–6 (N-YHS) and P-KC (OCA).

51. CG to HCK, March 31, 1906, P-KC, Box: 30, F: 1906 (OCA).

52. Several of the trustees wanted to keep nearly all the buildings away from Tappan Square. Others were concerned about the proposed demolition of older buildings, such as Talcott Hall, Baldwin Cottage, and Spear Laboratory. Many faculty, in contrast, generally supported Gilbert's plan as it was proposed in the blueprint. Yet another group of trustees and faculty was critical of Gilbert's placement of two buildings to the east of Warner Gymnasium and its proposed twin. Another group questioned the provision that had been made for nonscience departments to use the building cluster around Warner Gymnasium. Presumably these departments were con-

cerned about getting a share of space and facilities that would be comparable to those suggested in the plan for the science quadrangle in the northwestern section of the campus. Noted in the *New York Globe and Commercial Advertiser* as one of the most important features of the plan, this quadrangle was situated where there would be "four large laboratories to house the departments of geology, physics, zoology, and botany," as well as "a series of fully-equipped greenhouses." See *New York Globe and Commercial Advertiser,* May 7, 1912, p. 7, and *Springfield (Massachusetts) Republican,* May 10, 1912, both in CGC, oversize-SB, p. 180 (N-YHS).

53. HCK to CG, April 20, 1912, CGC, PC, Box: OC 1912–29/no. 1, F: 1912 (N-YHS).
54. CG to Lewis S. Gillette, May 27, 1907, CGC, CGP-LB 11/06–6/07 (N-YHS).
55. See correspondence, CGC, 1907–17 (N-YHS) and (LCMSS), about the delays and Gilbert's frustrations because of them. The project began with a budget of $600,000, which grew quickly to more than $2 million. Although Gilbert prepared several presentation drawings in the spring of 1907, the design was not officially chosen until two and a half years later. Further complications occurred when the railroad encountered difficulty in obtaining the land that had been chosen for the project. Change in leadership occurred in 1913, when Howard Elliott became the new president, having come from a post at the Northern Pacific Railroad. His administration was short-lived; he was forced out in 1917, only months after Gilbert's original design had been radically stripped down. The onset of World War I was also a factor in the delays; some of Gilbert's other work (such as the U.S. Army Supply Base) was focused on contributing to the war effort.
56. Robinson, *Modern Civic Art,* pp. 59–80; "The New Depot," *New Haven Journal Courier,* February 6, 1909, in CGC, SB (1905–12), p. 76 (N-YHS). Other regional papers addressed this same issue as columnists called for stations to be built in small New England communities so visitors would obtain the best possible impression of the place where they were arriving. See "New Haven Railway Stations," *Providence (Rhode Island) Journal,* February 11, 1909, in CGC, SB (1905–12), p. 74 (N-YHS).
57. CG to FLO, June 2, 1908, CGC, Misc.-LB 1/08–8/08 (N-YHS).
58. "Designer of a New Station," *New Haven Palladium,* February 1, 1907, in CGC, SB (1905–12), p. 74 (N-YHS).
59. The project encountered financial difficulties as production costs rose. When Mrs. Ives died in 1908, part of her $86,000 estate had to be used for the building fund; CG to George D. Watrous, April 25, 1907, CGC, CGP-LB 11/06–6/07 (N-YHS); GDS to CG, November 16, 1907, CGC, Box: 7 (LCMSS), and numerous clippings from November 1907 in CGC, SB

(1907–10) (N-YHS); on budget problems, see "Joint Conference on Library Plans," *New Haven Register,* December 8, 1908, and "Library Plans Must be Changed," *New Haven Journal-Courier,* n.d. in CGC, SB (1907–10), n.p. (N-YHS).

60. Gilbert even sent blueprints of the St. Louis project on to the New Haven Library Committee for review; CG to GDS, August 1, 1907, CGC, CGP-LB 2/07–12/07 (N-YHS) and GDS to CG, August 20, 1907, CGC, Misc., Box: 1907–12, F: 6 (N-YHS).
61. CG to GDS, June 4, 1907, CGC, CGP-LB 2/07–12/07 (N-YHS).
62. CG to HCK, September 10, 1909, P-KC, Box: 30, F: 1909 (OCA).
63. CG to HCK, April 18, 1914, CGC, OC-LB 3/12–11/15 (N-YHS).
64. In one set of drawings, Gilbert envisioned the college hotel-inn as a Craftsman-inspired design; see AMAM holdings and CGC, VF, OC (N-YHS) for a photographic reproduction of one of these drawings. For information with respect to the need for a new high school, see *Oberlin News,* editorials, 1915–6.
65. From its earliest stages the Art Building was intended to house a museum. The primary impetus for this project was the lack of appropriate storage or display space for a fine arts collection that had been given to the institution. Touted as "the best in Cleveland," this collection represented a valuable acquisition for the college but one that exposed the college's lack of adequate facilities for it. Gilbert was instructed to develop plans for a $65,000 museum that could be enlarged in the future. Funds for this project were donated by Cleveland physician and Oberlin alumnus Dr. Dudley P. Allen; GHW report, July 5, 1905, CGC, PC, Box: OC 1903–19/no. 1, F: 1905 (N-YHS).

    The auditorium was funded by the bequest of Charles M. Hall, an Oberlin College alumnus and substantial donor to the college. Hall had made his fortune by discovering the process for the industrial manufacture of aluminum. He was a trustee of the college from 1905–14. Upon his death, Hall left Oberlin College $800,000, of which $500,000 was earmarked for auditorium construction. His will stipulated that the college could use three-quarters of his donation for the construction and maintenance of a new auditorium. This large influx of funds stimulated discussion about the development of the eastern campus, which ultimately produced the blueprint master plan that Gilbert presented to the college in February 1915. The auditorium project became a complicated venture that was not realized until 1953, according to the designs of Wallace K. Harrison, of the firm of Harrison and Abramowitz; HCK to CG, February 25 and March 11, 1914, CGC, PC, Box: OC 1914–25, F: K (N-YHS); news clipping from *New York Sun,* January 13, 1915, CGC, oversize-SB, p. 180 (N-YHS); "Will of the Late Charles M. Hall," *Oberlin News,* February 24, 1915, p. 8; and

"Complete Text of President's Address on the Bequest of Charles M. Hall," *Oberlin News,* June 23, 1915, pp. 1–2, in CGC, PC, Box: I. OC 1915–8/no. 2, F: Art Building 1915 (N-YHS), and detailed report on Hall's will (OCA). See also HCK to CG, January 28, 1915, CGC, PC, Box: I. OC 1915–8/no. 2, F: Art Building 1915 (N-YHS).

66. CG to HCK, January 16, 1914, CGC, OC-LB 3/12–11/15 (N-YHS). For other sketches illustrating this building arrangement, see one version, dated ca. February 28, 1915 (ADE 11-A-Gilbert 238 recto) and another version dated November 29, 1915, (ADE 11-A-Gilbert 43), both from LCPP.

Gilbert surely was thinking about the demolition of the Methodist Episcopal Church (which stood on land in this eastern area) as well as that of Peters Hall (which stood just west of Tappan Square), since both buildings were located near the central, unifying axis he envisioned.

67. CG to HCK, January 16, 1914, CGC, OC-LB 3/12–11/15 (N-YHS).

68. This idea is suggested by the subject of recent studies by architectural historians Gail Fenske and Sharon Irish. See Fenske, "The 'Skyscraper Problem' and the City Beautiful"; and Sharon Irish, "A 'Machine That Makes the Land Pay': The West Street Building in New York," *Technology and Culture* 30 (April 1989): 376–97.

Gilbert's Memorial Tower (1916), as well as later works such as the Graduate School of Theology (1916–31) and the Recitation Quadrangle (ca. 1930), make use of a multistory tower that would have served as the focal point for the entire campus and the town. Joseph Lyman Silsbee's designs served as a precedent; Gilbert was probably quite familiar with these designs through his close working relationship with Silsbee and with Henry Churchill King. Gilbert may also have been acquainted with these proposals since Silsbee was a cousin of one of Gilbert's close associates, Thomas Gannett Holyoke; Thomas G. Holyoke to CG, April 15, 1901, CGC, Chron., Box: 1887–1901, F: 1 (N-YHS).

69. Photographic reproductions of the series that is labeled "A" through "G" can be located in VF, OC (N-YHS). Most of the original drawings in the sequence are housed in the AMAM collections. Scheme "A" is AMAM 83.132.7, Scheme "B" 83.132.15, Scheme "D" 83.132.3, Scheme "E" 83.132.5, Scheme "F" 83.132.2, and Scheme "G" 83.132.16.

70. CG to HCK, June 9, 1916, P-KC, Box: 81, F: 1916 (OCA) and copy in CGC, OC-LB 11/16–5/24 (N-YHS). Six of these schemes (probably "A" through "G," were sent to King on this date.

On Gilbert's visit to Oxford in 1905, he was particularly impressed by the architecture and grounds of the university campus and also the village, calling the latter "one of the loveliest places I have ever seen." The British tower, however, was neither "a commanding feature in the landscape" nor did it "dominate the entire College," as he hoped his own design would; Diary, June 25–28, 1905, CGPprs, Box: 1, F: 2 (LCMSS).

71. Noted renderer Chesley Bonestell (1888–1986) possibly completed these views, ca. 1923 (VF, OC [N-YHS]) as well as the 1923 painting *Proposed Recitation Quadrangle* (OCA). A photographic reproduction of this painting, with a September 30, 1925, graphite study on top of the photo, can be found in VF, OC (N-YHS). Bonestell likely completed these studies and paintings when he was based in London, where he worked as a commercial designer. His better-known work includes paintings depicting nuclear holocausts and scenes in outer space.
72. CG to Warren P. Laird, August 26, 1912, CGC, CGP-LB 7/12–10/13 (N-YHS). Gilbert's letter to Laird was prompted by Pope herself; CG to Theodate Pope, August 26, 1912, CGC, CGP-LB 7/12–10/13 (N-YHS).
73. Early photographs of the chapel (through ca. 1940) illustrate the lamp posts Gilbert designed for the small plaza in front of the building. Batelli furnished the columns, which Gilbert completed between late 1907 and early 1908; R. Batelli to CG, December 19, and 27, 1907; January 27 and 30?, April 17, and May 1908; HCK to CG, January 2, 1908 (sketches included); CGC, PC, Box: OC 1903–19/no. 2, F: 1907–8 (N-YHS); CG to HCK, December 24, 1907 and January 6, 1908; CG to Batelli, January 8, 1908; P-KC, Box: 30, F: 1907 (OCA).
74. CG memo, November 21, 1908, CGC, Misc. Box: 1907–12, F: 5 (N-YHS).
75. CG to George D. Watrous, November 19, 1907, CGP-LB 2/07–12/07 (N-YHS).
76. CG to GDS, June 4, 1907, CGC, CGP-LB 2/07–12/07 (N-YHS). For a general discussion of the history of the other churches located on the green, see Rollin G. Osterweis, *Three Centuries of New Haven, 1638–1938* (New Haven and London: Yale University Press, 1964), p. 480. Gilbert also took into account the proportions and portico design of Yale University's Byers Hall for his proposal for the library.
77. CG to GDS, August 1, 1907, CGC, CGP-LB 2/07–12/07 (N-YHS).
78. "Cass Gilbert Will Submit Final Sketches of the Ives Library: Style to be Colonial," [newspaper unnamed], clipping in CGC, SB (1907–12), n.p. (N-YHS); "Cass Gilbert Interested," *New Haven Journal-Courier,* December 9, 1909, in CGC, SB (1907–10), n.p. (N-YHS).
79. "Library Plans Are Accepted," [newspaper unnamed], clipping in CGC, SB (1907–10), n.p. (N-YHS). Regarding his record drawings of the church, see GDS to Glenn Brown, April 10, 1911, GDS Papers, RG 801, SR 5, Box: 4, F: 8 (AIA).
80. GDS, in "Would Restore Center Church," *New Haven Journal-Courier,* December 9, 1909, in CGC, SB (1907–10), n. p. (N-YHS).

81. Gilbert's lecture was reprinted in several local newspapers, including the *New Haven Register,* December 11, 1907, as listed in a scrapbook of clippings kept by Gilbert (N-YHS). The 1907–8 Trowbridge series also included Frank M. Day (then president of the AIA), John M. Carrère, Walter Cook, Frederick Law Olmsted Jr., and Charles Howard Walker.

82. Cass Gilbert to a reporter of the *New Haven Register,* June 5, 1907, CGC, CGP-LB 11/06–6/07 (N-YHS).

83. For more general discussion of this area, see Osterweis, *Three Centuries of New Haven,* p. 387.

84. Under similar circumstances today, surely the demolition of a historic house for the purpose of a civic project would be more seriously considered by historic preservation advocates. But Gilbert's own sensibilities about the subject in 1903 seem in keeping with general preservation attitudes of the period. He presented the entrance porch of the Bristol mansion to the Metropolitan Museum of Art in 1915; it was placed on exhibition and eventually sold several years later at auction. For sketches of the plan and elevation of the portico, see Gilbert's notes attached to CG to F. W. Seagrist Jr., October 5, 1907, CGC, CGP 1909–19, F: 1907 *[sic]* (N-YHS); "An Example of the Work of a Connecticut Architect," *Bulletin of the Metropolitan Museum of Art* 22, no. 10 (October 1927).

CHAPTER FIVE

Gail Fenske

CASS GILBERT'S SKYSCRAPERS IN NEW YORK: THE TWENTIETH-CENTURY CITY AND THE URBAN PICTURESQUE

The three major skyscrapers that Cass Gilbert designed in lower Manhattan between his arrival in the city in 1899 and World War I—the Broadway Chambers Building, the West Street Building, and the Woolworth Building—were all critically acclaimed.[1] They were considered especially successful solutions to "the skyscraper problem," widely regarded as the most challenging architectural problem of the day; the noted architectural critic Montgomery Schuyler judged each design as "the last word" in the evolution of a particular approach.[2] The West Street and the Woolworth Buildings were also significant, as Schuyler and others noted, for their contribution to the new and controversial skyline of the city. The view, pictured in countless contemporary illustrations and photographs, was in the process of definition at the nineteenth century's turn as the earliest modern "signature" skyline (fig. 5.1). Few architects, other than George Post of the previous generation, were presented with such a rich array of opportunities to contribute to New York's new urban identity as the nation's busiest port, center of business and finance, indeed the "capital of capitalism," and to its architectural representation as a modern world metropolis. Cass Gilbert, an architect strongly inclined toward the picturesque from his early career and later a leading exponent of the City Beautiful, made a special effort to relate the architecture of his skyscrapers to their urban surroundings—regardless of the skyscraper's characteristic independence as a building type,

FIGURE 5.1

New York Skyline, 1901. G. P. Hall and Sons, photographer.

which tended to isolate it from all adjacent construction. He, like his contemporaries, would develop a heightened consciousness of the skyscraper's potential for shaping the views of the city.[3]

Commercial buildings made up a significant component of Gilbert's early architectural practice in St. Paul, Minnesota. After his arrival in New York in 1899, however, he was faced with an especially formidable challenge. His colleagues in the profession, many of whom trained at the Ecole des Beaux-Arts in Paris—Charles McKim, Stanford White, Thomas Hastings, and Ernest Flagg among them—considered the modern commercial skyscraper an especially troublesome and undesirable building type, as both an architectural and an urban phenomenon. They made their criticisms public in numerous discussions and debates. These began with two forums sponsored by the Architectural League of New York in 1894, held for the purpose of examining proposals to restrict building heights, and culminated with the essays written for the *Report of the Heights of Building Commission* of 1913, which formed the basis for the Zoning Resolution of 1916. Architects had a professional interest in controlling the mania for building ever higher, but speculators in urban real estate were more determined to build exactly as they pleased—at least before the construction of the aggressively bulky Equitable Building (1913–5), which was instantly recognized as a threat to property values.[4]

Most New York architects were dismayed by the city's extremely rapid modernization process, and few building types signaled that process more blatantly than the upstart commercial skyscraper. As a manifestation of forces identified with the profit motive of the land speculator, skyscrapers seemed to architects to be a sign of the cultural impoverishment of the community, indeed of a city violated by disturbing, incomprehensible, and cataclysmic change. Such a commercial building type was not truly architecture as the beaux arts architect defined it: significant works of art that represented a society's noblest cultural aspirations. Moreover, this new architecture, as visually forceful and dramatic as it appeared in the many skyline views of lower Manhattan, was questioned by critics such as Montgomery Schuyler for its social meanings—whether these implied excessive individualism or unbridled prosperity—and hence for its suitability to the architectural identity of the nation's new metropolis.[5]

Modern New York, governed by the "mood of the moment," or "of things lately and currently done" as Henry James described the city in 1904, stood in stark contrast to the growing desire among architects and planners to aesthetically improve the city. Their model was the paradigm of visual

FIGURE 5.2
Endicott Building, St. Paul, ca. 1900. Unidentified photographer.
(From the collections of the Minnesota Historical Society)

order and unity that characterized European cities of international stature. Ideally, New York would have a comparable beauty. Community leaders such as the lawyer John De Witt Warner and organizations such as the Municipal Art Society were determined after the turn of the twentieth century to make New York the "world's capital for all time to come." The Municipal Art Society, architects, and the city's other art societies immediately generated a range of proposals for New York as a City Beautiful. These culminated in the New York City Improvement Commission's plans of 1904 and 1907.[6] As a center of finance, big business enterprise, and speculative land development, however, New York faced a formidable challenge if it were to become the equivalent of the widely esteemed and unified European capital, graced with architectural monuments, grand boulevards, parks, sculpture, and greenery. Such obstacles, however, while troubling to Cass Gilbert's contemporaries, did not prevent him from conceiving his own vision for the future of New York. He thought it entirely possible to create a modern city that also had beauty, monumentality, and a distinctive architectural identity. New York, inevitably, would distinguish itself among the great cities of the world.

Cass Gilbert and the Skyscraper as a Modern Building Type

Gilbert arrived in New York in 1899 as an optimistic practitioner from the midwestern city of St. Paul. He did not study at the Ecole des Beaux-Arts but was nonetheless strongly influenced by beaux arts principles of design during his education at the Massachusetts Institute of Technology in 1878–9 and his apprenticeship with McKim, Mead, and White in 1880–2. Gilbert's practice in St. Paul provided him with the opportunity to design the Minnesota state capitol—the project that established his national renown as an architect—along with a range of commercial buildings. These included office buildings, stores, warehouses, and of greatest importance to establishing his career in New York, his first skyscraper, the eleven-story Brazer Building (1894–7) in Boston. Gilbert's special interest in commercial building types was evident early in his student days. In 1879, while working for the U.S. Coast and Geodetic Survey in New York after his year at MIT, he came across a "factory office building" in Cold Spring and immediately proceeded to design twenty improved versions.[7] While traveling in London in 1880, he sketched "some very good modern store fronts."[8] Numbering among his commercial buildings in the St. Paul area were the Endicott Building (1888–90), the Bowlby and Company Store (1895; demolished), the Luther S. Cushing Store and Office Building (1895), the Gotzian Ware-

BOWLBY & CO.
RELIABLE
HATTERS.
FURNISHERS.
CLOTHIERS.
MEN AND BOYS
RELIABLE
OUTFITTERS.

house (1894–5), and two warehouses for the Boston Realty Company (1893, 1895–7).

The Endicott Building and the Bowlby and Company Store were the two key commercial projects of Gilbert's early career. Both were published in professional journals and represented for Gilbert advances he had recently made in his commercial practice, albeit advances of two very different kinds. The seven-story Endicott Building, designed for William and Henry Endicott of Boston (fig. 5.2), showed Gilbert's sophisticated command of a "Renaissance" architectural vocabulary—of the sort recently used by his friend Joseph Morrill Wells from the McKim, Mead, and White office for the Villard Houses in New York (1882–5). Gilbert created an office building of such refined distinction that for the critic Montgomery Schuyler it stood out in the Midwest as "ostentatiously discreet," like a "small voice of scholarly protest," conspicuous evidence of Gilbert's eastern architectural training. Gilbert could have used any one of McKim, Mead, and White's arcaded office buildings as his model, among them the New York Life Insurance Building in Omaha, Nebraska (1887–90). Instead, he chose to adapt Wells's more conservative Renaissance palazzo imagery to the problem of the office building, creating a surprisingly unified scheme, organized in a clear tripartite composition with authoritative Renaissance detailing. The Endicott had thick exterior walls of finely detailed red sandstone and brick, with deeply set windows, and an internal frame of iron. Its spacious L-shaped interior arcade, roofed with arches of iron and glass, boasted thirty shops and a foyer with a variety of imported marbles, "combined to please the eye with a harmony of color." Modern amenities included five elevators and an independent heating, lighting, and ventilating plant. Altogether, the Endicott Building had the character of a luxurious "home" for business.[9]

The Bowlby and Company Store was another type of commercial proj-

FIGURE 5.3
Bowlby and Company Store, St. Paul, 1895. Unidentified photographer.

modern steel-framed structure sheathed in cast stone and glazed white terra-cotta, with accents of opaque blue in the Della Robbia-inspired medallions of the upper stories. He was at the forefront among American architects in using glazed white and colored terra-cotta to enclose and decorate the exterior of a steel-framed building. Gilbert's experimentation with colored terra-cotta would continue, and he would find the material absolutely essential to his success with the design of modern commercial skyscrapers in New York.[10] Given the Bowlby and Company's purpose as a store, broad expanses of glass were required for illumination and for the dis-

CASS GILBERT, ARCHITECT.

play of goods in show windows. Gilbert met those needs with "Chicago" windows, that is, tripartite windows with operable sidelights, which extended the full width of a structural bay. Gilbert's allegiance as a young architect was to New York and to McKim, Mead, and White, but he was also fascinated by the recent work of Chicago architects.

Gilbert considered a partnership with Daniel Burnham in the early 1890s, participated in judging the architecture exhibits for the World's Columbian Exposition of 1893, and frequently traveled through Chicago by rail, so he had several opportunities to see the city's new commercial architecture.[11] Still, he refused to wholeheartedly adopt Chicago's modern commercial idiom. The highly ornamental character of the Bowlby and Company Store's top story—with medallions, swags, and figures modeled by the sculptor Johannes Gelert of Chicago—jarred with the open, gridlike clarity of the stories below, and suggested a lack of resolution in the direction that Gilbert intended to proceed with his commercial practice. Nevertheless, the Endicott Building and the Bowlby and Company Store demonstrated two very different approaches that Gilbert favored for the design of a commercial building in St. Paul. It could be on the one hand a prestige office building on East Fourth Street in the heart of the downtown or alternatively, a steel, terra-cotta, and glass store on Robert Street, a major shopping area, which required rapid construction for immediate occupancy and use.[12]

The eleven-story Brazer Building on State Street in Boston, on which Gilbert began design in 1894 and then supervised construction in 1896–7, was the architect's first skyscraper (fig. 5.4). It showed Gilbert attempting to reconcile his allegiance to New York with his knowledge of Chicago design and construction. Its tripartite columnar composition, rusticated shaft, Renaissance and baroque detailing, and gilded bronze cheneau all suggested that he had carefully studied Bruce Price's highly regarded American Surety Building in New York (1894–6).[13] Gilbert's design, however, contrasted with Price's skyscraper in three important ways. First, it showed a greater clarity and sophistication in its proportions. Second, the exterior, while "classical," also had a skeletal, modern openness, especially in the base and capital. Finally, Gilbert chose to locate large windows at the curved corners of the Brazer's terra-cotta enclosure, as opposed to "solid" enclosed corners as in Price's design—placing the openings precisely where an observer would expect to find heavy walls concealing diagonal wind bracing and primary structural supports. Such open corners were structurally feasible only with an inventive approach to wind brac-

FIGURE 5.4
Brazer Building, Boston, rendering of final design, 1894. Unidentified artist. Presentation drawing, ink on paper, 26 in. × 42¾ in.
(Cass Gilbert Collection, courtesy New-York Historical Society, neg. no. 72882)

ing; portal arches ran crosswise to the Brazer's orthogonal grid of columns.[14] Gilbert's careful study of the visual relationships between structure and enclosure would be central to his success with the design for the Woolworth Building.

More generally, Gilbert was weighing in his design for the Brazer Building the trade-offs between tradition and modernity. Tradition, expressed in the exterior's tripartite organization and Renaissance-baroque detailing, provided an office building in the heart of old Boston—fronting the main commercial axis of State Street at Devonshire and catercorner from the recently restored old State House—with the expected level of urban decorum and "image" that would appeal to tenants. The potential for achieving openness afforded by the Brazer's portal-braced steel frame and thin terracotta envelope, by contrast, gave Gilbert the opportunity to investigate his developing conception of the modern. Still, Gilbert made every possible effort to relate what was widely known as an unruly building type to the character of its urban surroundings. He was simply quite incapable of conceiving of any work of architecture in isolation. Consequently, he chose off-white for the Brazer's limestone base and terra-cotta cladding, which was to match the adjacent Worthington Building's (Carl Fehmer, 1894), and he aligned the Brazer's cornice and stringcourses with the Worthington and with Peabody and Stearns's Stock Exchange (1889–91) farther down State Street. Combined, the three light-colored buildings formed a "neutral" backdrop for the old State House.[15]

The Brazer Building project was significant in Gilbert's career as an architect of the skyscraper for yet another key reason: it was here, working with Thomas H. Russell and the Brazer Building Trust, along with the George A. Fuller Construction Company's Harry S. Black, that he began to develop an in-depth understanding of the mechanisms for financing large-scale speculative real estate development projects. As a result, Gilbert developed the habit of providing professional architectural advice, along with complete sets of architectural drawings, years in advance of actually receiving the commission for a commercial project. He also acquired skills and savvy about matters of real estate finance that rivaled those of the clients and investors to whom he provided his services. This would serve him especially well in New York. After he finally secured the commission for the eighteen-story Broadway Chambers Building in 1899 and set up his practice in the city that year, he used his knowledge about finance to conceptualize and initiate potentially lucrative development schemes that would bring new and important commercial projects into his office.[16]

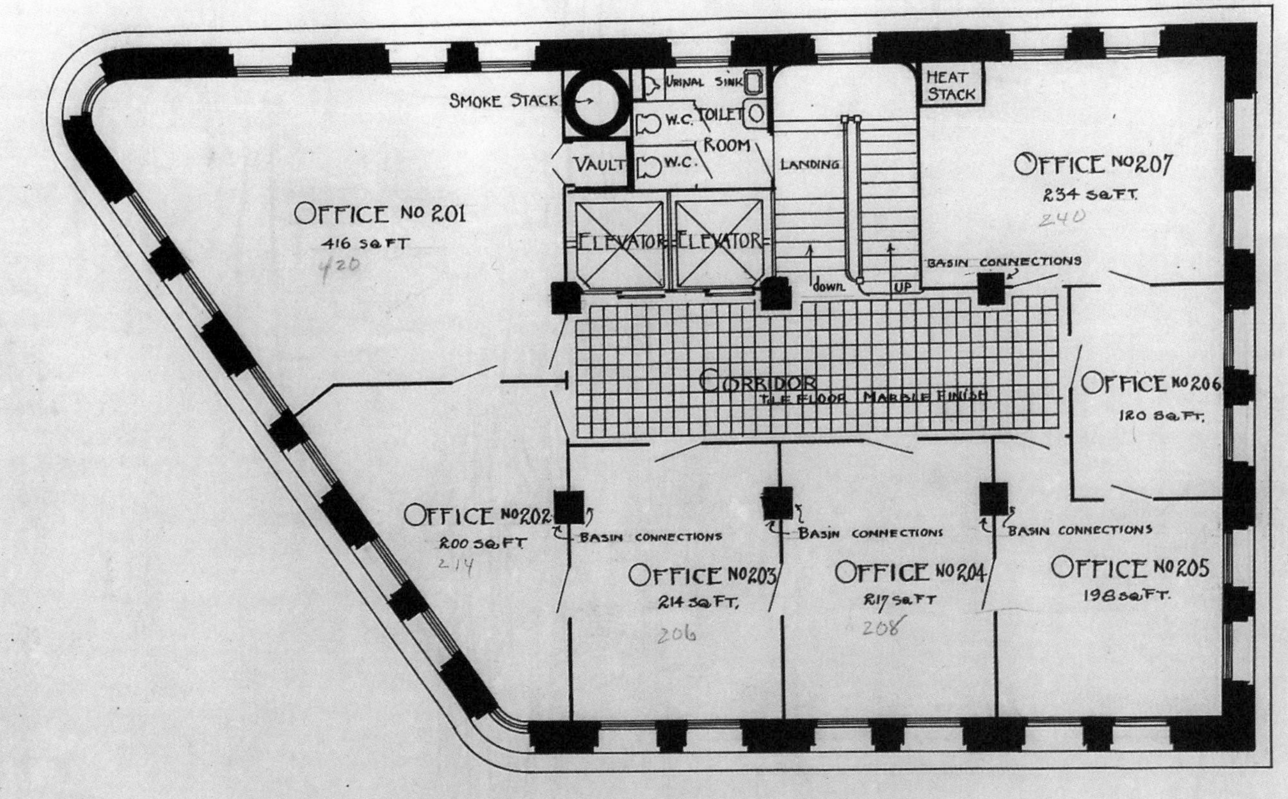

FIGURE 5.5
Brazer Building, Boston, typical floor plan, ca. 1894. Unidentified artist. Ink and graphite on tracing paper, 14 in. × 21 in.
(Cass Gilbert Collection, courtesy New-York Historical Society, neg. no. 72883)

Equally significant, Gilbert's design for the Brazer Building clarified his own understanding of the relationship between the *plan* of an office building and its *value* as a commodity for "sale" in the marketplace for downtown commercial space. According to industry experts such as George Hill, the office building's plan, in order to produce income for its owner, had to meet tenant expectations regarding dimensions, flexibility, quality of natural illumination, heating and ventilation, and services such as efficient elevators and the proper number of toilet facilities.[17] The typical upper story of the Brazer Building showed that Gilbert had completely mastered those planning criteria. It had offices surrounding a central elevator core, which avoided the inefficiencies of long corridors and so made every office an "outside office"; these, in turn, provided the generous exposure to natural illumination that all tenants had come to value (fig. 5.5). The Brazer's ground story had a lobby with a dome of colored mosaic, offices for banking purposes, and a first story that boasted a spacious banking hall. In the upper stories were marble toilet rooms on every floor, corridors with marble wainscots, and offices finished with "quartered oak."[18] Gilbert had produced one of the finest first-class office buildings of his day.

FIGURE 5.6
Brazer Building, Boston. Small conceptual sketches, 1894. Cass Gilbert, artist.
(Cass Gilbert Collection, courtesy New-York Historical Society, neg. no. 69631)

Gilbert further refined his knowledge of the close relationship between office building financing and planning while working on the Broadway Chambers project in New York. He honed his skills in finance while working with his client, Edward R. Andrews, and once again, much more closely, with the Fuller Company's Harry S. Black. After preparing detailed plans and elevations for the project in 1896, Gilbert was able to convince Andrews to lease his property to developers in return for a fixed percentage of the project's net income. Subsequently, he and Black prepared two detailed financial scenarios illustrating the project's potential earnings. Both assumed an average rental rate of two dollars per square foot and total earnings of seven thousand dollars per story. However, Black proposed a twenty-story office building, whereas Gilbert suggested it be nineteen stories at most. Then, in early 1897, Gilbert approached the Guaranty Construction Company of Chicago and other possible investors about subscriptions to purchase stock in the project.[19] As construction of the eighteen-story Broadway Chambers Building neared completion in 1900, Gilbert could proclaim with authority that the office building was "merely a machine that makes the land pay."[20]

Cass Gilbert and the Urban Picturesque

Gilbert's early conceptual designs for the Brazer Building showed a highly picturesque "medieval" tower with projecting turrets, gables, and a steeply

FIGURE 5.7

Zwinger Towers, Dresden, travel sketch, 1898. Cass Gilbert, artist. *(National Museum of American Art, Smithsonian Institution)*

sloping roof that would have enlivened its Boston urban surroundings with an ornamental crown (fig. 5.6). Gilbert's initial idea for the skyscraper as a picturesque entity within the city can be attributed, first of all, to his fundamental outlook as a designer. As a student he was strongly oriented toward the picturesque; his first choice of an architect with whom to apprentice was the Victorian architect George Edmund Street of London.[21] He ultimately chose McKim, Mead, and White, a firm that in the early 1880s was in the process of disciplining the picturesque toward the goal of classical order exemplified by Joseph Morrill Wells's design for the Villard Houses of 1882. The Brazer Building's client, Thomas H. Russell, similarly was seeking "fashionable" Renaissance design of the sort exemplified by McKim, Mead, and White's recently completed Boston Public Library (1887–95).[22] Gilbert, to please his client, decided to tame the Brazer's high picturesque exuberance through a comparable process. Gilbert's earliest medievalizing conceptual designs, nonetheless, decisively established the direction he would take in exploring the tall building as a potentially picturesque entity within the city. Every major skyscraper he designed for lower Manhattan—that is, the Broadway Chambers, the West Street, and the Woolworth Buildings—Gilbert initially conceived as either a picturesque tower in its own right or as an office block sporting a picturesque tower with a memorable skyline silhouette.

Gilbert's ongoing fascination with the picturesque was especially evident during his sketching tours of Europe, which became more frequent beginning in the late 1890s. He began devoting increasing study to the profile views of cities, typical among them his *Zwinger Towers, Dresden* (1898; fig. 5.7). For Gilbert, the character of a city was determined in large part by the ways in which individually prominent buildings—often sporting towers, pinnacles, and domes—enhanced such profile views. Gilbert's early sketches for the Broadway Chambers Building showed a steeply sloping picturesque roof that resembled Cyrus L. W. Eidlitz's new Washington Life Building (1897–8), an architectural reference for his design, also prominently sited on lower Broadway (fig. 5.8).[23] Equally important, an image of the Campanile of St. Mark's, Venice, appeared in the background among the sketches. Gilbert produced over the years several pencil studies and watercolors of European towers and campaniles; they became a special subject of study during his tour of Italy in 1898. In these, Gilbert found inspiration for the composition, the proportions, and the modeling of mass in light and shade of his skyscrapers, along with the lesser details of textural patterns and ornamental motifs. All contributed to Gilbert's conception of the sky-

scraper as a potentially lavish, lively, and colorful architecture that would effectively call attention to itself in New York's visually competitive and increasingly strident modern urban surroundings.[24]

Gilbert's design for the Broadway Chambers Building also demonstrated the depth to which he understood European architecture—a tradition he came to know intimately through his sketching tours. Gilbert employed this historical knowledge intuitively to refine for the Broadway Chambers Building a simplified and exquisitely proportioned tripartite design, a memorable image for a prestige office building in the city (fig. 5.9). Crucial to the image was Gilbert's increasingly sophisticated and "truthful" handling of materials—whether the rusticated rose-colored granite that he chose for the base, the dark red, rough-textured "Harvard brick" for the shaft, or the sculptural terra-cotta sporting accents of color that enlivened the crown. In this new approach to materials, Gilbert was inspired in part by Bruce Price, in particular by the variegated brick and terra-cotta exterior of Price's recently completed Saint James Building (1896–7) on Broadway at Twenty-sixth Street.[25] Gilbert's design, however, had a heightened level of texture, color, and ornamental exuberance, and it met the sky with a vigorously crested copper cheneau. In office planning and in the quality of the services it provided tenants, the Broadway Chambers Building was as up-to-date as the Brazer—it also claimed such modern amenities as a mail chute for every story, washbasins in most offices, and an independent electric lighting plant (fig. 5.10).[26] The Broadway Chambers Building did not house a bank in the lower stories, but Andrews briefly considered a rathskeller in the basement and proposed, but later abandoned, a downtown club for the crown.[27] Consequently, if Gilbert was unable to realize his vision of the picturesque roof as culmination, he could at least compensate for its absence with a deeply modeled two-story loggia, which sheltered balconies, was modulated by tall rhythmic pilasters, and was highlighted with a rich array of sculptural embellishments.

For Gilbert, color served as an especially important device for augmenting the skyscraper's picturesqueness in the city's profile views. Later, he would also call attention to color as the architect's essential modeling tool. In skyscraper exteriors, he believed, color could compensate for the typically thin walls that functioned as mere envelopes for the steel frame and so were devoid of depth and shadow, or what he called the "third dimension, such as is so potent an element in the older forms of architecture." "Color," he added, "may be invoked to aid in the desperate need of thickness by an architect if he be an artist . . . for the effect it may produce in

FIGURE 5.8
Broadway Chambers Building, New York City, conceptual sketches, November 1896. Cass Gilbert, artist. *(Cass Gilbert Collection, courtesy New-York Historical Society, neg. no. 69632)*

B WASSERMAN CO
CIGARS

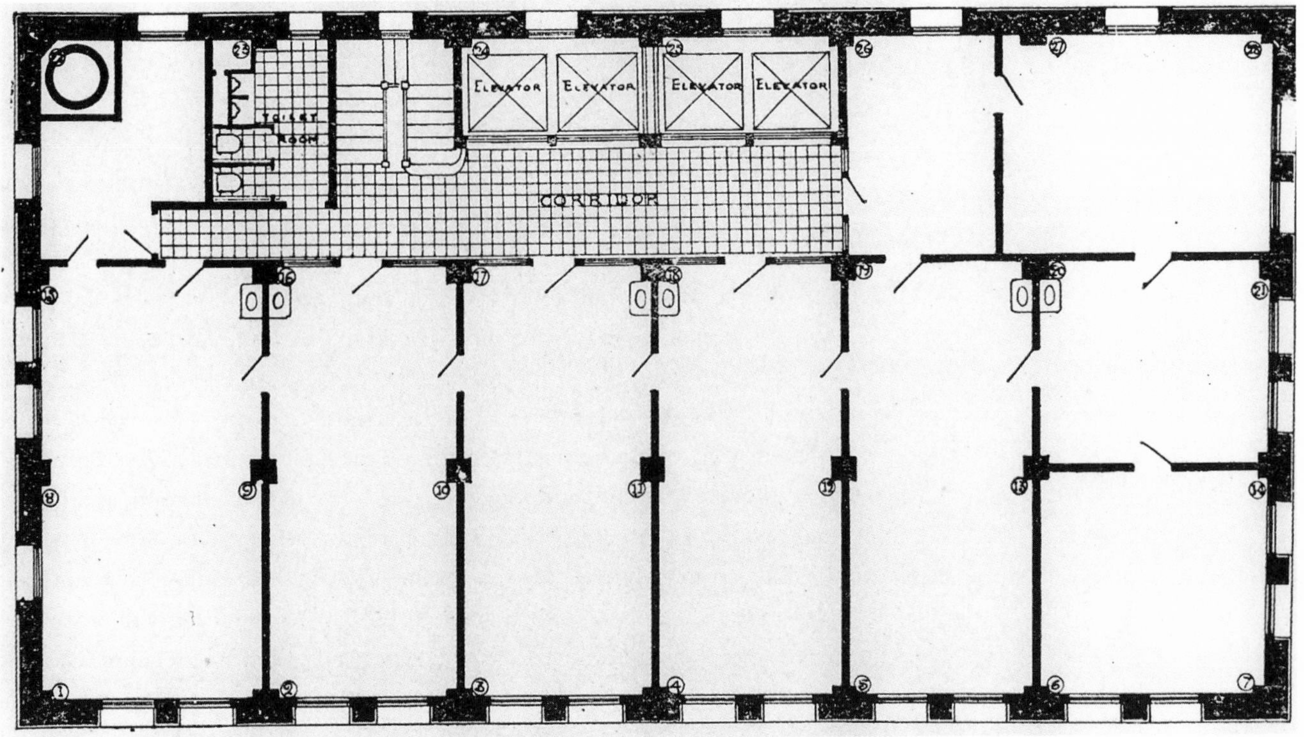

FIGURE 5.9

Broadway Chambers Building, New York City, ca. 1905. Unidentified photographer. Photograph, 17 in. × 10 in.

(Cass Gilbert Collection, courtesy New-York Historical Society, neg. no. 58803)

FIGURE 5.10

Broadway Chambers Building, New York City, typical floor plan, 1900. From George A. Fuller Company rental brochure, "Broadway Chambers: A Modern Office Building."

(Cass Gilbert Collection, courtesy New-York Historical Society, neg. no. 72884)

emphasizing form."[28] But color served other important purposes as well. For Gilbert, ever the artist and watercolorist, color was an especially effective device for relating New York's modern towers to the city's distinctive atmospheric setting, a "brighter, more sparkling, more luminous," background of clouds and sky.[29] Gilbert's general fascination with color can also be traced to his admiration for the writings of John Ruskin, the picturesque compositions of London Victorian architects such as George Edmund Street, and to the nineteenth-century craft ideal of "constructional polychromy." Even the beaux arts public buildings that Gilbert designed during these years, among them the Minnesota state capitol and the U.S. Custom House, contrasted with those of his beaux arts contemporaries on account of their rich color schemes. In creating these, Gilbert used colored granites, fine imported marbles and mosaics, gilding for sculptures, roofs, and finials, and on interiors, marble overlays and elaborate programs of mural painting.

Gilbert's skyscrapers dating from the mid-1890s became increasingly sophisticated in their color schemes. In the Brazer Building, Gilbert introduced jewel-like highlights of polychromatic glazes in the upper stories. For the Broadway Chambers Building two years later, he used the background colors of the rosy gray granite, dark red brick, and cream-colored terra-cotta to clarify his composition. In addition, he introduced darker, richer colors for depth and shadow, especially in the soffits of the skyscraper's crowning loggia. Finally, at key points in pilasters and paneling, he overlaid the background colors with polychromatic highlights in light greens, yellows, and ivories. Color, Gilbert discovered, could be employed to achieve a wide range of compositional as well as ornamental ends.

Gilbert's emphasis on a richness of color, as well as texture and ornament, was most pronounced in the skyscrapers he designed for lower Manhattan. He seemed to have a heightened consciousness of how their exteriors would be perceived in the many views of the city. Beginning in the late 1890s, an increasing number of images showing the city from the surrounding waterways were produced for popular consumption by illustrators, view book publishers, and by the makers of postcards such as the Detroit Publishing Company.[30] These, in turn, helped shape popular perceptions of the skyline. In addition, New York City's community of modern artists, among them Alfred Stieglitz, the Whistler-inspired Joseph Pennell, and John Marin, began engaging themselves with the sustained examination of the skyscraper as the emblem of the modern city. Such a continuing obsession with picturing the city for all observers was symptomatic of the larger need for a structured mode of understanding its physical character, particularly in the face of the disorientation, even chaos, brought on by the modernization process.[31] Gilbert was not only sensitive to such concerns but also fully attuned to New York as a modern world phenomenon in the making. His skyscrapers were to be picturesque and, as such, to enrich the experience of the city for all observers. New York had become a bewildering city, a scene of jarring contrasts. But it was also a city of individual builders determined to "package" their enterprises architecturally—to advertise the city internationally—and Gilbert was delighted to be a part of the process.

Cass Gilbert and the Skyscraper Gothic: The West Street Building

With his design for the twenty-three-story West Street Building project of 1905, Gilbert reconciled his intuitive understanding of the skyscraper as a modern building type with his growing convictions about the significance of the skyscraper as a picturesque tower in New York's profile views (fig. 5.11). The sudden and startling appearance of the West Street Building's skyscraper Gothic seems unusual at first—Gilbert had never made previous use of such a "Gothic" vocabulary for the skyscraper.[32] In light of his earlier inventive explorations of the modern, however, and of his elaboration of the crowns of his skyscrapers with sculptural embellishments and color, Gilbert's crafting of a distinctive medievalizing imagery for the West Street Building seems logical. Furthermore, Gilbert conceived each of his skyscrapers as being wholly unique in its own right, like his favorite European towers that he sketched and painted. On the one hand, such a quest for uniqueness reflected Gilbert's determination to find the desired architectural image for a particular client or business organization. On the other hand, modern New York was already distinguished by the heterogeneity of its architecture—the architectural incongruities reflecting "a million people with a million tastes and perfect freedom to express them as they please."[33] Gilbert had to have believed that the resulting collective differentiation among the city's urban buildings—indeed, the city's kaleidoscopic array of styles and colors—only added to its urban splendor, indeed, to its memorability as a modern world metropolis.

The skyscraper Gothic style Gilbert developed for the West Street Building was far more than a superficial ornamental scheme—it was, rather, his proposal of a complete and integrated architectural vocabulary for the tall office building. As such, it represented a significant advance over the earlier skyscraper Gothic designs of his contemporaries in both Chicago and New York, and placed Gilbert at the forefront among them in the re-

FIGURE 5.11

West Street Building, New York City, 1907. Irving Underhill, photographer. Photograph, 25 in. × 21 in.

(Cass Gilbert Collection, courtesy New-York Historical Society, neg. no. 32071)

finement and resolution of a particular approach to the problem of the skyscraper. Gilbert's early design drawings, and their development by members of his office staff, show that at the outset of the West Street Building project, he carefully studied Louis Sullivan's designs for skyscrapers, in particular, Sullivan's Bayard-Condict Building in New York (1898–9). He chose Sullivan's verticals, with their alternating pattern of piers and colonettes, for the purpose of calling attention to what he considered the skyscraper's essential character as a building type—the type's modernity, he decided, should be boldly expressed in design. To enhance the image of the skyscraper as a picturesque entity within the city, Gilbert enlivened the West Street Building's upper six stories with a tall, deeply set arcade, accents of color, and a vigorous encrustation of medievalizing ornament—corbelled colonettes, canopies, dormers, crockets, and tourelles. He crowned the composition with a steeply sloping copper roof, the silhouette bristling with cresting and finials.

Gilbert's ability to craft a unified architectural vocabulary for the West Street Building owed a special debt to an existing tradition of Gothic-inspired skyscrapers built of steel and terra-cotta. Chicago architects, among them William Le Baron Jenney, who wrote "An Age of Steel and Clay" in 1890, viewed terra-cotta as the ideal material for sheathing the exteriors of steel-framed office buildings, on account of its lightness and plasticity. By the mid-1890s Chicago architects had conceived terra-cotta as a complete system of cladding and ornament for the commercial office building. Charles Atwood's designs for the Reliance Building of 1894 and the Fisher Building of 1896 were enclosed throughout in off-white glazed terracotta accented with "Gothic" details. In 1894 Louis Sullivan designed for the Guaranty Building in Buffalo, New York, a fully integrated system of ductile, thin-skinned ornamental terra-cotta cladding, its surfaces energized and pulsating with his abstracted nature-inspired ornament. Gilbert's 1895 Bowlby and Company Store in St. Paul showed that he was intrigued by the Chicago approach to construction in steel and terra-cotta, although for a low structure with horizontal proportions he found little need for the verticality of skyscraper Gothic.[34]

Equally significant for Gilbert's development of the West Street Building's skyscraper Gothic style were the medievalizing vocabularies of his New York contemporaries Francis Kimball and Cyrus L. W. Eidlitz. The West Street Building's crowning arcade was indebted to that of Eidlitz's New York Times Building (1903–5), and its tourelles echoed those of Kimball's Trinity Building (1904–5) and City Investing Building (1906–7). More

WEST STREET BLDG
Copyright 1907 By
UNDERHILL New York

generally, however, Gilbert's sources were also European; he particularly admired the monuments of medieval Flanders, both secular and ecclesiastical—favorites were the *hotels des villes* of Brussels, Middelburg, and Audenaarde, the trade hall in Bruges, and the soaring yet monumental verticality of the cathedral tower in Malines. Ultimately, it was this European Gothic tradition that for Gilbert legitimated his synthesis of the West Street Building's bold verticality with an elaborate crowning ornamental scheme. As a consequence, critics such as Montgomery Schuyler and Claude Bragdon instantly recognized Gilbert's skyscraper Gothic as a remarkably convincing and coherent language of form, indeed a singular and highly successful solution to the problem of the skyscraper. Such stylistic coherence was also indebted in no small part to terra-cotta's capacity as a material for fluidity of form, modeling and color, and bold sculptural effects.[35]

Gilbert elucidated the thoughts behind his design for the West Street Building in 1907 in a talk he delivered at the West Point Military Academy, "The Architecture of Today." Gilbert asserted that what concerned him, first of all, was the formal expression of the skyscraper's modernity as a building type, and second, the design of a proper cladding for the steel frame. On account of the skyscraper's modernity, Gilbert reasoned, its height should be expressed with "aspiring verticals." For this treatment of skyscraper elevations, he emphasized, he looked to the example of the skyscrapers of Louis Sullivan and to Sullivan's well-known dictum, "form follows function." A skyscraper's cladding, Gilbert also observed, should be thin and light, like an envelope or veneer, thus essentially revealing of its nonstructural purpose. Ideally, the cladding would be a thin facing of marble, brick, or terra-cotta, with colors intrinsic or added, and so would reveal its true nature as a rich and polychromatic garment for modern, steel-framed construction. In his West Street Building project Gilbert found both the artistic vocabulary and the philosophical justification for his own version of the skyscraper Gothic. Significantly, the project also fulfilled his artistic vision for the skyscraper's role in the city.[36]

Gilbert's success with the West Street Building can also be ascribed in no small part to the ambitions of his client, Howard Carroll, vice president of the Starin Transportation Company. Carroll chose a Hudson River waterfront site for the project, at West Street's intersection with Cedar and Albany Streets, which provided high visibility, and he was willing to pay for a skyscraper that stood out from the city's ordinary commercial vernacular. He envisioned catching the attention of the ferry traffic on the river and, at the docks, that of the bustling shipping-related crowds. In this Carroll set himself apart from Gilbert's earlier clients, who viewed their skyscraper projects foremost as potentially lucrative investments and so were seeking a distinctive street address, such as State Street in Boston or Broadway in New York, and the right combination of efficient office planning, economical construction, and attractive exterior. Carroll wanted more. Gilbert's first design for the West Street Building showed an ornate office block sporting a majestic central tower (fig. 5.12). The design composition was modeled on the secular architecture of medieval Flanders, in particular on the *hotel de ville* of Audenaarde. Such a design would have given Carroll's project the monumentality typically associated with important public buildings—that is, buildings with a capacity for representing a society's nobler community or cultural aspirations—and significantly, the desired prominence, if not showiness, in the view of lower Manhattan from the Hudson River.[37]

Gilbert also probably intended to invest the West Street Building project with what he considered the proper "corporate" character. Carroll initially called the project the "Railroad and Iron Exchange Building" and envisioned a tenantry of interrelated coal, iron, rail, and steamship concerns. Among them were the building's main tenant, the Delaware, Lackawanna, and Western Railroad Company, which occupied the seventeenth through the twentieth stories, and Carroll's own Sicilian Asphalt Paving Company. Together, the tenants would comprise a community of shared business interests at work. Gilbert had to have assumed that such a community, housed under a single roof, was worthy of a distinctive form of architecture. That architecture, in turn, would serve as an effective means of representing a collective identity while providing a memorable business address.[38]

For the West Street Building's interior, Gilbert designed a spacious groin-vaulted lobby on the ground story and flexible office space for the typical stories above (figs. 5.13, 5.14). The offices were arranged around a central utilities core, with elevators, stairs, and bathrooms, and all were open to light and to sweeping views of the Hudson River. On the top story, Carroll installed the Garrett Restaurant. The restaurant would offer those who worked in the building a distinctive space in which to gather informally, along with an elevated outlook over the industrial landscape on which their businesses depended—the waterfront's piers, terminals, and warehouses, and the railroad and shipping enterprises on the New Jersey side of the river. Carroll chose not to build the tower. Nonetheless, in the final design Gilbert treated the crown as a highly picturesque, colorful, and memorable feature on the skyline—it met Carroll's representational re-

FIGURE 5.12

West Street Building, New York City, perspective showing tower, 1905.

(Museum of the City of New York, Wurts Collection)

FIGURE 5.13
West Street Building, New York City, lobby, ca. 1907. Unidentified photographer.

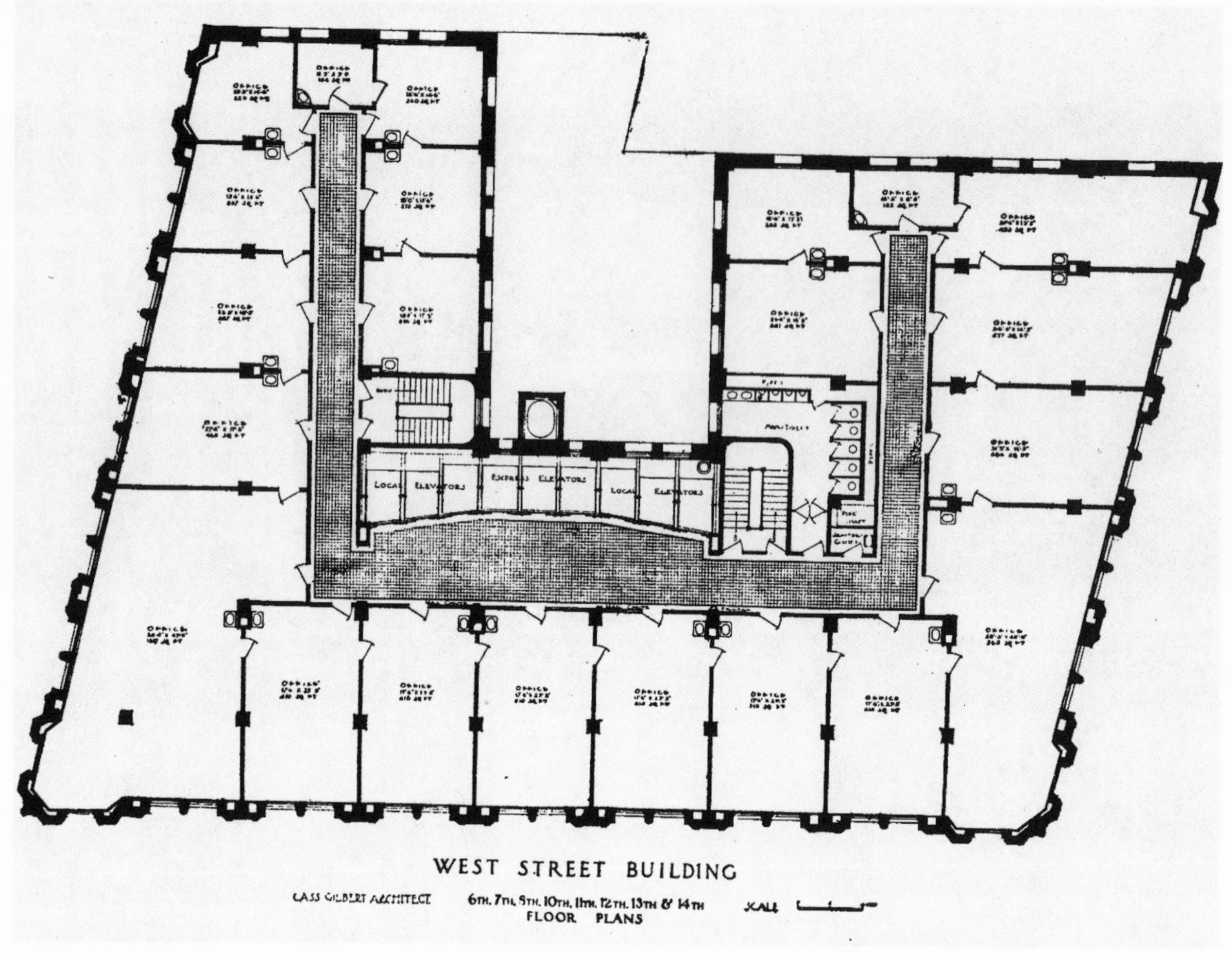

FIGURE 5.14

West Street Building, New York City, ca. 1905. Typical floor plan.

quirements for "address," while enhancing the view of the city from the Hudson River. The crown's "rich pinnacles relieved against the roof of sky" were instantly recognized and heralded as "the thing" by Montgomery Schuyler. "In a nearer or more distant view," he wrote, it made the beholder "glad and grateful."[39]

The West Street Building represented an important turning point in Gilbert's career as an architect of the skyscraper. His development of a modern Gothic vocabulary, his conception of the skyscraper as a showy monument to business enterprise, and his contribution to the view of the city from the Hudson River all forcefully impressed the client of his next big and important project, Frank Woolworth. Woolworth came to Gilbert looking for a skyscraper something like the West Street Building—modern, Gothic, theatrical, and capable of providing the F. W. Woolworth Company with an office building as a profitable speculative enterprise, a corporate headquarters, and a renowned business address. Gilbert, on account of his earlier experiences with the skyscraper as a modern steel-framed building type, his vision of the urban picturesque, and his recent development of an original and full-fledged skyscraper Gothic vocabulary for the West Street Building, had the architectural tools to serve his client well.

The F. W. Woolworth Company Building

The Woolworth Building represented the convergence and culmination of a series of themes Gilbert was exploring in his career as a designer of the modern skyscraper and especially of the skyscraper in New York (fig. 5.15). These included from the mid-1890s the evolution of the skyscraper as a building type of greater height and greater structural sophistication—particularly in the engineering of foundations and systems of wind bracing—and, as already suggested by Gilbert's designs for the Broadway Chambers and the West Street Buildings, greater internal complexity of use.[40] They also included Gilbert's own continued architectural experimentation with the skyscraper Gothic style and the peculiarly New York phenomenon of building slender, isolated towers to increasingly competitive heights—as exemplified by the Singer (1906–8) and the Metropolitan Life Insurance (1908–9) Towers—for the sake of advertising and "show."[41]

When Frank Woolworth first met with Gilbert in 1910, the skyscraper he was seeking for the headquarters of the F. W. Woolworth Company in New York was to be a theatrical work of architecture far more striking and magnificent than any ordinary office building.[42] That "requirement" was central, regardless of Woolworth's initial intention to build a structure of a

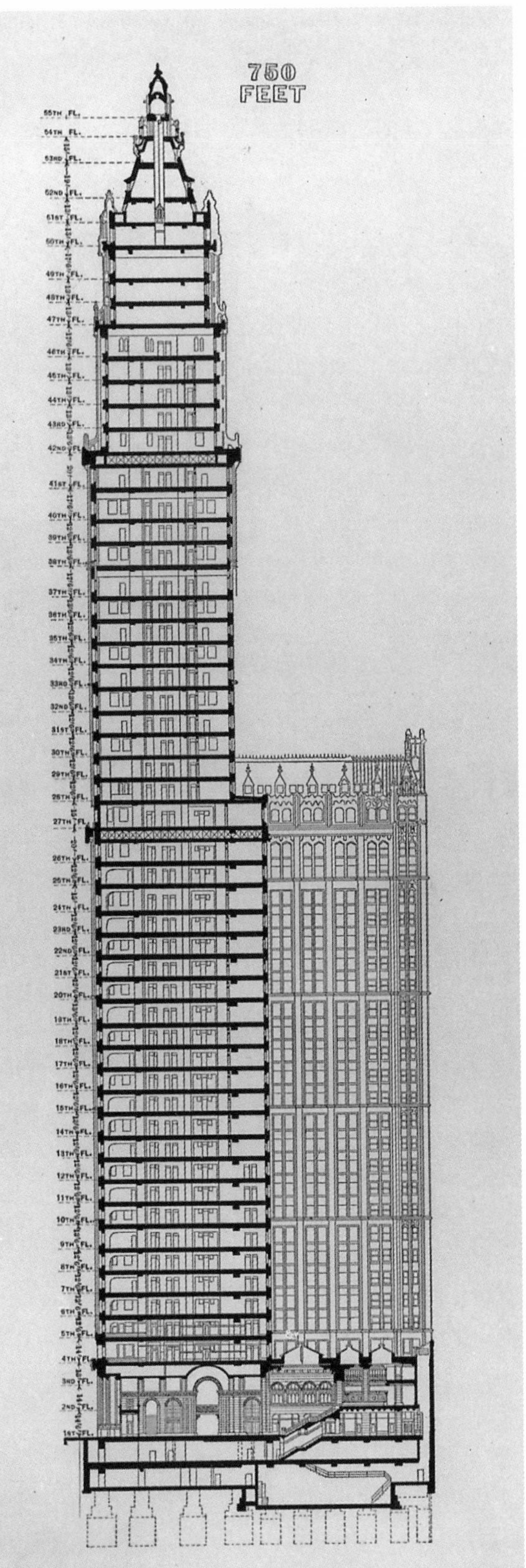

FIGURE 5.15

F. W. Woolworth Company Building across City Hall Park, New York City, 1913. Unidentified photographer. Photograph, 13 in. × 8 in.

(Cass Gilbert Collection, courtesy New-York Historical Society, neg. no. 46309)

FIGURE 5.16

F. W. Woolworth Company Building, New York City, sectional view, 1912. From rental brochure, "Woolworth Building, Highest in the World," 14 in. × 17 in.

(Cass Gilbert Collection, courtesy New-York Historical Society, neg. no. 72150)

FIGURE 5.17

F. W. Woolworth Company Building, New York City, view of lobby-arcade, 1913.

(Museum of the City of New York, Wurts Collection)

mere twenty stories at Broadway and Park Place, opposite the southwest corner of City Hall Park. Woolworth, in fact, only needed a single story of office space to house his corporate headquarters. Moreover, he viewed the project as a convenient vehicle through which he and its initial investors, the F. W. Woolworth Company and Irving National Bank, would be assured of a profitable financial return. The typical speculative office building was by 1910 a tried-and-true architectural as well as financial phenomenon, its parameters fully understood by investors such as Woolworth, Gilbert, and his architectural contemporaries in New York. George Hill, who had already established precise standards for the plan of and services in an office building, turned in 1904 to the question of "economical" height. He based his analysis of height on a detailed examination of the trade-offs between the construction costs per story of an office building and each story's potential rental income. He concluded that sixteen to twenty stories would be the favored "economical height," but that twenty-five stories would probably become the "average height" for all investors seeking an acceptable financial return. The prohibitive costs of construction twice as high would cancel out the benefits.[43]

Gilbert and Woolworth chose to deviate significantly from the standard formula for a profitable office building in a number of important ways. Such differences are, ultimately, what made the Woolworth Building truly exceptional. First of all, within three weeks of the project's beginning in April 1910, they proposed a startling jump in size and height—from the thirty stories and approximately 420 feet of the first design to a design that occupied the entire Broadway block front and soared to an unprecedented fifty-five stories and 750 feet (plate 12). Then, within six months, Gilbert and Woolworth developed a wholly new concept for a skyscraper interior—the Woolworth Building was to house a rich and varied internal world, an aggregate of distinctive yet complementary public spaces, dispersed throughout the building, and supportive of an office community at work (fig. 5.16).[44]

As the project evolved, Gilbert and Woolworth continued to refine and elaborate its internal spaces. For the first level below grade, they designed a health club with a Turkish bath and swimming pool, a large barbershop, a rathskeller for dining that seated five hundred, safe deposit vaults, and a direct connection, on axis, through bronze doors to the IRT and BRT subway lines. Irving National Bank would have a magnificent banking hall, Elizabethan in character, preceded by a great forecourt, or "Marble Hall," with a sweeping monumental stair. The quarters of a downtown club, the New Amsterdam Club, were planned for the Woolworth Build-

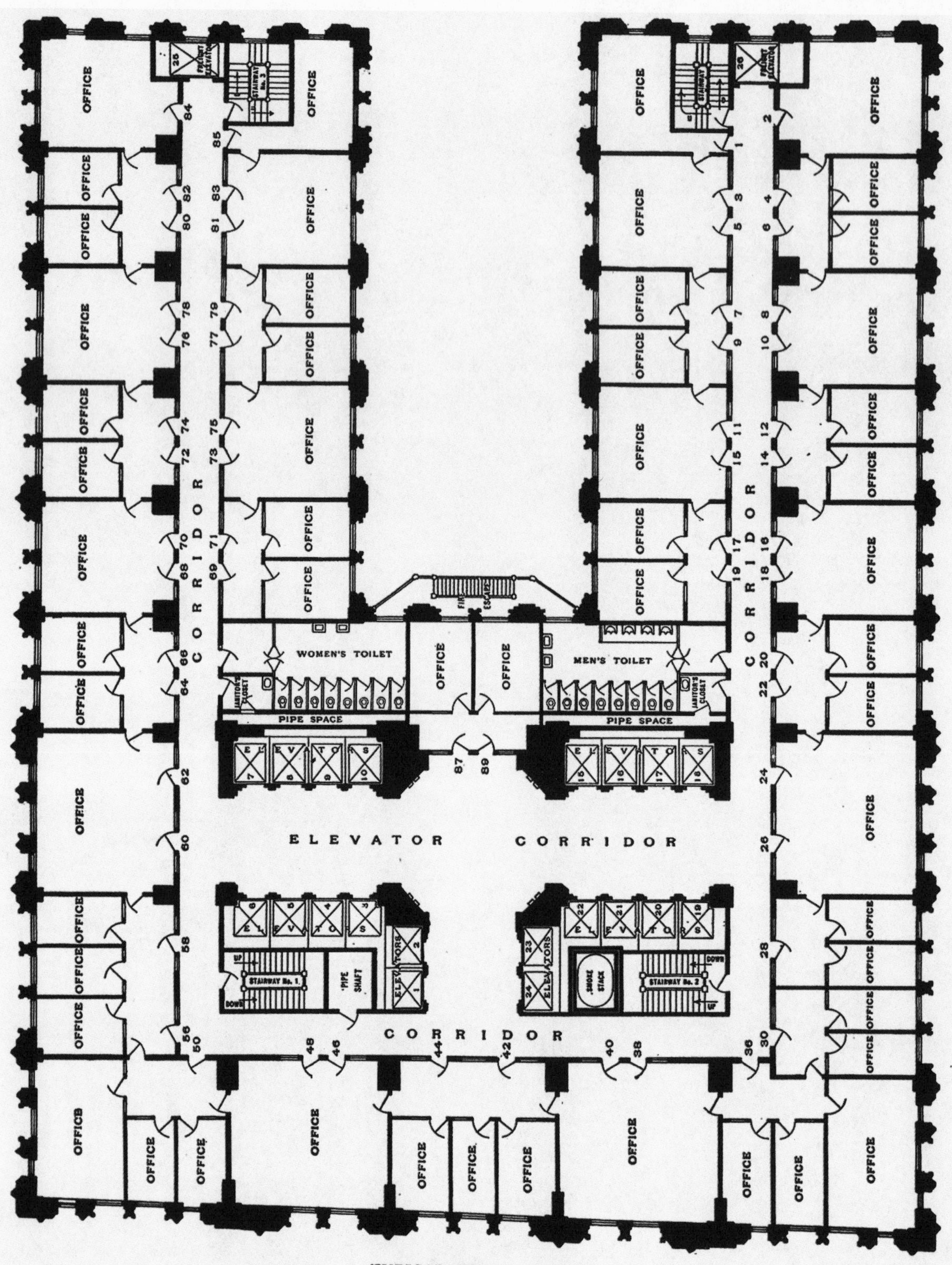

TYPICAL FLOOR PLAN

WOOLWORTH BUILDING

Cass Gilbert, Architect

ing's twenty-sixth, twenty-seventh, and twenty-eighth stories. Near the top of the tower there was to be a tearoom, from which a visitor could take a shuttle elevator or climb a spiral stair to a spectacular pinnacle observatory. The headquarters of the F. W. Woolworth Company—with an office in the Empire style, surrounded by offices for Woolworth's key executives—was perched high in the twenty-fourth story. Woolworth had a private office and apartment in the tower's fortieth story. Collectively, the spaces comprised a rich internal environment, a series of discrete worlds within a world, superbly tailored to meet any prospective tenant's needs for work, amusement, and pleasure.[45]

FIGURE 5.18
F. W. Woolworth Company Building, New York City, typical floor plan, 1913.

The lobby of the Woolworth Building—designed to outshine that of Ernest Flagg's recently completed Singer Tower—had a splendor, color, and opulence previously unknown in New York office buildings (fig. 5.17). Serving as a grand entrance vestibule for the F. W. Woolworth Company and Irving National Bank, as well as a shopping arcade, it was organized around an axial, nave-like space of tall, Romanesque proportions. This was intersected by a cross-axis for the elevator lobbies, with balconies modeled on the mausoleum of Galla Placidia, Ravenna. The balconies were trimmed with gilded Gothic ornament, the elevator doors with arabesque patterns in etched steel set off against gold-plated backgrounds, and all the vaults surfaced with sparkling and colorful Byzantine mosaics. In addition to the interior's amenities, Woolworth provided his tenants with premium office space (fig. 5.18). Floor-to-floor heights, many of which were twenty feet, far surpassed the standard, so that the offices, never more than twenty-six feet deep, were flooded with light. Large bathrooms for both men and women appeared in every story, and six batteries of high-speed elevators, a total of twenty, provided both express and local service. Corridors were wide; the elevator lobbies were spacious and monumental; and the marbles of floors and wainscots varied story to story.[46]

In choosing to build the highest skyscraper in the world, at fifty-five stories and 792 feet, Woolworth was convinced that a structure of such prodigious height—a striking and wonderful vertical cynosure in the city—was the surest way to achieve an international address as well as international renown. His decision to advertise the F. W. Woolworth Company in such a way was based on his discovery, while on one of his buying trips abroad, of the popularity among Europeans of the new Singer Tower. Most significantly, however, New York's market for office space was overbuilt in 1910, and Woolworth was keenly aware of the competition.[47] He decided he had to make his office building so attractive that prospective tenants simply

FIGURE 5.19

Houses of Parliament, London, showing Victoria Tower, after 1867. Unidentified photographer. Photograph.

FIGURE 5.20

F. W. Woolworth Company Building, New York City, preliminary design, April 26, 1910. Cass Gilbert, delineator. Graphite on tracing paper, 23 in. × 14 in.

(Cass Gilbert Collection, courtesy New-York Historical Society, neg. no. 72148)

could not turn him down. He was determined to accomplish no less than the seduction of tenants away from their existing quarters in other, slightly older and less desirable, office buildings. This he did indeed accomplish—one of those tenants, the law firm Beach and Pierson, chose to move out of the recently completed Singer Tower and into the Woolworth Building.[48] As a result of his savvy development strategy, which entailed besting the boom and bust cycles of New York's real estate market, Woolworth's showy landmark headquarters would ultimately end up paying for itself. Woolworth had developed the concept of the "luxury" office building. His skyscraper would rival not just New York's finest office buildings but also the city's most elegant hotels, restaurants, and other notable "palaces" of public amusement. The Woolworth Building, like a men's club, rapidly became synonymous with exclusivity.

Gilbert's skill with the skyscraper Gothic was an equally important consideration in Woolworth's conception for his theatrical skyscraper—as Montgomery Schuyler put it, "no Gradgrind of a projector would dare attack 'the record' without some thought as to how his record-beater was going to look." Woolworth, having spent a lifetime buying attractive goods from European cottage industries and displaying them equally attractively in his stores, was already highly attuned to the financial importance of beauty. For his skyscraper that beauty was to be all at once European, Gothic, and "modern." As a consequence, the skyscraper's Gothic imagery—and Woolworth's perception of its advertising value—had a critical role in the project from its very beginning. Woolworth admired Gilbert's West Street Building, but also, as he told Gilbert, the nineteenth-century perpendicular Gothic of the Victoria Tower, Houses of Parliament, in London. These served as the starting point for Gilbert's design (figs. 5.19 and 5.20).[49] When Gilbert finally completed the project that fulfilled the requirements of Woolworth's increasingly grander vision in February 1911, however, it had evolved significantly to become a much more sophisticated version of the skyscraper Gothic style he developed for the West Street Building. Gilbert expanded his array of Gothic sources to include cathedral forms and ornamental details, among them, the crossing tower of the Benedictine Abbey Church of Saint-Ouen, Rouen—which served as the model for the Woolworth Building's picturesque crown—and the flamboyant Gothic detail of the choir at Mont-Saint-Michel. They also included a full range of secular Gothic sources, from the *hotel de ville* at Compiègne, on which Gilbert patterned the building's composition, to the octagonal roof of the Guild Hall in Cologne, the model for the pinnacle observatory's circumambient balcony.[50]

FIGURE 5.21

F. W. Woolworth Company Building, New York City, view of upper stories, 1913. Unidentified photographer. Photograph, 13 in. × 8 in.

(Cass Gilbert Collection, courtesy New-York Historical Society, neg. no. 72885)

The Woolworth Building's verticals, a more sophisticated version of the West Street's, were composed with syncopated rhythms modulated by major piers. The piers' angular projections, the boldest of which were found in the tower, forthrightly expressed the structural loads they had to carry. A complete system of portal bracing, to maintain the rigidity of the steel frame against the forces of the wind, was designed by the structural engineer Gunvald Aus. Now greatly elaborated and advanced over any of Gilbert's earlier skyscrapers, the Woolworth Building's portal braces—those in the first twenty-eight stories of the tower actually portal arches—obviated the need for the more typical cross bracing or knee bracing. Gilbert, as a consequence, was able to achieve an even greater openness and perpendicular Gothic delicacy in the Woolworth Building's elevations.[51] In few skyscrapers before or since has there been contrived such a close and complementary relationship between structure and cladding. The verticals soar straight upward from the sidewalk with a force and energy unprecedented in earlier skyscrapers; they echo the dynamism of New York as a modern city in the making.[52]

The adventuresome modernity of the Woolworth Building's verticals did not in any way preclude Gilbert's larger goal of urban high picturesqueness. His design was conceived in reference to a multiplicity of viewing angles within the metropolis and beyond.[53] Gothic canopies, dormers, giant gables, buttresses, and outriggers, along with a tower that telescoped in three setback stages, its composition culminating in a crown embellished with four tourelles, a steep octagonal roof, and pinnacle observatory surrounded by buttresses—all contributed to Gilbert's increasing refinement of the skyscraper's exterior as a modern yet carefully composed picturesque entity within the city. Gilbert's skyscraper Gothic now had heightened qualities of the illusory and the pictorial—the "crystalline tower" especially, in Schuyler's words, "in the dwindling bulk of its upper stages . . . flatters and satisfies the eye" (fig. 5.21). Gilbert made the most sophisticated use of color to date for the sake of heightening those pictorial qualities. The Woolworth Building's general color was a light ivory terra-cotta; to this Gilbert added a darker buff-colored terra-cotta in all the spandrels—these were to appear recessed by contrast to the lighter-colored verticals of the colonettes and piers. Beneath the canopies and on their undersides, Gilbert used dark blues and bronze greens to heighten the effect of cavernous depth and shadow in the tower's upper stages; this he intensified with glimmering pinpoints of gold. Where appropriate, Gilbert applied lighter shades of blue,

FIGURE 5.22
Photograph taken from F. W. Woolworth Company Building tower, ca. 1913. Unidentified photographer. Photograph, 8 in. × 10 in.
(Cass Gilbert Collection, courtesy New-York Historical Society, neg. no. 73194)

FIGURE 5.23

View of lower Manhattan, ca. 1912. "Bird's Eye View of Lower Manhattan." Unidentified artist. Chromolithograph, 7 in. × 17 in.

(Courtesy New-York Historical Society, neg. no. 63652)

yellow, and green to relate the tower's telescoping mass effectively to the clouds and the sky.[54]

The Woolworth Building's pictorial qualities were especially important in what were becoming increasingly picturesque city views—"in its white spectrality, 'it shines over city and river,' " Schuyler wrote in 1913—as well as in the numerous contemporary etchings, illustrations, and paintings produced of those views (fig. 5.22). The artist Joseph Pennell was especially intrigued by the Woolworth Building's contribution to New York's new skyline. His *New York from Hamilton Ferry* (1915), one of many similar etchings, showed a magical, modern city on the water, with the Woolworth Building's tower commanding neighboring skyscrapers like a cathedral spire. Both Gilbert and Woolworth appreciated the responses to their project by critics and artists but also expected their skyscraper to be popular, to play to the urban thousands, and in turn, to those crowds' perceptions of the skyline as emblematic of New York's new status as a twentieth-century commercial metropolis. Indeed, as the Woolworth Building neared completion in 1912, Gilbert called the skyline "the most picturesque thing in architecture in all the world." Both men were conscious of the pivotal role they played in shaping the skyline and hence the city's new urban identity. That skyline—an image of America, progress, and from a distance, picturesque beauty—they, along with the many others who financed, designed, and built New York's skyscrapers, conceived piece by piece, fragment by fragment to rival the capital cities around the world.[55]

Cass Gilbert's Skyscrapers of the 1920s and the 1930s

After World War I, Gilbert, as a designer of skyscrapers in New York, was faced with a wholly new set of challenges. The city was perpetually changing. As the new center of construction activity moved uptown, it increasingly took its visual identity from the imaginary and prophetic drawings of Hugh Ferriss—who apprenticed in Gilbert's office during the Woolworth Building project—and to a lesser extent, Harvey Wiley Corbett.[56] Both envisioned a future city of great setback skyscrapers, these inspired in turn by a new set of images and ideas—from the Zoning Resolution of 1916 to Ferriss's own sublime mountain imagery, ancient Babylon, and the pre-Columbian architecture of Central America.[57] Gilbert disapproved of at least one of Ferriss's published drawings showing a future New York—his illustration of Raymond Hood's *City of Needles* (1924)—and may have considered him a protégé who wandered astray.[58] Gilbert's vision for New York as a modern city of towers, it was clear, did not accord with Ferriss's. Gilbert

CASS GILBERT INC ARCHITECT

superbly expressed this in his 1920 skyscraper project for the General Electric Company in Augusta, Georgia, which showed that he continued to refine his personal version of the skyscraper Gothic (plate 13).[59] Here Gilbert proposed an even slenderer composition than the Woolworth Building, with a profusion of Gothic ornament at the upper stages of the tower and an overall brightness, lightness, and delicacy that surpassed other contemporary uses of the Gothic, among them Howells and Hood's winning entry for the Chicago Tribune Tower competition of 1922.

FIGURE 5.24
New York Life Insurance Company Building, New York City, preliminary design, May 1926. F. G. Stickel, delineator. Graphite and charcoal on board, 33 in. × 24 in.
(Cass Gilbert Collection, courtesy New-York Historical Society, neg. no. 72896)

Gilbert's design for the New York Life Insurance Company Building, by contrast, which he began in 1919, might be viewed as his effort to reconcile the ethereal Gothic idiom that he developed for the West Street Building and refined for the Woolworth Building with the weighty and earthbound step-back massing prescribed for skyscrapers by the Zoning Resolution of 1916 (fig. 5.24). Although initially projected at fifty stories, New York Life's headquarters, as finally designed at thirty-four stories and 610 feet, did not rise as high as the Woolworth Building. Still, it had a block-long shopping arcade joined to a tall, vaulted lobby, which surpassed the Woolworth Building's in size and rivaled it in grandeur. Located near Madison Square, on the site of the old Madison Square Garden, the New York Life Building, like the Woolworth Building, reaped the advantages of distant viewing angles. Its exterior and lobby-arcade had a staid and conservative air nonetheless, and it seemed regressive by comparison to the Woolworth's atmosphere of experimentation, novelty, and color.

Reportedly, Gilbert turned the planning of New York Life's offices over to Frederick Stickel, who had assisted him with the development of the floor plans for the Woolworth project.[60] The typical office floor plans of the second through the fifth stories paled by comparison to the humanly scaled and well-illuminated environments of the Woolworth Building—even though they may have met the insurance industry's requirement for deep loft spaces housing clerical work. In its internal pattern of uses, however, the New York Life Building was much more ambitious, although less diversified, than the Woolworth Building—the executive offices and the boardroom were located in the tower, and the mail room, file storage, security vaults, and mechanical equipment in five stories below grade. The first basement had a subway concourse lined with shops and restaurants, along with two huge company-operated cafeterias. The interior altogether resembled a huge mechanism for processing insurance claims—it had some 75 million items on file, received mail through six terminals, and circulated paperwork through the world's largest pneumatic tube system.[61] If Frank

THE TRUE ADMINISTRATION OF JUSTICE IS THE FIRMEST PILLAR OF GOOD GOVERNMENT

Woolworth was attempting to attract and retain tenants with his masculine, clublike interior, then the New York Life Insurance Company, proud of its "employee welfare program," strove paternalistically to create the domestic atmosphere of a home away from home for its employees, its huge clerical staff composed mostly of young women. Consequently, New York Life, while still a skyscraper, posed for Gilbert another sort of architectural problem entirely.[62]

FIGURE 5.25
U.S. Courthouse, Foley Square, New York City, 1936. Unidentified photographer.
(Courtesy of the Library of Congress)

In 1923 Gilbert became involved with the planning of New York's civic center at City Hall Park, at the request of Charles Dyer Norton and the Advisory Committee on the City Plan. Gilbert's committee, like many that preceded it, proposed clearing City Hall Park of all buildings except the city hall and supported the demolition of the old federal post office and courthouse. By 1930 Gilbert secured the commission for the proposed new federal courthouse at Foley Square—an extension of the civic center directly to the north of City Hall Park, slated to be surrounded by monumental buildings serving various government purposes.[63] Gilbert's U.S. Courthouse of 1934–6, which he conceived as the key public building in the complex and designed as a version of Saint Mark's campanile, Venice, was based on his conviction that buildings for government purposes should express timeless classical ideals (fig. 5.24).[64] Gilbert's tower, strikingly similar to Bruce Price's unbuilt project for the Sun Building in New York City (1890), was also reminiscent of Bertram Goodhue's recently completed Nebraska state capitol (1922–32) and Peabody and Stearns's Custom House Tower in Boston (1913–5). But it, too, grew out of Gilbert's earlier Europe-inspired vision for lower Manhattan as picturesque city of towers, however strongly classical, weighty, and massive it may have appeared by comparison to his strikingly ethereal Gothic skyscrapers.[65] As far as Gilbert was concerned, the U.S. Courthouse, a public building, had to have the character of a monument. As such, it lacked the adventuresome modernity that characterized his earlier commercial designs, from the Bowlby and Company Store in St. Paul to the Woolworth Building in New York. Although completed after his death by his son, Cass Gilbert Jr., it was still in basic conception Gilbert's project. As such, it seemed to demonstrate that Gilbert was at his best as an artist when faced with a speculative program as flexible as Woolworth's and when aggressively challenged by New York's powerful and conflicting forces of modernity.

I thank Sharon Irish, Barbara Christen, and Margaret Heilbrun for reading earlier versions of this essay and making thoughtful comments. I am also grateful to Mary Beth Betts for her expert assistance with the Cass Gilbert Collection at the New-York Historical Society.

1. Montgomery Schuyler and Claude Bragdon, among the most-noted critics of the day, hailed Gilbert's designs as especially successful "solutions" to the "problem" of the skyscraper. Both were critical of the building type generally. See [Montgomery Schuyler], "The West Street Building, New York City," *Architectural Record* 22 (August 1907): 102–9; Claude Bragdon, "Architecture in the United States: 3. The Skyscraper," *Architectural Record* 26 (August 1909): 96; Montgomery Schuyler, "The Woolworth Building [1913]," in William H. Jordy and Ralph Coe, eds., *American Architecture and Other Writings by Montgomery Schuyler,* vol. 2, (Cambridge, Mass.: Harvard University Press, 1961), pp. 605–21.
2. Schuyler, "The Woolworth Building," p. 611.
3. Schuyler wrote at length about the contribution of Gilbert's designs to the "artistic" enhancement of New York's skyline; [Schuyler], "West Street Building," p. 108, and Schuyler, "Woolworth Building," pp. 606, 608. On the "skyline view" as it emerged at the end of the nineteenth century and on the skyline as the "signature" of the modern city, see William R. Taylor, "New York and the Origin of the Skyline: The Commercial City as Visual Text," in William R. Taylor, ed., *In Pursuit of Gotham: Culture and Commerce in New York* (New York: Oxford University Press, 1992), pp. 23–9.

   "Capital of capitalism" is Kenneth Jackson's phrase. See Kenneth Jackson, "The Capital of Capitalism: The New York Metropolitan Region," in Anthony Sutcliffe, ed., *Metropolis, 1890–1940* (Chicago: University of Chicago Press, 1984).

   Two entirely different ways of seeing and conceiving the built environment, the picturesque point of view and the City Beautiful, both emphasized the importance of a strong visual relationship between a building and either the natural surroundings or adjacent buildings. On the picturesque, an aesthetic sensibility that persisted in the Anglo-American world through the early years of the twentieth century, see, for example, Richard Payne Knight, "An Analytical Inquiry into the Principles of Taste" [1805] and Sir Uvedale Price, "An Essay on the Picturesque" [1794], both excerpted in John Dixon Hunt and Peter Willis, eds., *The Genius of the Place* (New York: Harper and Row, 1975) pp. 348–50, 351–7. On the City Beautiful, see

Charles Mulford Robinson, *Modern Civic Art* (New York: G. P. Putnam's Sons, 1903).

4. Bills proposed to restrict building heights failed three times before passage of the Zoning Resolution of 1916: twice in the New York State Legislature, in 1896 and 1897, and then before the New York City Board of Alderman, in 1908. For a more extended analysis, see Gail Fenske, "The 'Skyscraper Problem' and the City Beautiful: The Woolworth Building," Ph.D. diss., MIT, 1988, pp. 28–42. See also Sarah Bradford Landau and Carl Condit, *Rise of the New York Skyscraper, 1865–1913* (New Haven: Yale University Press, 1996), pp. 187–90, 293–7, 347–53. See also *Report of the Heights of Buildings Commission to the Committee on the Height, Size, and Arrangement of Buildings to the Board of Estimate and Apportionment of the City of New York* (New York, 1913).

5. Especially perceptive essays criticizing the tall building were A. D. F. Hamlin, "The Difficulties of Modern Architecture," *Architectural Record* 1 (October–December 1891): 137–50, and Ernest Flagg, "The Dangers of High Buildings," *Cosmopolitan* 21 (May 1896): 70–9. Both Hamlin and Flagg studied at the Ecole des Beaux-Arts.

   Schuyler wrote in 1897 that the New York skyline was, on one hand, an "index of the national prosperity" and, on the other, that it "looks like business"; Montgomery Schuyler, "Sky-line of New York, 1881–1897," *Harper's Weekly* 41 (March 20, 1897): 295. In 1907 Schuyler viewed the densely built-up business district as an architectural manifestation of the less desirable aspects of American individualism: "There is so much 'ensemble' even of individualism that the individuals are merged in a riot"; Montgomery Schuyler, "Some Recent Skyscrapers," *Architectural Record* 22 (September 1907): 161.

6. Henry James, *The American Scene* (1907; reprint, Bloomington and London: Indiana University Press, 1968), p. 73; John De Witt Warner, "Matters That Suggest Themselves," *Municipal Affairs* 2 (March 1898): 123.

   Proposals for New York as a City Beautiful ranged from the architect Julius F. Harder's large-scale plan for the city of 1898 to Ernest Flagg's plan of 1904. The Municipal Art Society produced a block plan for the civic center in 1902. Art societies such as the National Society of Mural Painters and the National Sculpture Society proposed beautifying the city with mural and sculptural embellishment in public buildings and public parks; Fenske, "The 'Skyscraper Problem' and the City Beautiful," pp. 22–4, 44–6, 119–20.

   Report of the New York City Improvement Commission (New York: New York City Improvement Commission, 1904); *Report of the New York City Improvement Commission* (New York: New York City Improvement

Commission, 1907). See also Harvey A. Kantor, "The City Beautiful in New York," *New-York Historical Society Quarterly* 58 (April 1973): 153–71, and Robert A. M. Stern, Gregory Gilmartin, and John Montague Massengale, *New York, 1900* (New York: Rizzoli International Publications, 1983), pp. 30–1.

7. Cass Gilbert to Clarence Johnston, November 17, 1879, Clarence Johnston Papers, Minnesota Historical Society. Gilbert added that the building "was noticeable only for its utter lack of design and beauty." Gilbert's proposed designs were "Richardsonian Romanesque," highly picturesque, and sported central towers.

8. Gilbert to Johnston, January 30, 1880, Clarence Johnston Papers, Minnesota Historical Society. Gilbert sketched one of the storefronts from memory (a three-story building with gridded arrangements of windows, grouped by story). He added that "the beauty of it was its simple arrangement of forms."

9. The Endicott Building appeared in the short-lived *Architectural Reviewer;* "Cass Gilbert," *Architectural Reviewer* 1 (June 1897): 44–8. For the Bowlby and Company Store, see, "Building Owned by E. D. Chamberlain, Esq., St. Paul, Minn.," *American Architect and Building News* 51 (March 21, 1896): 135, plate 1056. Montgomery Schuyler, "Glimpses of Western Architecture: St. Paul and Minneapolis [1891]," in William H. Jordy and Ralph Coe, eds., *American Architecture and Other Writings by Montgomery Schuyler,* vol. 1 (Cambridge, Mass.: Harvard University Press, 1961), pp. 150–1. The Endicott Building is described in detail in Pioneer Press Company, ed., *Saint Paul, History and Progress: Principal Men and Institutions* (St. Paul: Pioneer Press, 1897), pp. 80–1. Gilbert chose to locate his architectural office on the fifth floor. See also Sharon Irish, "West Hails East: Cass Gilbert in Minnesota," *Minnesota History* 53, no. 5 (spring 1993): 201–4.

10. Susan Tunick, *Terra-Cotta Skyline* (New York: Princeton Architectural Press, 1997), p. 54, calls attention to Gilbert's early experimentation with colored glazes.

11. Gilbert served on the National Jury of Selection for the Department of Fine Arts of the World's Columbian Exposition. Cass Gilbert to Julia Finch Gilbert, March 6, 1893, Box 6, Cass Gilbert Papers, Library of Congress. Gilbert met with Burnham and then corresponded with him regarding their proposed partnership. See, for instance, Cass Gilbert to Daniel Burnham, February 18, 1891, Box 17, Minnesota Historical Society.

12. The Bowlby and Company Store was constructed in 129 days; "Building Owned by E. D. Chamberlain," p. 135.

13. Gilbert traveled to Providence, R.I., New York City, and Washington, D.C., in November 1895 to study classical precedents for his Minnesota state

capitol (among them the Rhode Island state house, Low Library, and the U.S. Capitol). In New York he may have seen Bruce Price's American Surety Building, which was nearing completion at the time. See Cass Gilbert, Diaries, Box 1, Cass Gilbert Papers, Library of Congress.

14. Henry S. Pritchard, "Design of Structural Frame with an Explanation of Method of Determining Wind Stresses As Devised by Engineering Department of New Jersey Steel and Iron Company, Trenton, N.J.—September 1896," Box 2, Cass Gilbert Papers, Minnesota Historical Society, illustrates the details of the Brazer Building's portal arch wind bracing. The structural engineer for the project was Louis E. Ritter of Chicago, who was recommended to Gilbert by both Daniel Burnham and William Le Baron Jenney; Gilbert to Professor F. W. Chandler, June 14, 1897, Box 2, Cass Gilbert Papers, Minnesota Historical Society. Gilbert wrote that "the owners of the building, being very conservative people . . . requested me to design the building with a view to exceptional strength." While working with the Chicago-based Ritter and the George A. Fuller Construction Company, however, Gilbert lightened the building's steel construction for the sake of greater economy.

15. Boston's building law at the time limited the height of all new construction in the city to two and a half times the width of the widest street on which a building stood, not exceeding 125 feet in height; Peabody and Stearns to Cass Gilbert, April 12, 1897, Box 2, Cass Gilbert Papers, Minnesota Historical Society. When the directors of the neighboring Merchant's National Bank protested that the Brazer's cornice and cheneau projected too much, Gilbert modified his design to conform strictly to the height limitation; Thomas H. Russell to Cass Gilbert, May 21, 1897, Box 2, Cass Gilbert Papers, Minnesota Historical Society.

16. Gilbert was introduced to Thomas H. Russell through Henry Endicott, his client for the Endicott Building in St. Paul, in June 1894. By that October, Gilbert had prepared detailed plan drawings, and he and the George A. Fuller Company were investigating the financial potential of a speculative office building on the Brazer site. Gilbert signed the contract for his services much later, in June 1896. In September 1896 he and Harry S. Black explored methods of reducing the project's construction costs. For correspondence related to the Brazer Building project, see Box 2, Cass Gilbert Papers, Minnesota Historical Society.

    In the Broadway Chambers project, as in the Brazer Building project, Gilbert spent a considerable amount of time producing preliminary drawings and arranging financing before he signed the contract in 1899 for his architectural services. Many examples documented in his personal letter books show that he continued to use the same strategy while in practice in

New York. In 1906, for instance, he mailed plan studies to a local developer for a loft building on Market Street in New Jersey, accompanied by a cost estimate per story for all possible heights between eight and twelve stories, and indicated that if he were retained as an architect, he would charge the standard 5 percent fee; Cass Gilbert to Mr. Bierman, June 11, 1906, Personal Letter Books, Cass Gilbert Collection, New-York Historical Society.

17. Gilbert was as well-versed as the experts of his day regarding the tall office building as a financial, technical, and planning problem. Foremost among the experts was the architect and engineer George Hill, who wrote "Some Practical Limiting Conditions in the Design of the Modern Office Building," *Architectural Record* 2 (April–June 1893): 446–68. On the evolution of the office building as a financial and planning problem, see Carol Willis, *Form Follows Finance: Skyscrapers and Skylines in New York and Chicago* (New York: Princeton Architectural Press, 1995).
18. "Brazer Building, Boston," *American Architect and Building News* 56 (May 22, 1897): 64, plate 1117.
19. H. S. Black to Cass Gilbert, November 12, 1896, Box 3, Cass Gilbert Papers, Minnesota Historical Society; Cass Gilbert to Guaranty Construction Company, February 22, 1897, Box 3, Minnesota Historical Society. On the backgrounds of the key individuals involved with the Broadway Chambers project, see Sharon Irish, "Cass Gilbert's Career in New York, 1899–1905," Ph.D. diss., Northwestern University, 1985, pp. 146–208.
20. Cass Gilbert, as quoted in "Building Skyscrapers—Described by Cass Gilbert," *Real Estate Record and Builders' Guide* 65 (June 23, 1900): 1091.
21. Cass Gilbert told his boyhood friend Clarence Johnston that "I have pronunciation for Street first, Waterhouse second, Shaw third, and Burges fourth as my choice; and I have held to Street as my man"; Gilbert to Johnston, July 21, 1879, Clarence Johnston Papers, Minnesota Historical Society.
22. As part of their commission, McKim, Mead, and White also redesigned Boston's Copley Square. Their concern for the Boston Public Library's urban setting can be credited with affirming a "new professional and municipal desire to shape and improve the urban environment," or what would eventually become known as the City Beautiful. See Leland Roth, *McKim, Mead, and White, Architects* (New York: Harper and Row, 1983), p. 130.
23. Office memorandum by Cass Gilbert, February 24, 1899, Cass Gilbert Papers, Minnesota Historical Society, states that "I told him [Edward R. Andrews] the building would not be as ornamental in finish as the Washington Life, but would be very much better than the Cheseborough Building."

24. Pencil studies for towers and campaniles appear in Gilbert's sketchbooks, which are housed at the New-York Historical Society, the Library of Congress, and the National Museum of American Art. Gilbert's watercolors, most of which can be found at the National Museum of American Art, include *Tower of the Cathedral, Utrecht, Holland* (1889); *Tower at San Francisco Romano, Rome* (1898); *San Giorgio Maggiore, Venice* (1898) (showing St. Mark's campanile); *Cathedral Tower, Pistoia, Italy* (1898); and *Church Tower, Italy* (1898).

25. Sarah Bradford Landau compared Gilbert's Broadway Chambers Building with Price's Saint James Building in "Cass Gilbert and the New York Skyscraper before 1914," a talk delivered at the symposium "Cass Gilbert, Life and Work: From Regional to National Architect," New York, November 13, 1998.

26. "The Broadway Chambers, New York, N.Y.," *American Architect and Building News* 67 (February 24, 1900): 63, plate 1261. George A. Fuller Company, *Broadway Chambers, A Modern Office Building: Exhibited by Models at the Paris Exposition, 1900* (New York: George A. Fuller Company, 1900), pp. 18–23.

27. One early sketch shows a rathskeller in the basement, and a set of drawings to scale, dated October 21, 1897, includes a plan showing the proposed downtown club; Broadway Chambers Building, Cass Gilbert Collection, New-York Historical Society.

28. Cass Gilbert, "Response on the Occasion of the Presentation of the Gold Medal for Architecture to the Society of Arts and Sciences," in Julia Finch Gilbert, ed., *Cass Gilbert: Reminiscences and Addresses* (New York: privately printed, 1935), p. 51.

29. John C. Van Dyke, *The New New York: A Commentary on the Place and the People* (New York: Macmillan, 1909), p. 23, describes the city's atmospheric setting. Gilbert would later write that he used color on the upper stories of the Woolworth Building's tower to "relate it to the color of the sky, whether blue or grey"; Cass Gilbert, "The Tenth Birthday of a Notable Structure," *Real Estate Magazine of New York* 11 (May 1923): 345.

30. Neil Harris, "Urban Tourism and the Commercial City," in William R. Taylor, ed., *Inventing Times Square* (Baltimore and London: Johns Hopkins University Press, 1991), pp. 69–73.

31. Van Dyke, *The New New York,* p. 7, wrote that "the buildings are eruptive and the whole city abnormal—something apparently 'just happened.' " On the effort of photographers such as Alfred Stieglitz to "find in photography itself a principle of picturing and thus ordering urban life," see Alan Trachtenberg, "Image and Ideology: New York in the Photographer's Eye," *Journal of Urban History* 10 (August 1984): 453–64.

32. Gilbert's "Gothic" skyscrapers incorporate many non-Gothic sources, mod-

ern and historical. His contemporaries, the critic Montgomery Schuyler among them, nonetheless viewed them as "Gothic."

33. Van Dyke, *The New New York,* 10.

34. W. L. B. Jenney, "An Age of Steel and Clay," *Inland Architect and News Record* 16 (December 1890): 75–7. Jenney wrote that "with cheap steel of a very superior quality and a light, dull glazed terra cotta and a strong, light fire-proofing, we are ready to build as never before. . . . We enter upon a new age—an age of steel and clay." Terra-cotta, as a plastic material for sheathing the steel frame, was especially well-suited to the expression of Sullivan's organic philosophy: "All things in nature have a shape, that is to say, a form, and an outward semblance that tells us what they are"; Louis Sullivan, "The Tall Office Building Artistically Considered," in *Kindergarten Chats and Other Writings,* rev. ed. (1947; reprint, New York: Dover Publications, 1979), p. 207.

35. Gilbert had been sketching in Flanders since at least 1897. His trip to Flanders of that year was part of a four-month-long sketching tour in Europe. At age thirty-nine he sailed from New York in November, arrived in Antwerp, sketched the cathedral tower, and then went to Malines, where he wrote an extended description of the Cathedral of Saint Rombout's tower. From Malines, he went to Brussels, Ghent, and Bruges in early December, and then on to the Netherlands, and afterward to continental Europe. On a trip to England and France in 1905, he visited the cathedrals at Exeter, Lincoln, York, Gloucester, Durham, and Reims, and Notre Dame in Paris. See Cass Gilbert, Diaries, Box 1, Cass Gilbert Papers, Library of Congress.

    Schuyler wrote: "It is not frequent for a designer of skyscrapers to attain this double success. But Mr. Cass Gilbert, having attained it once in the Broadway Chambers, has scored again with the West Street Building, where he had a larger opportunity"; [Schuyler], "The West Street Building," p. 103. Claude Bragdon called Gilbert's design "the work of a master mind, the last word in New York skyscraper architecture"; Bragdon, "Architecture in the United States: 3. The Skyscraper," p. 96.

36. Cass Gilbert, "The Architecture of Today" [lecture delivered at the West Point Military Academy], May 4, 1909, Box 16, Cass Gilbert Papers, Library of Congress, pp. 9, 4–5, 26–8. Gilbert added that in animal life and plant life, "form adapts itself to the use it is intended to serve."

37. On the West Street Building's client, General Howard Carroll, and the relationship of the project to its waterfront site, see Sharon Irish, "A 'Machine That Makes Land Pay': The West Street Building in New York," *Technology and Culture* 30 (April 1989): 378–80, 390–1. See also Landau and Condit, *Rise of the New York Skyscraper,* p. 321.

38. See West Street Building tenant list, West Street Building, incoming correspondence, Cass Gilbert Collection, New-York Historical Society. On the name of the building, see Hugh Bonner and Howard Constable to Cass Gilbert, April 29, 1905, West Street Building, incoming correspondence, Cass Gilbert Collection, New-York Historical Society. New York's Coal and Iron Exchange was located near the West Street Building, at the southeast corner of Church and Cortlandt Streets.

39. The Delaware, Lackawanna, and Western Railroad Company and the Starin Transportation Company jointly owned Pier 13, which extended into the Hudson River directly in front of the West Street Building. On the opposite bank was Lackawanna's Hoboken rail and ferry terminal; Irish, "A 'Machine That Makes Land Pay,' " p. 391. [Schuyler], "The West Street Building," pp. 108, 109.

40. Skyscrapers higher than sixteen stories required concrete pier foundations carried to bedrock by the caisson method. They also required more elaborate systems of wind bracing (portal bracing, full-bay cross bracing, knee bracing) to combat the higher wind stresses associated with greater height. On the evolution of the structural technologies used to build higher buildings from the mid-1890s, see Landau and Condit, *Rise of the New York Skyscraper,* pp. 233, 238–41, 252, 289–93, 303, 312–3, 358–9, 364–5. See also Gail Fenske, "Gratte-ciel," in Antoine Picon et al., comps., *L'Art de l'ingeneur: constructeur, entrepreneur, inventeur* (Paris: Centre de creation industrielle, Centre Georges Pompidou, 1997), pp. 167–8.

41. Another advantage of the tall, slender, and isolated towers was a "perpetual supply of excellent light"; "The Newest Thing in Skyscrapers," *Architectural Record* 19 (May 1906): 398. "Skyscraping Up to Date," *Architectural Record* 22 (January 1908): 74, noted that "now we possess genuine tower architecture as an advertising feature on a rental basis."

42. Later, Woolworth would declare the skyscraper "the grandest and most beautiful erected by man"; Frank Woolworth, "General Letter to All Stores: United States, Canada, and Great Britain," February 20, 1914, Woolworth Building, Cass Gilbert Collection, New-York Historical Society.

43. Frank Woolworth set up the Broadway–Park Place Company in April 1910 for the purpose of purchasing the site and constructing the building. Both he and the bank owned shares in the company. In May 1914, after the building was constructed, Woolworth purchased the bank's five thousand shares, so that he owned the building outright; Frank Woolworth to Board of Directors of the Irving National Bank, April 19, 1910, Bank of New York Archives. See also Robert Holmes Elmendorf, "Evolution of Commercial Banking in New York City, 1851–1951," in "Which Is Recorded the Story of the Irving Trust Company," typescript, 1951, pp. 124–6.

George Hill, "The Economy of the Office Building," *Architectural Record* 15 (April 1904): 316. See also Landau and Condit, *Rise of the New York Skyscraper,* pp. 289–91. Landau and Condit note that in Hill's essay "the economy of the office building was discussed at some length—and apparently for the first time."

44. All that remains to document Woolworth and Gilbert's initial exploration of the proposed skyscraper at 750 feet high are a complete set of plans titled "scheme 17," dated May 17, 1910. The earliest remaining perspective drawing illustrating the exterior of the new and larger design is "scheme 26," dated July 6. Its tower, however, rises only about 580 feet.

Woolworth's new conception for the interior of his skyscraper was described in "New Woolworth Building Will Eclipse Singer Tower in Height," *New York Times,* November 13, 1910. Lincoln Steffens, "The Modern Business Building," *Scribner's* 22 (July 1897): 57–8, noted that the following uses either appeared in or were being proposed for New York office buildings in 1897: banks, stores, storage rooms in the basement, libraries, restaurants, clubs, bachelor apartments, and roof gardens with variety stages. What distinguished Woolworth's project was that it included not only a few such ancillary uses but many, and collectively they created a self-sustaining as well as opulent interior environment for the skyscraper's diverse tenantry.

45. The rich array of public and semipublic spaces proposed and designed for the Woolworth's interior are described in office memorandums dated 1912 to 1915 and in Frank Woolworth's "General Letter to All Stores," both in Woolworth Building, Cass Gilbert Collection, New-York Historical Society. See also in office scrapbooks the many newspaper accounts describing the building after it opened, Cass Gilbert Collection, New-York Historical Society. The New Amsterdam Club, a personal project of Woolworth's, reached an advanced stage of design development but was eventually abandoned. The tearoom proposed for the fifty-second story of the tower's crown was replaced with ice cream and souvenir stands on the fifty-first floor.

46. Lobbies and arcades of a grand scale had been identified with New York office buildings since George Post's design for an addition to the Equitable Building (1886–9). See Landau and Condit, *Rise of the New York Skyscraper,* pp. 71–5. The lobby Woolworth had in mind when thinking about his own skyscraper, however, was that of the Singer Tower. Whereas the Singer lobby was sheathed with light-colored Italian marble and flooded with light from glazed saucer domes, Woolworth and Gilbert purposely introduced in the Woolworth lobby a contrasting dark and shadowy Byzantine atmosphere, drenched in color.

47. Woolworth stated: "While in Europe a few years ago, wherever I went the men with whom I came in contact asked about the Singer Building and its famous tower. That gave me an idea"; Frank Woolworth, as quoted in Leo Redding, "Mr. Woolworth's Story," *World's Work* 25 (April 1913): 663. Later, Woolworth told the builder Louis Horowitz that he intended to erect a "giant signboard to advertise around the world a spreading chain of five and ten cent stores"; Earle Schultz and Walter Simmons, *Offices in the Sky* (Indianapolis and New York: Bobbs-Merrill Company, 1959), p. 66.

"Rents in Downtown Office Buildings," *Real Estate Record and Builders' Guide* 138 (July 29, 1911): 118, stated that "at present there appears to be more office space on the market than can be readily absorbed," a condition that "has prevailed since the panic of 1907." Harry S. Black, interviewed in 1911, declared that "New York is overbuilt"; Schultz and Simmons, *Offices in the Sky,* p. 74. Woolworth wrote to Gilbert in 1911 about his concern over having to compete with the vacant space in office buildings in the vicinity of City Hall Park. They were at the time occupied by various city departments, which soon would be moving into the new Municipal Building, scheduled to be completed in 1913; Frank Woolworth to Cass Gilbert, December 27, 1911, Woolworth Building correspondence files, Cass Gilbert Collection, New-York Historical Society.

48. Edward Hogan to Cass Gilbert, September 13, 1913, Woolworth Building Correspondence Files, Cass Gilbert Collection, New-York Historical Society. Hogan told Gilbert that Beach and Pierson would willingly pay higher rental rates for space in the Woolworth Building.

49. Montgomery Schuyler, " 'The Towers of Manhattan' and Some Notes on the Woolworth Building," *Architectural Record* 33 (February 1913): 103. The drawings associated with the Woolworth project's first design (April 21–May 12, 1910) showed Gilbert and the office's chief designer, Thomas R. Johnson, seeking a synthesis between the astylar verticality of a modern commercial skyscraper and the desire for picturesqueness, especially in the crown.

50. The Woolworth project developed from May 12, 1910, over the next nine months in three distinct stages, to become, in the end, larger and taller. The fluctuating size and height of the project can be ascribed in part to the difficulties Woolworth faced in acquiring parcels to complete the building site. Some of the sources for the design are documented in scrapbooks and in Gilbert's drawings from his European tours. For instance, Gilbert produced a detailed pencil drawing of the Benedictine Abbey Church of Saint-Ouen, Rouen, in 1880.

51. Gunvald Aus was born in 1860 in Haugesund, Norway, received a degree in civil engineering from the Polytechnic Institute in Munich in 1879, and

immigrated to America in 1883. Before working on the Woolworth project, he advised Gilbert on the structural design of the Minnesota state capitol, the West Street Building, and the St. Louis Public Library. On account of the conservatism of the New York building code, of which Aus was highly critical, the Woolworth Building was structurally overdesigned. Gilbert, however, was proud that the tower "*does not sway at all,* so far as we can detect by the most careful measurements"; Gilbert, "The Tenth Birthday of a Notable Structure," p. 345.

52. Schuyler, " 'The Towers of Manhattan,' " p. 104, observed that "the Woolworth most unmistakably denotes its skeleton. . . . The uprights of the steel frame are felt throughout and everywhere." Manfredo Tafuri, "The Disenchanted Mountain: The Skyscraper and the City," in *The American City: From the Civil War to the New Deal,* trans. Barbara Luigia La Penta (Cambridge, Mass.: MIT Press, 1979), p. 391, cited Schuyler's essay and viewed Gilbert's design for the Woolworth Building as a pivotal example of the "primacy of structure and the subordination of style."

53. As Montgomery Schuyler put it, "there is no point of view from which it 'comes in wrong,' which means that there is no point of view from which the designer has not been beforehand with the observer"; Schuyler, "The Woolworth Building," p. 606.

54. Ibid., p. 606. Gilbert described his use of color in the Woolworth Building's design in Gilbert, "The Tenth Birthday of a Notable Structure," p. 345.

55. Schuyler, "The Woolworth Building," p. 606; Cass Gilbert to Emily and Cass Gilbert Jr., October 8, 1912, Box 8, Cass Gilbert Papers, Library of Congress.

56. Hugh Ferriss worked in Gilbert's office from 1912 to 1915. For the Woolworth project he produced a large, detailed pencil perspective of Irving National Exchange Bank's main banking hall. Gilbert encouraged Ferriss to establish himself independently as an architectural delineator. See Carol Willis, "Drawing towards Metropolis," in Hugh Ferriss, *Metropolis of Tomorrow* (1929; reprint, New York: Princeton Architectural Press, 1986), p. 153. In 1922 Ferriss and Corbett published their famous drawings showing the four stages of design for a skyscraper in accordance with the Zoning Resolution of 1916. The popular Titan City Exhibition of 1925 featured Ferriss and Corbett's designs for a future metropolis.

57. Robert A. M. Stern, Gregory Gilmartin, and Thomas Mellins, *New York, 1930: Architecture and Urbanism between Two World Wars* (New York: Rizzoli International Publications, 1987), pp. 510–3; Willis, "Drawing towards Metropolis," pp. 161, 164–5. For one interpretation of the historical significance of pre-Columbian architecture to the 1920s American metropolis, see Francisco Mujica, *The History of the Skyscraper* (Paris: Archaeology and Architecture Press, 1929).

58. Gilbert scrawled harshly critical comments across Ferriss's illustration. See scrapbooks, Cass Gilbert Collection, New-York Historical Society. Later, he asked Ferriss to produce a rendering of his New York Life Insurance Building.

59. The early studies for the General Electric project show a skyscraper with massing resembling that of the Woolworth Building. Gilbert also proposed an alternate design, with highly abstracted verticals not unlike those of Howells and Hood's much-later Daily News Building (1929). Gilbert's drawings included detailed calculations of square footage. He described the site for the project as "Broadway and downtown." See GE Project, Cass Gilbert Collection, New-York Historical Society.

60. Paul Starrett with Webb Waldron, *Changing the Skyline* (New York: Mc-Graw-Hill, 1938), pp. 268–73. See also Stern, Gilmartin, and Mellins, *New York, 1930,* pp. 542–3, and *American Architect* 135 (March 20, 1929): 350–414, the entire issue of which is devoted to the New York Life Insurance Company Building.

61. "The Story of the Design for the New Home Office of the New York Life Insurance Company, Told by Working Drawings from the Office of Cass Gilbert, Inc., Architect," *American Architect* 135 (March 20, 1929): 383–96; Stratford Corbett, "An Office Building of a New Era: Science Contributes to Efficiency, Employee Comfort, and Convenience in a 'New York Sky-scraper,' " *Scientific American* 141 (December 1929): 484–6. The two cafeterias served six thousand employees in four shifts.

62. About twice as many women as men worked for the New York Life Insurance Company; the dining room for women seated 975 and that for men 450. According to "Planning for Employees' Welfare in the Design of the New York Life Insurance Company Building," *American Architect* 135 (March 20, 1929): 401, "the attention given to the welfare of employees is particularly noticeable in the case of insurance companies. . . . The large institutions dealing in life insurance understand the importance and value of safeguarding the health and mental fitness of their employees and view it as a good investment." On the insurance industry and the "domestic office," see Angel-Kwolek Folland, *Engendering Business: Men and Women in the Corporate Office, 1870–1930* (Baltimore: Johns Hopkins University Press, 1994), pp. 94–128, and for the industry's "feminized office culture," see Olivier Zunz, *Making America Corporate, 1870–1920* (Chicago and London: University of Chicago Press, 1990), pp. 116–21.

63. For Gilbert's own record of his involvement with New York's civic center in the early 1920s, see "City Plan: City Hall and Court House Region [1923]," Box 17, Cass Gilbert Papers, Library of Congress. See also Stern, Gilmartin, and Mellins, *New York, 1930,* pp. 93–9. On the relocation of the

federal courts from the old federal post office and courthouse to the new federal courthouse and Gilbert's commission for the project, see John B. Kenney and Elliott B. Nixon, *The Federal Courthouse at Foley Square* (New York: Second Circuit Historical Committee and the Federal Bar Council, 1985), pp. 1–2, 5–6. Gilbert won the commission after he began work on the U.S. Supreme Court in Washington, D.C.

64. In 1909 Gilbert wrote that he viewed commercial office buildings and public buildings as two different architectural problems altogether. "I believe that our modern problems such as the skyscraper and the railroad building should be wrought out in harmony with the needs and the structural materials and that out of this will grow a beautiful architecture. I believe that in our public buildings, where the problems are not dissimilar to those of former times, we may well study the serious and noble proportions of the old buildings"; Cass Gilbert to Francis Swales, [autobiographical letter], September 24, 1909, Box 17, Cass Gilbert Papers, Library of Congress.

65. As far as Gilbert was concerned, towering buildings were appropriate for New York but not for European cities, and most especially not for Rome. In October 1924 he wrote to Premier Benito Mussolini advising him against the construction of a thousand-foot skyscraper in Rome, which was reported to be influenced by the Woolworth Building. "If then a tower 1,000 feet high should be erected in Rome, a great and glorious thing it might be in itself, it would inevitably be detrimental to the city from an aesthetic point of view." Gilbert added that he hoped Mussolini "will reconsider the whole subject and that your architect will be asked to design some other type of structure which will not be excessively high, something that will be in harmony with the beauty of Rome"; Cass Gilbert to Premier Benito Mussolini, October 16, 1924, Box 10, Cass Gilbert Papers, Library of Congress.

CONTRIBUTORS

Mary Beth Betts

Mary Beth Betts is director of research at the New York City Landmarks Preservation Commission and former curator of architectural collections at the New-York Historical Society. She received her Ph.D. in art history from the Graduate Center, City University of New York. Her previous publications include an essay in *The New York Waterfront* (New York: Monacelli Press, 1997).

Barbara S. Christen

Barbara S. Christen is currently a research associate at the Center for Advanced Study in the Visual Arts at the National Gallery of Art in Washington, D.C. She was executive director of the Committee on Cass Gilbert Projects in New York, where she coordinated a series of exhibitions, building and walking tours, and a symposium devoted to Gilbert. She received her Ph.D. in art history from the Graduate Center, City University of New York; her dissertation was entitled "Cass Gilbert and the Ideal of the City Beautiful: City and Campus Plans, 1900–1916."

Gail Fenske

Gail Fenske is an architect and historian. She received her Ph.D. from MIT, is a professor of architecture at Roger Williams University, and has taught as a visiting professor at Cornell University and MIT. She has published essays in *The Education of the Architect,* edited by Martha Pollack (Cambridge, Mass.: MIT Press, 1997), *L'Art de l'ingénieur: constructeur, entrepreneur, inventeur,* compiled by Antoine Picon et al. (Paris: Centre de creation industrielle, Centre Georges Pompidou, 1997) and *The Landscape of Modernity,* edited by David Ward and Olivier Zunz (Baltimore: Johns Hopkins University Press, 1997). She has recently completed a book on the Woolworth Building.

Betsy Gotbaum

Betsy Gotbaum is president of the New-York Historical Society. Previously, she served as New York City's commissioner of parks and recreation. She has also worked as Mayor John V. Lindsay's assistant for education, as the executive director of the New York City Police Foundation, and as executive director of the National Alliance Against Violence. She has a master's degree in education from Columbia University.

Hugh Hardy

Hugh Hardy cofounded Hardy Holzman Pfeiffer Associates, one of the nation's leading planning, architectural, and interior design firms, in 1967. In recognition of its versatility, the firm has been honored by architectural, civic, and preservation groups with well over one hundred design awards. Mr. Hardy has been responsible for important restoration projects, including the New Amsterdam Theater, the Rainbow Room, and Radio City Music Hall in New York City, and the St. Louis Art Museum. He has participated in significant urban renewal projects such as the planning and design for Bryant Park in New York City and the development of a master plan for the New Haven cultural district. He is part of the team converting the Farley Post Office Building into the new Pennsylvania Station. Mr. Hardy has contributed numerous articles to professional journals and general magazines.

Margaret Heilbrun

Margaret Heilbrun is director of the library, which includes the department of prints, photographs, and architecture, at the New-York Historical Society. The former curator of manuscripts at the society, she has an M.L.S. in archives and rare books from Columbia University and an M.A. in American civilization from New York University.

Sharon Irish

Sharon Irish is affiliated with the School of Architecture at the University of Illinois, Urbana-Champaign, where she has been since receiving her Ph.D. in art history from Northwestern University. She has written on sanitary engineering and performance art in public spaces; with Edward Kaufman she compiled a book-length bibliography on medievalism in the art and architecture of Great Britain and North America. She recently published *Cass Gilbert, Architect: Modern Traditionalist* (New York: Monacelli Press, 1999).

INDEX

This book was set in 10/14 Bembo, licensed from Monotype/Adobe, a facsimile of a typeface cut in 1495 by Francesco Griffo (1450–1518) for the Venetian printer Aldus Manutius (1450–1515). The face was named for Pietro Bembo, the author of the small treatise *De Ætna,* in which it first appeared. The companion italic is based on the handwriting of the Venetian scribe Giovanni Tagliente from the 1520s. The present-day version of Bembo was first introduced by the Monotype Corporation in 1929, under Stanley Morison's supervision. Serene and versatile, it is a typeface of classical beauty and high legibility.

This book was designed by Linda Secondari.
Composed at Columbia University Press by William Meyers.
Printed and bound at Edwards Brothers.